From the CRADLE *to the* CROSS

A 365 DAY MORNING PRAYER DEVOTIONAL

GEORGE H. BROOKS

WESTBOW
PRESS®
A DIVISION OF THOMAS NELSON
& ZONDERVAN

WestBow Press books may be ordered through booksellers or by contacting:

WestBow Press
A Division of Thomas Nelson & Zondervan
1663 Liberty Drive
Bloomington, IN 47403
www.westbowpress.com
844-714-3454

ISBN: 978-1-6642-2473-5 (sc)
ISBN: 978-1-6642-2474-2 (hc)
ISBN: 978-1-6642-2472-8 (e)

Library of Congress Control Number: 2021903602

Print information available on the last page.

WestBow Press rev. date: 05/17/2021

Preface

George H Brooks, George is one of the most loving and compassionate people I have ever met. I met him when I was practicing as a Christian Counselor in 1982 when he lived in Texas. George was fighting demons that I could only begin to imagine. He grew up in a family that was abandoned by his father. This forced him to spend some of his childhood in a children's home. He grew up on the streets of Brooklyn, New York City.

George proudly wore the uniform of the United States Army. While in the military, he served with medical services both in Korea and Vietnam. His military service brought him to several military bases in Texas, where he served as a Clinical Specialist (LPN). A failed marriage left him with two lovely young daughters to raise by himself.

Through it all, he remained faithful to the Lord, Jesus Christ. It was that faith that had given him the ministry of prayer and the strength to survive and stand.

Through it all, he remained faithful to the Lord, Jesus Christ. It was that faith that had given him the ministry of prayer and the strength to survive and stand. When I first met him, I could not have imagined ever writing an introduction to a book written by George. Here is his second book of prayers and devotionals. Today I cannot imagine him not doing this and even greater things.

I am proud and honored to be asked to give this new work a gentle nudge into existence and recommend it to become a part of your library and your life.

Pastor Jerry Bullock
Texas Country Church
Colonel (Ret) USAF

Dedication

There are so many people I need to dedicate this book to. After a dream that was the catalyst for writing "From the Cradle to the Cross, A 365 Day Devotional," I began writing daily prayers that I posted on Facebook and shared with many friends and family. Over the months that followed, I received many compliments on the prayers with suggestions to write a book. This was the beginning of the First Edition that was published in 2018. Since then, the book was instrumental in speaking to inmates' hearts at the Hamilton County Jail in Noblesville, Indiana. Many of them shared their stories and how the prayers spoke to them and then led them to accept Jesus Christ as their Savior.

With this Second Edition, my desire has grown to touch more and more people, not just inmates, with the Gospel of Jesus Christ. During this process, one thing became crystal clear, this book could not have been written without the Holy Spirit's presence. Without His guidance, I would have floundered to find the words and truths of God's Word.

Also, a great debt of gratitude is given to Jerry M. Bullock, Pastor of Texas Country Church, Texas Country Church, Colonel USAF, (Ret). Jerry has had a profound impact on my life, dating back to the 1980s. Without his love and spiritual guidance, I might not be here today. Thank you, Jerry, for your selfless love and sacrifice during a tumultuous period of my life.

I also realized the deep debt of gratitude I owe to White River Christian Church in Noblesville, Indiana, and Pastor Fred Knoll and Pastor Tim Brock. A special thanks to Chaplain Mark Fidler, who facilitates volunteers with the Hamilton County Jail Ministry. Finally, I have a deep appreciation for the readers of my prayers and those who encouraged me in this endeavor. I will always be indebted to them.

This book is dedicated to all the individuals I mentioned: my precious wife, Nancy Brooks, and our daughters, Tammy Brooks, Misty Chastain, Natalie Ramirez, and Mandy Grace. It is also dedicated to my sister Bev. Leckie who was there for me when I needed her spiritual guidance. Without their encouragement and long-suffering as I frequently shared my excitement for the book, the writing and challenge of preparing this devotional would have increased. My deepest heartfelt thanks to all of you. God Bless each one of you.

Foreword

By Fred Knoll, Pastor

I have long admired George's deep and sincere love for Jesus Christ and those who do not yet know Him. Throughout my years of ministry, I have met countless people. People who are seeking to find that place where God's will intersect with their spiritual giftedness. That sweet spot where they indeed come alive inside. George Brooks has found it. He continues to impact lives for the kingdom of God through his writing and teaching. One place he does this is through the jail ministry through our local church. Through this book, God has used George to bring a powerful light into a dark place. He continues to have more requests from those behind bars, thirsty for the truth, honesty, and freedom for captives so eloquently communicated in this book.

The book you are holding in your hands was written from a place of brokenness and humility. George exposes his pain and shares from a place of sincere and warm vulnerability. The Holy Spirit has uniquely gifted him to weave the powerful truth of scripture into his pain to create a beautiful tapestry of healing for the reader.

The Holy Spirit has uniquely gifted him to weave the powerful truth of scripture into his pain to create a beautiful tapestry of healing for the reader.

I have read this book while sitting in silence on my deck in my backyard. I have read it in my sunroom during a soft rain. It has spoken to me in front of the fireplace on many cold mornings. And on the beach, while my chair sank ever so slowly into the sand. Find your quiet place and set a time to read the insightful, encouraging, and challenging devotions in this book every day for a year. I trust you will hear God's voice speak to your heart and find yourself walking more closely with Jesus at the end of the year.

Fred Knoll
Missional Living Pastor
White River Christian Church
1685 North 10th Street
Noblesville, Indiana 46060

Special Introduction

By Chaplain Mark Fidler

When I first met George, he talked about a book he had written, "From the Cradle to the Cross." He gave me a copy to read and see if I would approve it for distribution in the jail to inmates who would like a copy. I am always looking for writings that will speak to the incarcerated heart about the need for a love relationship with Jesus Christ and not just another book to sit on the shelf. As I read "From the Cradle to the Cross," I first read a Scripture passage, the Word of God. Still, when I read the prayer that followed, I soon realized that I was reading the words penned from the heart of a servant to his Lord, Jesus Christ. It was as though the power of the heartfelt words of prayer reminisced the Words of the psalmist when he prayed, "Let the words of my mouth and the meditation of my heart be acceptable in your sight, O Lord, my strength and my Redeemer." (Ps. 19:14 NKJV)

> *As I began to read "From the Cradle to the Cross," I first read a Scripture passage which is the Word of God, but when I read the prayer that followed, I soon realized that I was reading the words penned from the heart of a servant to his Lord, Jesus Christ.*

In George's prayers, one will find God speaking to the reader through scripture and the reader speaking to God through personal prayer. The prayers are filled with Praising the Lord for who He is and what He has done and is doing even now in the servant's life. It includes prayer for Protection, as God is a Providential Care Giver. It includes prayer for Guidance of the Holy Spirit in our daily life and for the Power and Strength to live a life that would glorify God daily. After I distributed the first copy of George's book, the flood gates seemed to open, and requests frequently came for the book. As is usually the case, my fear was I want what he has, which is a jail mentality, but this was not the case. The inmates were actually reading the book as their daily devotional, and they shared how it spoke to them and helped them through the journey they were on.

George is a gifted writer and a faithful servant of the Living King, and I am honored to call him my brother.

Pastor Mark A. Fidler
Senior Chaplain
Hamilton County Sheriff's Office

Testimonials from Inmates

Hamilton County Jail
Noblesville, Indiana 46060

Anonymous Female Inmate: This devotional has been a great guide for me through prayer. The words give me encouragement for each day while I am on this journey, and I will continue reading them when I return to society. I have shared it with my bunkies, and now they have their own copy.

Anonymous Female Inmate: From the Cradle to the Cross gives me daily inspiration and helps me look at the day ahead with a positive attitude.

Anonymous Male Inmate: This devotional hit home with me in how it relates to daily life. I love the way it is worded because it is very easy to understand. I start my day off reading it and sometimes read it again later in the day as a reminder.

Anonymous Male Inmate: It is easy to read and understand. It is helpful to read, and it makes the day go by better.

Anonymous Female Inmate: I have been reading this book with my Bunkie every day. It is very inspiring and has brought me peace. I lost my dad last year, and my mom is dying from lung disease, and this book has helped me to keep my faith strong and intact. I read the passages before bed and certain passages repeatedly to stay encouraged. My favorite to read daily is January 13. I find it to be very peaceful and helpful. It is Amazing.

Written with God and Led by the Holy Spirit

How God Spoke to Me

In my dream, I was in a town square with people all about me. Suddenly, they began dropping to their knees, and I began blessing them in the name of the Father, Son, and Holy Spirit. At that moment, I awoke with a flood of heat coursing through my body from my head to my toes, and I found myself breathing very rapidly. Nothing like this has ever happened to me before or since. I knew then that God had laid that dream upon me. The following morning, I called a minister I knew and asked him what he thought the dream meant. He said, "It means you are supposed to bless people." After prayer and reflection, I embarked on the first edition of this book, "From the Cradle to the Cross, A 365 Day Devotional."

This book could not have been written without the direction of the Holy Spirit. He alone gave me the words to share with you, coupled with words that were laid upon my heart. Without Him, this devotional simply could not have been written. The Holy Spirit was present from the beginning when the book was born from a dream on my wife's birthday in 2016.

In my dream, I was in a town square with people all about me. Suddenly, they began dropping to their knees, and I began blessing them in the name of the Father, Son, and Holy Spirit. At that moment, I awoke with a flood of heat coursing through my body from my head to my toes, and I found myself breathing very rapidly. Nothing like this has ever happened to me before or since. I knew then that God had laid that dream upon me. The following morning, I called a minister I knew and asked him what he thought the dream meant. He said, "It means you are supposed to bless people." After prayer and reflection, I embarked on the first edition of this book, "From the Cradle to the Cross, A 365 Day Devotional."

This second edition has the same prayers as the first edition. However, it was published to enhance the written format, add additional material, improve the editing, and clarify the Holy Spirit's role in this book. The second edition includes a question or comments at the end of the prayer from which the reader can use as further study of the prayer. After completing the first edition, I soon realized that it was published not to make money but to bless people and lead them to a personal relationship with Jesus Christ. From a jail ministry at the Hamilton County Jail in Noblesville, Indiana, God blessed me with the opportunity to serve as a volunteer. I was able to touch the lives of many inmates who told me the prayers spoke to them as if the prayer was what was on their hearts and what they wanted and needed to pray to God. The jail ministry received hundreds of book donations from White River Christian Church in Noblesville, Indiana. My deepest thanks to Pastor Fred Knoll of White River Christian Church for his fantastic support and belief in this prayer devotional. My thanks also to Chaplain Mark Fidler of Hamilton County Jail, who supported my efforts and his belief that this book could impact the inmates' lives.

This book could not have been possible without the love and support of my wife, Nancy Marie Brooks. Her support during the many hours of writing and editing has been immeasurable. My wife suggested that I include "Authored with God and led by the Holy Spirit" in the book, acknowledging that the Holy Spirit was present in this devotional writing. Thank you, honey, for your wisdom and precious love, and support that has allowed me to bring this book to fruition.

And finally, to all my readers, thank you for letting me be an instrument of God that hopefully will lead you and others to have a personal relationship with Jesus Christ. My continuing prayer is that as you live your life for Christ, you will experience immeasurable joy and peace. God bless you.

George H. Brooks
Author

Testimonials

Blessings from the Holy Spirit

"George begins the year with humility and heart dependence, wanting to know his God better, wanting to silence the lies that can misguide, and wanting to hear the whispers of God's Spirit. He longs for the likeness of Christ in his own life and a reflection that will impact the lives of others. He begins that way, and he continues with prayers that can give others a voice with their own prayers. Be blessed ..."

Bev Leckie

"It is often difficult in today's busy world to find a few moments to sit quietly and pray. George's prayers get to the heart of each verse in a way that is simple and sincere. They provide you with a beautiful way to reflect on God's Word no matter where you are or how little time you have. I am very grateful for these heartfelt prayers."

Amy Shoremount-Obra

"From the Cradle to the Cross will help you understand the necessity of staying focused on Jesus throughout the day and compel you to make a deep commitment to the people in your life and to God -- it is surprisingly fresh each morning."

J. Timothy Brock, DMiss, MDiv
Senior Pastor, wrcc.org

"Thank you, George, for your latest Morning Prayer Devotional. I appreciate your sensitivity to the Holy Spirit as you have tendered these heartfelt prayers. Like the Psalms, you have touched all emotions that are common to all men and women. Congratulations."

Buck Nielsen

"George's book, 'From the Cradle to the Cross, A 365 Day Morning Prayer Devotional', has been a great inspiration to me. It has been a wonderful faith learning and building experience. I am blessed to start each morning with the daily prayers, and I am confident God was with him as he wrote these prayers. The prayers speak to my heart and empower me, through the Holy Spirit, to find the strength to live my life for Christ. Thank you for these daily blessings."

Lisa Randall

"The daily prayers are so powerful and pertinent to my daily life. I try hard to find silence and alone time, so I can read them out loud. It is my quiet time with God. It means a lot to me to have this prayer book to read each day. Thanks for all you do."

Charlotte Lynch

Why does Christ want a *Personal Relationship* with you?

The concept of having a personal relationship with someone you cannot see or touch is difficult to comprehend. We all have family, friends, and acquaintances we may have a personal relationship with. These are people we can see and feel and with whom we can develop relationships based on mutual interests. Some people may believe they have a personal relationship with a sports figure, such as Tiger Woods. They may watch every game he plays and keep track of all his statistics, but do they know him? Knowing someone *personally* involves much more than being familiar with statistics or knowing someone's favorite television show, food, color, or any number of things. Knowing someone personally is when you have shared intimate details of your life. Someone you confided in, someone you may have vacationed with, and other interactions where you can truly get to know someone.

> *Many may question why Christ would want to have a personal relationship with you. Someone who may be a wretched sinner, so vile, so hateful, so full of pride, and so full of demonic influences and temptations that offend God.*

Knowing God is even more personal. Through faith, you can hear His whisper, talk with Him, and share your innermost thoughts and fears. Having a personal relationship with Christ means you can go to Him anytime through prayer and know through faith that He will hear you. God wants you to have a personal relationship with His Son, Jesus Christ, because of the deep love He has for you. He wants you to trust Him and His Holy Word that he gave to us so we can have a blueprint for living our lives. Many may question why Christ would want to have a personal relationship with you. Someone who may be — a wretched sinner, so vile, so hateful, so full of pride, and so full of demonic influences and temptations that offend God. God knows who you are. He knows the attractions you have faced, and He knows *why* you succumbed to them. There is nothing you can keep from God. He knows everything about you.

God loves you so much that He sent His only Son, Jesus Christ, to die on the Cross of Calvary for all your sins. Not just those "soft sins" you may shrug off, but those deep shameful sins that cause extreme guilt that can destroy relationships you have with others. Christ is always there to walk beside you, to pick you up when you stumble on your Christian walk, and to give you the strength, through the Holy Spirit, to conquer the forces of Satan in all its forms. Christ knows you are weak and cannot have victory over Satan unless you rely on the Holy Spirit. God sent the Holy Spirit as your advocate so you can draw on His strength to end Satan's power over you. He gave you Jesus Christ, so you will always know that God is with you, and no matter what difficulty you encounter, you do not need to do it by yourself. Jesus is still with you!

According to GotQuestions.org:
https://www.gotquestions.org/personal-relationship-with-God.html

"This personal relationship with God is not as hard to find as we might think, and there is no mysterious formula for getting it. As soon as we become children of God, we receive the Holy Spirit, who will begin to work on our hearts. We should pray without ceasing, read the Bible, and join a Bible-believing church; all these things will help us grow spiritually. Trusting in God to get us through each day and believing that He is our sustainer is how to build a relationship with Him. Although we may not see changes immediately, we will begin to see them over time, and all the Truths will become clear."

When you accept Jesus Christ as your Savior, you have decided to let Christ into your heart so He can shape you into the person He wants you to be, not what you want to be, but what He has planned for your life. Giving your life over to Christ means forsaking things of this world and living for Him. It does not mean you will not experience disappointments, sadness, or tragedy in your life. It does not mean you will not have days when you are weak and vulnerable to the ways of the world. God's promise to you is that He will always love you. He will always be there to comfort you. He will always listen to your prayers. And, when you trust in His Word and the redeeming blood of His Son, Jesus Christ, you will enjoy eternal life with Him in Heaven. Why does Christ want a personal relationship with you? Because He loves you. It is that simple. Love!

Written by George H. Brooks
Author

Message from the Author "The Power of Prayer"

My friends and brothers and sisters in Christ, prayer is powerful! God wants to hear from you, not only when you are in an emotional or financial crisis that is overwhelming. Not just during a personal problem that has created enormous fear in you. God longs to hear your voice, your whisper to Him saying, "I love you, Lord Jesus." Devotion to prayer is a great witness of your faith. It is not only to our God but also to all those who witness your dedication.

> *We can never overcome our sinful nature — that was set in stone by Adam and Eve. We can never stop sinning because our human condition is too weak. But we can repent each day and free our-selves from the bondage that Satan uses to entrap us.*

God wants us to have this kind of relationship with His Son, Jesus Christ. Love is not one-sided. God wants to know we love Him just as we need to know the assurance of God's love for us. And we do that by having a personal relationship with Christ; through prayer, through devotion to His Word, by showing love and compassion to our fellow man, and by putting to death, each day, our sinful nature, willful disobedience, and our tendency to be consumed with ourselves. We can never overcome our sinful nature — that was set in stone by Adam and Eve. We can never stop sinning because our human condition is too weak. But we can repent each day and free ourselves from the bondage that Satan uses to entrap us. How might you ask? By picking up the cross of Christ. By shouting out to the world through our actions, our behavior, through prayer, and the direction of the Holy Spirit, that we are children of God. That we are so full of love for Christ that through Him, we can rejoice in a victory that frees our souls.

How do we fulfill God's purpose for us? We do that by listening to God's whisper. That soft yet firm voice we hear in our hearts and our heads speaks to us and guides us as we make choices that either honor God with our faithfulness to His Word or that brings sadness to His heart and tears to His eyes. Yes, our God has emotions too. He wants so much for us to live our lives in ways that glorify His name in all we say and do. God wants so much for us to know the Truth of His Word. He wants so much for us to speak with Him and share the frustrations, disappointments, and needs we have, whether for physical or spiritual healing or other concerns. God wants so much to hear your words and songs of praise and adoration. He loves you. He wants to talk to you, and he wants you to speak to Him. The question is, do you want a relationship with Christ that is so rewarding that by the end of your day, you can look back and say with all sincerity, "It is well with my soul."

The Key to this kind of relationship is so simple. Prayer! We can do nothing in our lives faithful to His Word unless we go to Him in prayer and allow the Holy Spirit to lead and guide our thoughts and actions.

As my life was pruned and shaped by God, I realized that I do not need to be a biblical or spiritual scholar to touch the lives of people in need of hope and the assurance of God's love. And neither do you. Finally, I realized the power of prayer. It starts with a life of faith and confidence that God's Word is the truth. And while Christ spoke about the importance of love, love does not justify sin! True love embraces the truth of God's Word!

Philippians 4:6-7 NIV. says ...
6 Do not be anxious about anything, but in every situation, by prayer and petition, with thanksgiving, present your requests to God. 7 And the peace of God, which transcends all understanding, will guard your hearts and your minds in Christ Jesus.

So, as you read the prayers in this devotional, open your heart so you may hear God's whisper. Listen to God. Allow yourself to be filled and guided by the Holy Spirit. Acknowledge Him as the Almighty God, the Father of our Redeemer, Jesus

Christ. Rejoice in your love for God and your ability to communicate with Him through prayer.

1 John 5:14-15 NIV. tells us, [14]This is the confidence we have in approaching God: that if we ask anything according to his will, he hears us. [15]And if we know that he hears us whatever we ask, we know that we have what we asked of him.

No matter who the person is praying, the passion behind the prayer, or the purpose of the prayer — God answers prayers in agreement with His will. His answers are not always yes but are still in our best interest. When our desires line up with His will, we will come to understand that in time, when we pray passionately and purposefully, according to God's will, God responds powerfully!

From "The Cradle to the Cross," A 365 Day Morning Prayer Devotional, has been a real labor of love. Without the presence of the Holy Spirit, it could not have been written. The Second Edition of "From the Cradle to the Cross, a 365 Day Morning Devotional" gives a voice to those that have difficulty finding words to share with our Almighty God. It allows them to tell Him the depth of their sinful nature and their gratitude for His sacrificial death on the Cross of Calvary. My prayer for you is that as you read the prayers in this devotional, you will come to know Jesus Christ as your personal Savior. I pray that the Holy Spirit will lead you to live each day of your life trusting in the redeeming blood of our Lord and Savior. In the right column of each prayer, you will find a question or comment that is an opportunity to reflect on a critical aspect of the prayer. Use this area to write down any thoughts or observations that speak to your heart. Remember, during any uncertainty in life, believe that you too can soar like an eagle, victorious over all the efforts by Satan to steal from you the joy of life in Christ.

George H. Brooks
Author

To the Reader of this Book of Prayers

May you be blessed as you look upon this new day
with hope and anticipation of joy in all that you do.

May you know the love of Jesus Christ so that your heart
will recognize the power of His redeeming blood
for the forgiveness of all your sins.

May the Truth of all God's Word and promises give you
the peace and contentment to live your life as a Holy vessel
filled with love and compassion for your fellow man.

May you face the difficulties of this world and your personal
daily struggles with the knowledge and assurance of eternal life
through God's Son, Jesus Christ.

May you be filled with the power of the Holy Spirit
so that you may touch the lives of others as you use
your unique gifts to God's s.

May you know in your heart and soul that you are a child of God
and that you are loved, just as you are, no matter what doubts
or uncertainty you may have.

Praise to you, O Christ, for your enduring love,
ceaseless grace, and forgiveness of all my sins.

Amen.

Written by George H. Brooks, Author

Simply Asking

By Bev Leckie

The following devotional was written by the Author's sister, Bev Leckie. As *a pastor's wife, Bev has been writing most of her adult life to augment ministry outreaches. In writing devotionals, though, she found the freedom to put her heart on paper, communicating the grace of God and practical insights for living. She continues to reach out through her "Thoughts for a Woman's Heart" and through "Thoughts Under the Umbrella," a weekly encouragement for moms who have suffered the loss of a child. This devotional illustrates the impact sin and guilt have over our lives. It also shows we have a loving and forgiving God, one that loves us no matter how grave or severe the sin is. As you read this devotional, think of the depth of your sin and how you can be freed from the guilt of it by having a personal relationship with Jesus Christ.*

Sin transgresses the character of God. Sin is what God is not. And there is something innately woven within us that self-judges our choices, our attitudes, our behaviors, our words, and much else. We are capable of silencing that self-judgment, and we are capable of that self-judgment screaming at us, tormenting us, and literally shredding our inner person. The haunting presence of sin that still shames destroys and cripples. We call it "guilt," but some sins carry the stigma that they are far greater than other sins, they merit the unmerciful judgment of others, and we question if even God could possibly "forgive" us. And as the haunting presence lingers, we find we cannot even forgive ourselves.

God does not assign the stigma to sin that we assign, or that others assign, or that we think they assign. To God, sin simply sins, and it separates us from Him, and He does use "guilt" in a healthy, productive way to give us awareness of our sins. With that awareness, God's choice is for us to lay those sins at the foot of the cross, with the knowledge that Christ's death became the judgment for our sins, and with the brokenness that allows His sacrifice to eradicate our sinful condition fully, completely, and eternally. It is that simple. Simply asking for forgiveness, and simply, but profusely, receiving that forgiveness.

But believers and non-believers alike can identify themselves as shameful, unworthy, and undeserving of forgiveness. For the non-believer, the message of the cross becomes a message for "someone else" because it could not possibly be a message God has for them. They have gone too far. The horrendous have mutilated their personhood, and they have nothing, absolutely nothing, to offer a Holy God. They fear to even speak of the things that are hidden in the darkness of secrecy. The believer hangs on to a "hope so" kind of Christianity, hoping against hope that maybe God will truly be merciful to her, and the memories that scream cripple her spiritually and emotionally.

I have known the shame of unspeakable sin, but I have also known, and I continue to know, the freedom and security of forgiveness. I sing the words of Amazing Grace, and I sing with a similar fervor that compelled John Newton to write its truth. Amazing grace! How sweet the sound That saved a wretch like me! I once was lost, but now am found, was blind, but now I see. It is a grace that exceeds the bounds of the horrendous and quiets the torment of guilt. A grace that was poured out in Christ's sacrificial death, a grace that is given, simply because I asked.

(Related Bible reading: Romans 3:23-25; Romans 5:1,2; 1 Corinthians 15:9,10; 2 Corinthians 8:9; Ephesians 2:1-10)

– Bev Leckie
Author, Thoughts for a Woman's Heart

January 1

Psalm 96:13 NIV.

[13] Let all creation rejoice before the Lord, for he comes; he comes to judge the earth. He will judge the world in righteousness and the peoples in his faithfulness.

Father in Heaven, Lord of all creation, you have given me the power to communicate with you in times of need through prayer. You have given me this gift to petition you for personal needs and intervene on behalf of others. Forgive me, Father, for not always using this same gift to praise you and to thank you for all the blessings you bestow upon me. You are my Almighty God, my Father, who cares about me and wants to assure me of your love and Salvation through your Son, Jesus Christ.

Lord, I need to hear your gentle whisper, the soft voice that through the power of the Holy Spirit guides me and leads me down the path of righteousness. Sometimes I close the ears of my heart and tune out your voice, allowing the voice of Satan to draw me away from your warm embrace to behavior and thoughts that dishonor your name. Surround me, O Lord, with an impenetrable hedge of guardian angels that will rise and defeat Satan when he beckons. Protect me through your divine mercies and endless grace, in the name of the Father, Son, and Holy Spirit. Amen.

REFLECTIONS

Have you ever closed the ears of your heart and mind to hear God's Word?

Please use the space below to write down any thoughts or comments you may have.

"May God Bless You,
As you live your Life for Christ,
Empowered by The Holy Spirit."

January 2

Romans 7:18 NIV.

[18] For I know that good itself does not dwell in me, that is, in my sinful nature. For I have the desire to do what is good, but I cannot carry it out.

Heavenly Father, Lord of the ages, thank you for your eternal blessings. Thank you for the love of Christ that heals my broken heart, and that gives me peace to weather any storm that may cross my path. Lord, you know the trials and challenges I face daily. You see the shortness of patience I show in response to frustrating situations. You see the fear that grips my heart when I violate the laws of your scripture and the teachings of Jesus Christ.

O Christ, my Savior and precious Redeemer free me from the sins of this world so I can truly reflect the love and life of Jesus Christ in all that I do. Purge my heart from evil thoughts. Purify them with your Holy Spirit, so I may walk in the footsteps of my Savior. Let me be secure in knowing that I can rise above my sinful nature as a child of God. Grant these things, I pray, in the name of Jesus Christ. Amen.

REFLECTIONS

What is one area where you have been short of patience, and how can God help you?

Please use the space below to write down any thoughts or comments you may have.

"May God Bless You,
As you live your Life for Christ,
Empowered by The Holy Spirit."

January 3

Galatians 5:10 NIV.

[10] I am confident in the Lord that you will take no other view. The one who is throwing you into confusion, whoever that may be, will have to pay the penalty.

Dear Jesus, each day, I am confronted with personal struggles that are too difficult for me to face with humility, love, and compassion. Although confronted with difficulties in life that test my faith and loyalty to your Word, I cry out with the pain of a broken heart. I have failed you with careless and thoughtless acts toward others. I have not helped your children who struggle with unforeseen challenges.

Help me, gracious Father, through your infinite mercy and unending grace, of my disobedience to your Word. Forgive me for failing to faithfully live out my life in your service and failing to be a faithful witness of your Word to my fellow man. Restore me, O Lord, on the path of righteousness for your name's sake. In the name of the Father, Son, and Holy Spirit, I pray. Amen.

REFLECTIONS

What is one personal struggle you will be facing today, and what can you do about it?

Please use the space below to write down any thoughts or comments you may have.

"May God Bless You,
As you live your Life for Christ,
Empowered by The Holy Spirit."

January 4

2 Corinthians 7:11 NIV.

[11] See what this godly sorrow has produced in you: what earnestness, what eagerness to clear yourselves, what indignation, what alarm, what longing, what concern, what readiness to see justice done. At every point, you have proved yourselves to be innocent in this matter.

Dear God, it is with a humble heart and contrite spirit that I come before you to praise you for all the blessings you have bestowed upon me. Lord, you know the areas of my life that have required your Divine Intervention. You know the sorrow and fear that grips me when faced with situations I cannot control. You know the pleas of my heart as it implores you to restore my physical, mental, and emotional health. My heart and soul are ever grateful for your continued blessings.

I thank you that through your Son, Jesus Christ, I can have the assurance that you will always be there to meet my needs. Let me always be worthy of your love, grace, and forgiveness as I keep my eyes on the love and teachings of Jesus Christ. Make me a steadfast witness of your love and grace to all those whose paths I cross today, and may I truly reflect the life of Christ as I live out my faith in Him. In the name of the Father, Son, and Holy Spirit. Amen.

REFLECTIONS

What is one area of your life where you need God's help?

Please use the space below to write down any thoughts or comments you may have.

"May God Bless You,
As you live your Life for Christ,
Empowered by The Holy Spirit."

January 5

Romans 16:19 NIV.

[19] Everyone has heard about your obedience, so I rejoice because of you, but I want you to be wise about what is good and innocent about what is evil.

Father in Heaven, Lord of my heart, grant your mercies upon me as I go forth this day in faithful obedience to your Word. Send along your Holy angels as faithful guardians as I attempt to live a fruitful and blessed life that will glorify your name. I will no longer allow myself to be confused by Satan's ploys full of lies and deception. Assure me that by being faithful and obedient to your Word, I will overcome any adversities that come my way. Instill in me a deep reverence and love for serving you so I may taste the joy of being one in Christ.

Unfortunately, Lord, this world has a way of turning your children away from godliness. Whenever I go about my day, I see people caught up in anger, caught up in wrongful behavior, and captivated by things that build a wall between them and our Lord and Savior, Jesus Christ. Your children are being deceived by the forces of Satan and encouraged to forsake the truths of your Word. Help us, Jesus. Let us take on the armor of the Lord to defend ourselves from insidious attacks on our character's spiritual and moral fiber. Grant these things, I pray, in your Son's name. Amen.

REFLECTIONS

What lies will Satan tell you today to try to separate you from God?

Please use the space below to write down any thoughts or comments you may have.

"May God Bless You,
As you live your Life for Christ,
Empowered by The Holy Spirit."

January 6

Proverbs 4:11 NIV.

[11] I instruct you in the way of wisdom and lead you along straight paths.

Precious Lord Jesus, hear my plea as I embark upon another day in service to you. Lift my heart so I may rejoice in love and charity to all those whose paths I cross today. Bless me with the spirit of wisdom and revelation. Let me see with clarity the truth of your Word and have the courage to proclaim it unabashedly to all whose hearts are open to your truth.

Lord, in this year and day in 2021, our nation was confronted by massive crowds of protestors and domestic terrorists who rushed the United States Capitol for the first time in our history. During the Capitol storming, our political leaders' lives, including our Vice President, were threatened. Amidst the property destruction, several lives were lost, and many people were injured. Father, forgive all those people who perpetrated these acts of violence. Speak to their hearts. Let them be convicted of their behavior. Give all our leaders the spirit of wisdom and revelation so they will have no question of the direction and of your will for our country.

Father, let me be a Truth sower to those who cling to our society's false teachings. Bless them with a spirit of love, forgiveness, and grace as they wrestle with the temptations of this world. I ask these things in the name of the Father, Son, and Holy Spirit. Amen.

REFLECTIONS

How can you show God's love to someone today?

Please use the space below to write down any thoughts or comments you may have.

"May God Bless You,
As you live your Life for Christ,
Empowered by The Holy Spirit."

January 7

Ephesians 6:14 NIV.

[14] Stand firm then, with the belt of truth buckled around your waist, with the breastplate of righteousness in place.

O Christ, my Prince of Peace, I praise you for your unending gifts of mercy, love, forgiveness, and grace. Lead me this day, O Father, in your footsteps as I embrace the challenges this day presents. Guide me and deliver me from all distractions I may encounter as I seek to follow your will for my life. Open my eyes and heart to see the truth of your Word. Give me the strength and perseverance to confront all conflicts with the assurance that I can overcome any adversity by placing my faith and trust in you.

Whenever I come across a conflict that attempts to tear down the stronghold of faith I have in your Word, let me put on the Breastplate of Righteousness so I can fend off all attacks by Satan. Send now your Holy Spirit, O Lord, to sanctify me and to infuse me with the fruits of the spirit so I may fulfill your calling for my life. Bless me with your divine grace and lead me down the path of righteousness. In the name of the Father, Son, and Holy Spirit. Amen.

REFLECTIONS

Describe a distraction you may come across today that could hinder your walk with Christ?

Please use the space below to write down any thoughts or comments you may have.

"May God Bless You,
As you live your Life for Christ,
Empowered by The Holy Spirit."

January 8

Acts 13:38 NIV.

[38] "Therefore, my friends, I want you to know that through Jesus the forgiveness of sins is proclaimed to you.

Blessed Father, Comforter of my heart, I come before you today knowing my heart is not full of forgiveness for those who have offended me. I come before you, bound by the shackles of fear that grip my heart and turn it away from doing your will. Lord, as much as I want to escape from this hardness of my heart, I find it difficult to shed this cloak of unforgiveness that keeps me from being in tune with your will. Father, forgive me. Lift me from the claws of Satan that seek to destroy my unity with the Father, Son, and Holy Spirit. Open my eyes, O Father, so I may see a clear picture of your forgiveness and what it cost you when you sent your only Son to die on the Cross of Calvary.

I love you, Lord, and want to be completely faithful in my service and devotion to you. I want to reflect your love to others no matter what pain they have caused me. I want to have that spirit of forgiveness that refuses to be tarnished by memories that have caused me grief. I want to forget those memories, my Lord, and only focus on extending love, grace, and forgiveness. Even when my sinful nature beckons me to react in a spirit of unkindness.

Build me up, O Christ, with a love that seeks no revenge. Let me have a love that aims to show compassion and keeps me in the light of your grace as I faithfully strive to reflect the love you continuously bestow on me. Grant these things, I pray, in the name of the Father, Son, and Holy Spirit. Amen.

REFLECTIONS

Think of a fear that has you shackled to your old sinful nature. What can you break free of it?

Please use the space below to write down any thoughts or comments you may have.

"May God Bless You,
As you live your Life for Christ,
Empowered by The Holy Spirit."

January 9

Revelation 3:8 NIV.

[8] I know your deeds. See, I have placed before you an open door that no one can shut. I know that you have little strength, yet you have kept my word and have not denied my name.

Precious Father, I arise this morning singing praises to your name. My heart is full of gratitude and love for the opportunity to serve you. Each day I seek your face knowing you will be with me to guide and direct my footsteps. Each day, I pray you will keep me aware of opportunities to share the message of your Gospel.

O Lord, bring to me Divine Opportunities to share my faith and demonstrate love, grace, and forgiveness to my fellow man. When I am weak and frustrated by life situations, renew my strength to continue my journey to love and serve you. Fill me with the spirit of wisdom and revelation to have the spiritual countenance that will reflect to others that I am a child of God. Grant me peace in my life, complete with the assurance and faith that I can be a faithful witness of your love. In Christ's name, I pray. Amen.

REFLECTIONS

As you seek to serve God, in what areas of your life are you grateful to Him?

Please use the space below to write down any thoughts or comments you may have.

"May God Bless You,
As you live your Life for Christ,
Empowered by The Holy Spirit."

January 10

1 Corinthians 10:13 NIV.

[13] No temptation has overtaken you except what is common to mankind. And God is faithful; he will not let you be tempted beyond what you can bear. But when you are tempted, he will also provide a way out so that you can endure it.

Blessed Father, Lord of my heart, I come before you on bended knees and with a contrite heart, knowing I will not be utterly faithful to you today. Lord, I am a sinner lost in this world of turmoil, struggling to cope not only with my failings but those of my neighbors, my family, and the strangers among me. Father, extend your arms around me. Bring me into your bosom where I can be kept safe from all harm, secure in the knowledge that through your Son, Jesus Christ, I can find the peace and comfort I need as I live my life for you.

Embrace me, O Lord. Soothe my wounded spirit and heal me from all emotional and physical afflictions that keep me from turning to you when I am in the clutches of Satan. Send your Holy Spirit to whisper to me the words I need to be firm in my devotion to you. Let me be earnest in my desire to serve you. Let me be full of the love, grace, and forgiveness you want me to share with others. Praise to you, Lord Jesus, for the example of your life that is the model for me to live. In your name, I pray. Amen.

REFLECTIONS

In what ways might you not be faithful to God today?

Please use the space below to write down any thoughts or comments you may have.

"May God Bless You,
As you live your Life for Christ,
Empowered by The Holy Spirit."

January 11

Hebrews 12:11 NIV..

[11] No discipline seems pleasant at the time, but painful. Later on, however, it produces a harvest of righteousness and peace for those who have been trained by it.

Gracious God, the truth of your Word is evident in my heart. You are my Lord, my Savior, and my hope for complete restoration of my body, mind, and spirit. You alone are the source of righteousness in this world that is full of deceit, wickedness, and all sources of evil. You stand alone as the one to turn to for guidance when I face the mayhem caused by humankind.

Dear Jesus, I give you thanks that I can always turn to you when I am lost and bewildered by situations in life that are of my doing and those beyond my control. Lord, let me be a vessel of hope and righteousness, an ambassador of your Truth to others that may not know you. Cleanse me from all impurities of my heart and mind that may impede my ability to touch the lives of those that need your love, grace, and forgiveness. Let me be a blessing to all those who hear my words, who see my actions, whose lives I interact with, and to whom I share my faith. In your precious name, I pray. Amen.

REFLECTIONS

What truth of God's Word would you share today with someone who is seeking the truth?

Please use the space below to write down any thoughts or comments you may have.

"May God Bless You,
As you live your Life for Christ,
Empowered by The Holy Spirit."

January 12

1 Peter 5:5 NIV..

[5] In the same way, you who are younger, submit yourselves to your elders. All of you, clothe yourselves with humility toward one another, because "God opposes the proud but shows favor to the humble."

Most Holy God, King of my heart, enlighten me today in areas of service and love I can share with my fellow man. Help me to put aside all pettiness that can encumber my witness to others. Strengthen me in all areas where my gifts of the Holy Spirit are weak and not used to your glory. Embolden me to go forth confident of my victory in Christ so I can accomplish your will for my life. Let me be full of humility and grace so I do not become a victim of pride and thus hinder my service to you. Grant me the peace I need in my life to love others who are lost, distraught, and yearning for your love.

I am living in a world, O Christ, where the opportunities to bless others are boundless. I never know who may cross my path. I cannot know who is caught up with emotions that can make the strongest of us go weak. But you, O Gracious Lord, know the hearts and minds of all your children. You see the suffering that consumes them. I pray that you will shower blessing upon blessing upon them so that they will one day know that you are the Almighty God.

Bless me, Heavenly Father, as I go about my day in service to you and my fellow man. Surround me with a hedge of guardian angels, so I may persevere in my desire to love and serve you. In the name of the Father, Son, and Holy Spirit. Amen.

REFLECTIONS

- *How can your pride hinder you in reaching others with the truth of God's Word?*

Please use the space below to write down any thoughts or comments you may have.

"May God Bless You,
As you live your Life for Christ,
Empowered by The Holy Spirit."

January 13

Psalm 118:14 NIV

[14] The Lord is my strength and my defense; he has become my Salvation.

Gracious Lord Jesus, through your infinite grace, you have extended unlimited mercy to me. I praise you, O Lord, that I can always come to you with the petitions of my heart and know that in your time, you will impart your blessings upon me. Thank you, Lord Jesus, for being my strength in times of physical weakness. Thank you, Lord Jesus, for being the rock of my faith when I am in spiritual decline.

Guide me along the path of righteousness as I seek your face in all that I do. Speak to my heart and soul as I share with others the love of my Savior. Let me not forget that I am one of God's children, created in your image, to reflect the life of Christ to the world around me. Bless me, O Lord, as I lean on you for the spiritual sustenance to grow in love, grace, and forgiveness. Help me to love others as you first loved me. In the name of Jesus, I pray. Amen.

REFLECTIONS

How has Christ, as the rock of your faith, helped you in times of spiritual need?

Please use the space below to write down any thoughts or comments you may have.

"May God Bless You,
As you live your Life for Christ,
Empowered by The Holy Spirit."

January 14

John 7:18 NIV.

[18] Whoever speaks on their own does so to gain personal glory, but he who seeks the glory of the one who sent him is a man of truth; there is nothing false about him.

O Holy Father, thank you for revealing the truth of your Word to me. Thank you for your divine revelation that is instrumental in applying your Word to my life. In your infinite wisdom, you sent your Son, Jesus Christ, to teach me how to live my life in faithful obedience to your teachings. Lord, let me be a vessel of Truth and fill me with the power of the Holy Spirit so I may live out my Christian life in the manner Christ did while He was walking among us.

Lord Jesus, as I seek to be faithful in my walk with you, my heart is troubled by the ways of the world. I am sad in my inability to resist Satan's temptations that do nothing but undermine the Word of God. Lord, provide me through the power of your name and with the guidance of the Holy Spirit, the courage and moral fortitude to preserve my faith and devotion to you. I ask these things in the name of the Father, Son, and Holy Spirit. Amen.

REFLECTIONS

In what ways do the temptations of the world hinder your relationship with Jesus Christ?

Please use the space below to write down any thoughts or comments you may have.

"May God Bless You,
As you live your Life for Christ,
Empowered by The Holy Spirit."

January 15

Psalm 108:13 NIV.

[13] With God we will gain the victory, and he will trample down our enemies.

Almighty and most gracious Redeemer, I give you thanks for the bountiful blessings of love and mercies you have so generously bestowed upon me. O Lord, it is through you and your redeeming grace that I seek your continued guidance for all my life challenges. Stay ever so close to me, so I may not deviate from the path you have ordained for my life. Provide me the guidance and wisdom to make the right choices as I endeavor to walk down the path of righteousness.

Lord, I know that I am a sinner who never stops sinning. Each day I have burdened you with the transgressions of my sins; sins for which you bore the penalty of death on the Cross of Calvary. Yet, despite my sins, you have extended an unending supply of grace and love to free me from their penalty. Thank you, dear Jesus, for coming into my heart and for the privilege of being in your presence.

Father, the forces of Satan are determined to wage a battle to turn me away from your will for my life. Protect me with a hedge of blessings so I may be victorious over the forces of evil. I lift your name in praise for all those that have not yet come to know you. I ask you to make your presence known to those that remain lost so they too may receive the blessings of Salvation. Hear my prayer, O Lord, that I may always be deserving of your countless benefits. Let me be forever faithful in extending your love to my fellow man. In the name of Jesus, I pray. Amen.

REFLECTIONS

What are some of the blessings God has given to you?

Please use the space below to write down any thoughts or comments you may have.

"May God Bless You,
As you live your Life for Christ,
Empowered by The Holy Spirit."

January 16

Romans 12:1 NIV.

[1] Therefore, I urge you, brothers, and sisters, in view of God's mercy, to offer your bodies as a living sacrifice, holy and pleasing to God---this is your true and proper worship.

O God of everlasting love, in your mercy, you generously provide all things I need. You know the needs of mine and the timing for which to provide for those needs. Let me be forever grateful for the mercies for which you have blessed my life.

Father, there are times when I cry out for the love and compassion of my fellow man, but no one hears me. There are times when my heartaches and the burdens I carry seem so overwhelming. And there are times when I forsake the promises of your Word and look to find the answers to my problems through contrived efforts. Lord, in those times, restore my spirit and my hope in your scriptures.

Lord Jesus, when opportunities for me to show love and compassion to my fellow man are at my doorstep, let me not fail to respond to the call. When I see the wounded plight of others, I often close my eyes. In those times, O Lord, open my heart, ears, and mind to do your will. In the name of the Father, Son, and Holy Spirit. Amen.

REFLECTIONS

What are some of the struggles in your life where you cry out to God for His help?

Please use the space below to write down any thoughts or comments you may have.

"May God Bless You,
As you live your Life for Christ,
Empowered by The Holy Spirit."

January 17

Acts 28:31 NIV.

[31] He proclaimed the kingdom of God and taught about the Lord Jesus Christ---with all boldness and without hindrance!

Praise to you, O Lord, the Christ, and my Savior. I thank you for allowing me to bring glory to your name and for lifting me out of the darkness and into the light of your Holy presence. Lord, there are times when my attitude is a hindrance in my earthly relationships. Situations that should be opportunities for personal growth fester with ungodly emotions that cause discord and turmoil. In those moments, Lord, calm my heart so I can be a peacemaker. When I fail to love my neighbors as you love me, open my eyes and heart so I can see the goodness in all people. When someone hurts me, and I want to react in hurtful ways, I need to curb my tongue and behavior to not lose the bridge of understanding and love.

Grant me the wisdom, my Lord, to always look to you for guidance down the path of righteousness so I may remain in your favor. Forgive, O Christ, when I fail in my attempts to live in obedience to your Word. Assure me of your eternal love and forgiveness so, through repentance, I may once again be in harmony with your will. In the precious name of Jesus. Amen.

REFLECTIONS

When confronted with anger or a poor attitude, how can you be a peacemaker?

Please use the space below to write down any thoughts or comments you may have.

"May God Bless You,
As you live your Life for Christ,
Empowered by The Holy Spirit."

January 18

Romans 13:12 NIV.

[12] The night is nearly over; the day is almost here. So, let us put aside the deeds of darkness and put on the armor of light.

O Lord, my Jehovah. You are my rock, the cornerstone of my faith. Lead me down the path to eternal happiness with you in Heaven. Lord, your children, face so many difficulties in life, so many obstacles to living out their devotion to you in faithful obedience to your Word. There are so many fears I encounter when I do not have complete trust in you.

O Christ, remove from me all thorns that hinder the growth of your presence in my life. Remove from me the clouds of darkness that impair my vision when I lose sight of the promises of your kingdom. Let me always remember the eternal security you made to love and protect me when doubt and fear consume me. Give me the peace to move forward in my life, confident of your love, grace, and forgiveness as I wrestle with the temptations instigated by Satan. Bind the forces of the world that attempt to influence me to deviate from your Word. Send your Holy angels to protect and guide me as I live my life in faithful obedience to you. In the precious name of Jesus. Amen.

REFLECTIONS

What thorns in your life are keeping you from complete joy in Christ?

Please use the space below to write down any thoughts or comments you may have.

"May God Bless You,
As you live your Life for Christ,
Empowered by The Holy Spirit."

January 19

2 Corinthians 4:2 NIV.

[2] Rather, we have renounced secret and shameful ways; we do not use deception, nor do we distort the word of God. On the contrary, by setting forth the truth plainly, we commend ourselves to everyone's conscience in the sight of God.

O Gracious Lord, my Redeemer, and Savior, your Holy Word, the Bible, is the manna of my soul, the source of all righteousness and wisdom from which I find your Truth. Lord, reveal to me through the spirit of knowledge and revelation a deeper understanding of your Word. Please help me better understand how to be a faithful witness to all those who have not yet come to know you. And may I more fully grasp your teachings.

Father, so many of your children, look for contemporary language and instructions that fit what they want to perceive as their Truth in today's world. They do not see the Truth as revealed in your Word. Lead me to understand the validity of your Word. Show me it is the same today as it was in the beginning. Let the world know that your Word cannot be modified or changed. Let the world know that language more inclusive of social behaviors, activities, or perceptions not grounded in your Scriptures' Truth are in error.

Father, forgive me when I try to adapt your Holy Scriptures to meet my personal needs. Rather than adjusting my behavior, thoughts, and lifestyle to the world, let me be devoted to the Truths revealed in your Word. In Christ's name, I pray. Amen.

REFLECTIONS

What beliefs have you modified to be your truth rather than God's truth?

Please use the space below to write down any thoughts or comments you may have.

"May God Bless You,
As you live your Life for Christ,
Empowered by The Holy Spirit."

January 20

Luke 12:3 NIV.

[3] What you have said in the dark will be heard in the daylight, and what you have whispered in the ear in the inner rooms will be proclaimed from the roofs.

O God of Faithfulness, Redeemer of my soul, praise to you for the opportunity to worship my almighty God. Lord, you have been so faithful in your love and devotion to me. No matter the circumstance I may be facing in life. No matter what adversity is tearing my heart apart, you are there to heal me, comfort me, and love me despite my sinful condition. For all your love and devotion, know how much I love you. Know how much I cherish the warmth of your arms. Know how much I long to hear the whisper of your voice guiding me through the dark valleys of my life.

O, Father, I adore you. I exalt you. I honor you by surrendering my stubborn will. Thank you, Lord, for your faithfulness, love, grace, and forgiveness. Lead me this day in a true spirit of worship and submission as I strive to be a faithful reflection of Christ in my daily walk. At the end of this day, my Lord, let me look back in retrospect and humbly proclaim, "I have been obedient to your will." In the name of Christ Jesus. Amen.

REFLECTIONS

How can you exalt God today, so He will know you love Him unconditionally?

Please use the space below to write down any thoughts or comments you may have.

"May God Bless You,
As you live your Life for Christ,
Empowered by The Holy Spirit."

January 21

Romans 5:17 NIV.

[17] For if, by the trespass of the one man, death reigned through that one man, how much more will those who receive God's abundant provision of grace and of the gift of righteousness reign in life through the one man, Jesus Christ!

Most merciful Jesus, you are indeed an amazing God. You hear my prayers. You know the disappointments I face in life. You know the challenges I encounter as I try my best to live out my life in faithful obedience to your Word. Yet, despite all my shortcomings, you continually demonstrate your love for me.

Thank you, Father, for all your blessings that touch my life. Thank you for the grace you always bestow upon me. Thank you for knowing my needs and coming to my rescue with the divine assistance needed to bring hope and peace into my life. But most of all, Father in Heaven, it is with a grateful heart that I sing praises to your name.

Thank you for sending your Son, Jesus Christ, for paying the penalty for my sins as the Sacrificial Lamb. I praise you, O Lord! I give all glory to your name. I recognize I am lost without you and surrender my will to your Lordship. And I ask that you hear my continuing pleas to forgive my sins and to keep me on the path of righteousness. These things I ask, in the name of the Father, Son, and Holy Spirit. Amen.

REFLECTIONS

Recognizing you are lost without God, how can you honor Him today?

Please use the space below to write down any thoughts or comments you may have.

"May God Bless You,
As you live your Life for Christ,
Empowered by The Holy Spirit."

January 22

Acts 26:16 NIV.

[16] Now get up and stand on your feet. I have appeared to you to appoint you as a servant and as a witness of what you have seen and will see of me.

Heavenly Father, what a joy it is to wake up this morning to what promises to be a beautiful day. No matter what the weather conditions, it is a day you have made. Lord, as my day unfolds, let me be a faithful reflection of your light so someone who does not know you as Lord and Savior may come to know you.

Father, the gift of Salvation is offered to all who believe in you. It is a gift where I can enjoy eternal life with you in Heaven. For those who do not know your Son, Jesus Christ as their personal Savior, knock loudly on the door of their hearts so they may hear you, and with willing hearts, may they open the door, so they too may have the joy of life in Christ? For it is through you I have power over sin. It is through you that true love can radiate from my life. And Lord, it is through you that no matter what difficulty I may be facing, I can find the peace and comfort to face the storms of life.

Let me not falter in my witness to others less I lead them astray. Let me be a shining example of your love so I may be an effective instrument in leading others to know you. In the name of Jesus, I pray. Amen.

REFLECTIONS

What would you share with someone to let them know how much God loves them?

Please use the space below to write down any thoughts or comments you may have.

"May God Bless You,
As you live your Life for Christ,
Empowered by The Holy Spirit."

January 23

Psalm 40:11-12 NIV.

[11] Do not withhold your mercy from me, Lord; may your love and faithfulness always protect me. [12] For troubles without number surround me; my sins have overtaken me, and I cannot see. They are more than the hairs of my head, and my heart fails within me.

Heavenly Father, once more, I come before you with a burden of sins, sins that have been weighing heavily upon my heart. For the sake of your Son, Jesus Christ, my Lord and Savior, bury my guilt and punishment deep in His wounds.

Lord, my heart is tormented by the sins I willfully commit, sins that not only grieve your heart but impede my relationship with you. Each day I am confronted with personal struggles that are difficult for me to face with humility, love, and compassion. Each day, I face obstacles in my life that test my faith and loyalty to you and your Word. Each day, I cry out with the pain of a broken heart. At day's end, I know I have failed you with careless and thoughtless acts toward others.

I see children of yours who are wallowing in the pain and confusion of this world. Forgive me, gracious Father, through your infinite mercy and unending grace, of my disobedience, of failing to live out my life faithfully in your service, and of failing to be a faithful witness of your Word to my fellow man. In Jesus' name, I pray. Amen.

REFLECTIONS

Think of something that makes you feel incredibly guilty. How can you be free of that guilt?

Please use the space below to write down any thoughts or comments you may have.

"May God Bless You,
As you live your Life for Christ,
Empowered by The Holy Spirit."

January 24

2 Corinthians 7:1 NIV.

[1] Therefore, since we have these promises, dear friends, let us purify ourselves from everything that contaminates body and spirit, perfecting holiness out of reverence for God.

Lord, you are the light of the world, my hope, and my Salvation. I praise you, Jesus, that you are always there to guide my footsteps and lead me down the path of righteousness. From the beginning, your children had the power of free choice, the ability to choose what paths in life they will follow. Lord, unfortunately, I often fail to follow the way that would keep me in your light and basking in the presence of the Holy Spirit. Forgive me, O Lord, for those times I departed from my walk with you, forgive me for being weak in spirit, and forgive me for neglecting the Word of God that is the source of my strength.

Lord, it is in you that the hope for mankind rests. Please help me find a way to live my life preparing for the day when you shall return. Let me live my life full of expectation and with complete faith, where the promises spoke of in the scriptures will come to pass. Let me not be consumed with doubts and fears that undermine the truth of your Word. Let me be complete with the knowledge and assurance that you are the Living God, the source of my Salvation, and my confidence in eternal life. I praise you, dear Jesus. My faith and hope will always be in you. Reveal to me daily the truth of your Word, so I may continue down the path of righteousness and be in complete obedience and submission to your will for my life. In the precious name of Jesus, I pray. Amen.

REFLECTIONS

When you are spiritually weak, what should you do?

Please use the space below to write down any thoughts or comments you may have.

"May God Bless You,
As you live your Life for Christ,
Empowered by The Holy Spirit."

January 25

2 Chronicles 1:11-12 NIV.

[11] God said to Solomon, "Since this is your heart's desire and you have not asked for wealth, possessions or honor, nor for the death of your enemies, and since you have not asked for a long life but for wisdom and knowledge to govern my people over whom I have made you king, [12] therefore wisdom and knowledge will be given you...

O God, Lord of the Universe, and ruler of all principalities, through you all things are known. Father, grant me the wisdom of discernment to see the purpose you have ordained for my life. In your mercy, show me the purpose of my life so I may faithfully serve you through my Lord and Savior, Jesus Christ. Father, I want to be passionate about helping you and bringing honor to you in all things I do. Please show me the path of righteousness so I will have no doubt which leads to your glorious kingdom.

O Lord, sometimes I do things that do not please you and weigh heavily upon your heart. Convict my heart, in the name of your Son, Jesus Christ, to always honor you by pursuing those things that will bring you joy. Lord, you know the motive of my heart, and you know the secrets I try to hide from you. Cleanse my heart, O Lord, from all impure thoughts, hidden agendas, and desires to subvert the teachings of your Word. Sometimes I am weak and fail in my efforts to follow you faithfully. When I do not have the courage, strength, and integrity to push aside my weaknesses and claim the power, and the conviction of your Word, fill me with the Holy Spirit. Let me be faithful in my walk with you. Let your purpose for my life always be before me so I may know all you desire of me. For as long as you are still with me and my eyes and heart are focused on you, I cannot fail. In Christ Jesus's name, I pray. Amen.

REFLECTIONS

Is there a hidden secret in your life you have been trying to hide from your family, friends, or God?

Please use the space below to write down any thoughts or comments you may have.

"May God Bless You,
As you live your Life for Christ,
Empowered by The Holy Spirit."

January 26

Luke 12:32-34 NIV.

[32] "Do not be afraid, little flock, for your Father has been pleased to give you the kingdom. [33] Sell your possessions and give to the poor. Provide purses for yourselves that will not wear out, a treasure in heaven that will never fail, where no thief comes near, and no moth destroys. [34] For where your treasure is, there your heart will be also. ...

Gracious Lord Jesus, heartache and suffering abound throughout the world among your people. Lord, hear my plea that somebody may bring comfort to each of your children in need. In lands far off and here at home, many of your children live in squalor conditions without the resources to meet their basic needs. Hear my plea that they will receive appropriate food, shelter, water, and healthcare. Lord, without these provisions, without the help of your earthly angels, without angels of mercy called into the ministry of service, your children would suffer. Give me the desire and compassion to reach out to those who are less fortunate by sharing the blessings and gifts you have so generously bestowed on me.

Father, I do not always understand why there is so much suffering among your children. Lord, wake me up with a spirit of renewal to serve with love those that cannot help themselves. Hear my prayer that they may be comforted through their trials and tribulations. Let me not forget, precious Jesus, that none of my wealth and belongings will ever earn me greater rewards with you. Please help me realize it is only through devotion to your Word and a life of faith and grace in and through you that will bring me eternal peace. Let my happiness be in the kingdom of Heaven. Amen.

REFLECTIONS

What can you give to help those who are less fortunate?

Please use the space below to write down any thoughts or comments you may have.

"May God Bless You,
As you live your Life for Christ,
Empowered by The Holy Spirit."

January 27

Galatians 5:16-17 NIV.

[16] So I say, walk by the Spirit, and you will not gratify the desires of the flesh. [17] For the flesh desires what is contrary to the Spirit, and the Spirit what is contrary to the flesh. They are in conflict with each other so that you are not to do whatever you want. ...

O God, the Father of my Salvation, I thank you for the garden of life, a garden you have given to me to cultivate and to nourish with the fruits of the Holy Spirit. Lord, you are a Master Pruner, the one that knows the branches in need of pruning. You are the one that knows which fruit needs to be brought forth in my life.

Father God, you have promised if I need anything, you will be faithful in your provision. Grant me the spirit of wisdom and revelation so I may know the fruit I must bring forth in my life. Bearing the fruit of righteousness and living a life devoted to service in your name is one of the most incredible blessings I could have. Extend to me the freedom of grace and mercies so I may extend the same to all those in need.

Lord, there are days when I find it difficult to love others as you have loved me. There are days when I am frustrated with life, full of anxiety, and cannot bring forth the fruit of the Holy Spirit to touch the lives of others. In those times, Lord, you have granted me forgiveness and understanding of my weaknesses, so I may not lose favor in your eyes. Help me, Lord, to always have the assurance of my Salvation no matter how often I may fail to reflect to others the love of Christ.

As I remember the garden of my life, Lord God, provide me with spiritual discernment to see the withering branches and wilting flowers in need of nourishment. Grant me then, my Lord, the spiritual food to cultivate and sustain their growth in the light of your love and endless mercies. Amen.

"May God Bless You,
As you live your Life for Christ,
Empowered by The Holy Spirit."

REFLECTIONS

💡 *Is there someone in your life who is hindering your ability to grow stronger in your faith?*

Please use the space below to write down any thoughts or comments you may have.

"May God Bless You,
As you live your Life for Christ,
Empowered by The Holy Spirit."

January 28

1 Corinthians 4:21 NIV.

[21] What do you prefer? Shall I come to you with a rod of discipline, or shall I come in love and with a gentle spirit?

Heavenly Father, it is often easy to take you for granted. It is easy to think the blessings I have received have come from my own doing rather than from your Divine Intervention. All too often, I get caught up in a me-cycle. I think what I have accomplished in life, the blessings I have received – physical, relational, and spiritual, have come about by acts of my doing. Father forgive me for being misguided. You are the source of all that is good in this world. You have provided me hope when I have known despair. You had fed me when I was hungry. You had met my financial needs when I was lacking. You had given me people to love and care for when I was lonely. And you had given me the gift of your love when I was spiritually spent and needed to have my faith restored.

Lord, all this you have provided to me because of your infinite love. O Lord, sometimes I fail to take the time to thank you for a life that has been richly blessed by having a personal relationship with you. Please forgive me for not always praising you and expressing gratitude for the blessings you have bestowed upon my life. In Christ's name, I pray. Amen.

REFLECTIONS

If God is the source of all that is good in this world, who is the source of evil?

Please use the space below to write down any thoughts or comments you may have.

"May God Bless You,
As you live your Life for Christ,
Empowered by The Holy Spirit."

January 29

2 Peter 1:3 NIV.

[3] His divine power has given us everything we need for a godly life through our knowledge of him who called us by his own glory and goodness.

Holy Jesus, all glory to you, my Christ, my Lord, and my Redeemer; blessed are you, the chosen One, sent from God the Father to be a light unto the world. Blessed are you, whom through the sacrifice of your life on the Cross of Calvary gave the gift of eternal life to all who believe in your name. Let me be a faithful child of yours, obedient to your Word, and fulfilling the call of discipleship to proclaim your Gospel to all the earth.

Father, empower me with the fruits of the Holy Spirit so I may recognize Divine Opportunities to share your Word. Give me the gift of articulation so I may touch listeners' hearts with your gifts of love, mercy, forgiveness, and grace. In your Son's precious name, hear my prayer. Amen.

REFLECTIONS

In what areas of your life have you shown a lack of faith in God?

Please use the space below to write down any thoughts or comments you may have.

"May God Bless You,
As you live your Life for Christ,
Empowered by The Holy Spirit."

January 30

James 3:17 NIV.

[17] But the wisdom that comes from heaven is first of all pure; then peace-loving, considerate, submissive, full of mercy and good fruit, impartial and sincere.

Praise to you, O Lord. You are the Fountain of Life. Your love is as vast as the heavens, and your mercies never cease. Thank you for the gifts of grace you have so generously bestowed upon me. Lord, I know there is a time and season for every righteous activity. Grant me the wisdom and spiritual discernment I need to know when to implement changes in my life. I need to make wise decisions that impact my welfare and your children's lives. Please help me in all I do to make responsible and mature choices that will further your kingdom on earth. In all I do, Lord Jesus, let me speak and react to others in a Spirit of love that promotes harmony and peace among your people.

Father, there are countless life choices I am called upon to make during my daily walk with you. Let me be a faithful follower of your Word. Let my actions and attitude toward others mirror the love and grace you have extended toward me. I know I can do all things with my faith and trust placed in you. Provide me, dear Lord, with the emotional, physical, and spiritual strength to weather all storms in life and to be victorious in my witnessing of your Word. Amen.

REFLECTIONS

When storms in your life are brewing? How can you calm their fury?

Please use the space below to write down any thoughts or comments you may have.

"May God Bless You,
As you live your Life for Christ,
Empowered by The Holy Spirit."

January 31

John 16:13 NIV.

[13] But when he, the Spirit of truth, comes, he will guide you into all the truth. He will not speak on his own; he will speak only what he hears, and he will tell you what is yet to come.

Glorious Father, in your Word, you speak of being obedient not only to your teachings but to civil authorities on this earth as well. Lord, all too often, I focus my attention primarily on things of this world. I obey man's laws because they hold more of an immediate consequence to my behavior. Father, enable me with an obedient heart to always uphold the righteous laws of man. Empower me to further your kingdom on earth by embracing the teachings of Christ in all I say and do. But Lord, let me always be mindful I am your creation.

Above all the laws of man, I must first be obedient to your Word because of the eternal consequences it holds for my soul. Fill me and guide me through the power of the Holy Spirit so I may be discerning in all matters of faith. Fill me with an awareness of your spiritual Truths and their application in my life. Fill me, O Lord, with a genuine desire to love and serve you through the same, Jesus Christ, my Lord. Amen.

REFLECTIONS

When confronted with embracing God's truth or man's law, what should you do?

Please use the space below to write down any thoughts or comments you may have.

"May God Bless You,
As you live your Life for Christ,
Empowered by The Holy Spirit."

February 1

Ephesians 1:3 NIV.

[3] Praise be to the God and Father of our Lord Jesus Christ, who has blessed us in the heavenly realms with every spiritual blessing in Christ.

O Lord, the Light of my life, give me the words this morning to sing songs of praise to your name and to proclaim your love and endless grace to all whose paths I cross today. I give you thanks, dear Father, for the opportunity to bless others through my witness and to receive blessings of love from you despite my sinful nature. Lead me, Lord, through all the dark valleys of life into the presence of your Abiding Love. Let me rejoice in the correct interpretation of your Word and be spiritually fed with the nourishment of your Holy Scriptures.

Grant me, I pray, the anointing of the Holy Spirit. Feed me, my Father in Heaven, with your Holy Sacraments and sustain me when my flesh is weak and when I cry out in hunger and thirst for your Living Water. Praise to you, O Christ, for your living sacrifice, and may I always remember to crucify myself daily to your glory. Amen.

REFLECTIONS

What does it mean to crucify yourself daily to Christ?

Please use the space below to write down any thoughts or comments you may have.

"May God Bless You,
As you live your Life for Christ,
Empowered by The Holy Spirit."

February 2

Hebrews 10:22 NIV.

[22] let us draw near to God with a sincere heart and with the full assurance that faith brings, having our hearts sprinkled to cleanse us from a guilty conscience and having our bodies washed with pure water.

Through your Son, Jesus Christ, my God, whom I love, I have tried to comprehend the magnitude of your love, but I have failed. Through the power of the Holy Spirit, I have wanted to be a faithful instrument of your Word. Again, I have been unable to.

O Lord, my God, the true magnitude of your love can only be obtained through your Son, Jesus Christ, who gave his life obediently for the sins of humanity. Instill in me, and all your children, thirst, and desire to live our lives in faithful obedience to your Word. When I am facing adversities in my walk with your Son, rattle my feet and let me stumble so I can get up secure in the grip of Christ. Let His love and assurance steady me as I rely on the power of the Holy Spirit for my guidance.

O God, let me be faithful in my love for you, ever seeking and always acknowledging your Son as Lord of my life. And when I find my heart crying out in despair, when I long to feel the love of your Son, remove from me the thistles and thorns that are strangling me so I may feel the warm embrace of His love. Bless me, my precious Lord, so I can be free to receive and enjoy the magnitude of your passion. Amen.

REFLECTIONS

What does it mean to have a thirst for living your life for Christ?

Please use the space below to write down any thoughts or comments you may have.

"May God Bless You,
As you live your Life for Christ,
Empowered by The Holy Spirit."

February 3

2 Corinthians 12:10 NIV.

[10] That is why, for Christ's sake, I delight in weaknesses, in insults, in hardships, in persecutions, in difficulties. For when I am weak, then I am strong.

Heavenly Father, Lord of my life, I give you thanks that you have given me the health and strength to begin another day in your service. Thank you for all the blessings and mercies you have extended to me. Many of them unwarranted, except through your grace. Each day, my Lord, there have been personal struggles where I have failed to cry out your name for your Divine Intervention. Each day, there have been problems I have struggled with where I have tried to calm myself or to ease my pain through efforts of my own totally fruitless efforts. Each day, I deal with issues that have been too painful or sorrow-filled for me to cope effectively. Lord, help me to realize I cannot cope with life issues.

I cannot overcome the pain and sorrow in my life without calling upon the Holy Spirit's presence to guide and comfort me. Lord, you are a mighty God, one that is ever-present and ever willing to reach out to your children with love, mercy, and unending compassion. Father, into your hands, I commend my life, thoughts, behaviors, and stubborn will. Help me, my dear Lord, to bow down in submission to your will for my life. Help me to surrender all those things that are impediments to my life in Christ. Lord, I cannot do these things on my own. I cannot succeed in my walk with you without your guiding hand. Show me, Lord Jesus, the path to peace and contentment so I will finally be free of the anguish and sorrow that consumes my life. In the name of the Father, Son, and Holy Spirit, anoint me with your blessings. Amen.

REFLECTIONS

- *We all have struggles in life. What are some of yours you would like to share with God?*

Please use the space below to write down any thoughts or comments you may have.

"May God Bless You,
As you live your Life for Christ,
Empowered by The Holy Spirit."

February 4

Romans 15:13 NIV.

[13] May the God of hope fill you with all joy and peace as you trust in him, so that you may overflow with hope by the power of the holy spirit.

My Lord, my God, I come before you today seeking your divine guidance and the Spirit of wisdom and revelation. As I walk with you today, O Lord, give me precious opportunities to be a faithful ambassador of your Word. I want to carry your message of hope and freedom to all those who are lost and do not know your Son, Jesus Christ. Let me faithfully reveal your Word to those in need of spiritual enlightenment. Free me of personal impediments that can impede the delivery of Christ's Gospel.

When my heart is filled with distractions, purge me of them. Grant me opportunities to share my faith. Let me be a bridge of understanding and hope to those that are troubled, confused, and need the comfort and love of your Son. Let me be a dedicated vessel of your love so I can be a blessing to others. Help me instill in them a thirst to have a personal relationship with your Son, Jesus Christ, so they may experience the joy I have found in Him. In your Son's precious name, I pray. Amen.

REFLECTIONS

How can you be a bridge of understanding to someone in need of God's love?

Please use the space below to write down any thoughts or comments you may have.

"May God Bless You,
As you live your Life for Christ,
Empowered by The Holy Spirit."

February 5

Matthew 23:12 NIV.

[12] For those who exalt themselves will be humbled, and those who humble themselves will be exalted.

Lord Jesus, I come before you with a humble spirit reconciled that I am by nature sinful and in need of your redemption. Father, if I am to be truthful, I often fail in my prayer life. In your Word, you have taught me to pray, not just in bad times but in good times as well. So often, my heart is overwhelmed with fears, anxieties, and frustrations that tear down my will to live my life for you. Lord, I need you. Help me to overcome life situations that keep me from coming before you in prayer. I want my time with you in prayer to be my top priority, from the moment I wake until I go to sleep. Forgive me of all the excuses I make, dear Jesus, for not faithfully reaching out to you in prayer for your divine love and guidance.

Help me, dear God! In my heart, I cry out for your love and guidance every moment of my life but fail to utter the words. I endure personal struggles alone, needlessly, because you have promised to always be with me. Wake me up, O Christ, to the love and open arms that you extended to me from the moment you died on the Cross of Calvary. In prayer, let me claim all your promises. In the name of Jesus Christ, my Lord and Savior, I pray. Amen.

REFLECTIONS

- *When you find yourself caught up in turmoil, what promises of God can you claim?*

Please use the space below to write down any thoughts or comments you may have.

*"May God Bless You,
As you live your Life for Christ,
Empowered by The Holy Spirit."*

February 6

Matthew 17:5 NIV.

[5] While he was still speaking, a bright cloud covered them, and a voice from the cloud said, "This is my Son, whom I love; with him, I am well pleased. Listen to him!"

Gracious Father in Heaven, give me the words to express to all those whose paths I cross today the joy of knowing Jesus Christ. Lord, let me be a beacon of light where every action of mine, every word I utter, and every thought I think reflects the truth of your Word and the glory of your Son, Jesus Christ. Through the Holy Spirit's power, reveal to me Divine Opportunities where I may share the love of Christ with my fellow man. Stir within me the words to say, the compassion to understand, and the heart to listen so I may be a faithful witness of your kingdom.

Bless me in all my endeavors that seek to reveal your love, forgiveness, and grace. Bless those whose lives I touch this day, that they may genuinely know your Son and the power of His redeeming blood. In all things, my God, let me sing praises of your kingdom and rejoice in the peace that comes when I place my life in your hands. Grant all these things in the name of the Father, Son, and Holy Spirit. Amen.

REFLECTIONS

What do you think a Divine Opportunity is? How can you use it to bless someone?

Please use the space below to write down any thoughts or comments you may have.

"May God Bless You,
As you live your Life for Christ,
Empowered by The Holy Spirit."

February 7

1 Timothy 6:12 NIV.

[12] Fight the good fight of the faith. Take hold of the eternal life to which you were called when you made your good confession in the presence of many witnesses.

Lord Jesus Christ, Son of God, have mercy on me. Lord, in your infinite compassion, you laid down your life on the Cross of Calvary as an eternal sacrifice for the sins of humanity. Father, you know and can see all things. I come before you as a sinner stripped bare of any falsehood that would cloak my presence before you. Forgive me, O Lord, of all the trespasses that have disgraced me and have offended my Heavenly Father.

Lord, you desire all your children to trust in you and to confess matters that weigh heavily upon their hearts. Grant me the honesty to examine my heart, my behaviors, and my thoughts so they may conform to the laws of your commandments. Enable me, dear Lord, to recognize my sins and to feel the guilt of my transgressions, so I may not become insensitive to those things that offend your Word. Please give me the courage and humility to confess all my sins so the absolution I receive may bring glory and honor to your Holy Name. Amen.

REFLECTIONS

What word best describes what absolution means?

Please use the space below to write down any thoughts or comments you may have.

"May God Bless You,
As you live your Life for Christ,
Empowered by The Holy Spirit."

February 8

Galatians 2:20 NIV.

[20] I have been crucified with Christ, and I no longer live, but Christ lives in me. The life I now live in the body, I live by faith in the Son of God, who loved me and gave himself for me.

Gracious God, Lord of the earth, and Lord of my life. Thank you for the seeds of goodness you have placed in my heart. Thank you for your numerous blessings that have touched each area of my life. Thank you for your abundant grace and mercies you have seen fit to bestow upon me despite my sinful nature.

Father, I am no longer of this world. When I accepted Christ into my heart, my old self died with Christ. No longer can I live in this body. Through Christ, who preserves me through the resurrection of His body, His blood, and through the power of the Holy Spirit, I am alive. Father, the Son of God, Christ Jesus, now lives in me. I am still a wretched sinner caught up in the sins of this world with the forces of Satan consistently exploiting my weaknesses to further his reign on this earth. Shield me, God of Mercy, with coats of armor and a hedge of protection so I may fend off the forces of evil and be victorious in my battles over sin. In the precious name of Jesus, I pray. Amen.

REFLECTIONS

What does it mean to be in Christ and no longer of this world?

Please use the space below to write down any thoughts or comments you may have.

"May God Bless You,
As you live your Life for Christ,
Empowered by The Holy Spirit."

February 9

Genesis 17:1 NIV.

[1] When Abram was ninety-nine years old, the Lord appeared to him and said, "I am God Almighty; walk before me faithfully and be blameless.

O Holy Father, thank you for revealing the truth of your Word to me. Thank you for your Divine Revelation is instrumental in applying your Word's Truth to my life. In your infinite wisdom, Father, you sent your Son, Jesus Christ, to teach me how to use your Word in my life. Lord, let me be a vessel of Truth and fill me with the power of the Holy Spirit so I may live out my Christian life in the manner Christ did while he was walking among us.

O Father, living out my Christian walk-in faithful obedience to Christ is an ongoing challenge. The lessons in your Word taught by Christ are incredible examples of love and faithfulness. Yet, in my fallen state, being faithful in applying the teachings of Christ in my life and walking the road of the faithful is one in which I often fail. O Lord, let me not be discouraged in my Christian walk but lift me when I stumble and grant me the courage and desire to keep my heart on the will of Christ so I may bring glory and honor to your kingdom. Amen.

REFLECTIONS

Can you be a vessel of God's truth if the Holy Spirit is not in you?

Please use the space below to write down any thoughts or comments you may have.

"May God Bless You,
As you live your Life for Christ,
Empowered by The Holy Spirit."

February 10

Romans 12:3 NIV.

[3] For by the grace given me, I say to every one of you: Do not think of yourself more highly than you ought, but rather think of yourself with sober judgment, in accordance with the faith God has distributed to each of you.

Awaken my soul, O Christ, my Lord, and Risen King, and let me go forth in joyful song as I proclaim the wonders of your kingdom. Rescue me from the depths of despair so I may understand the majesty of your grace. Instill in me a passion for reaching out to unbelievers in Christ. Let me, through the power of the Holy Spirit, be a vessel that leads them to a personal relationship with their Savior, Jesus Christ.

Lead me to those that are lost and help me to be an effective witness who demonstrates the power of your love. Extend to them the same grace, the same forgiveness, and the same mercies you have bestowed upon all your children. Speak to their hearts' needs and minister to their physical, emotional, and spiritual needs so they may have no doubt you are the God of all creation.

Bless them with faith like a child's, open to your love with a trust that defies human understanding. Fill them with the anointing of the Holy Spirit so they may bear fruits in their lives that spur them onto love and service in your name. Bless them, Lord Jesus, as they live their lives for you. In your name, I pray. Amen.

REFLECTIONS

- *Describe a situation in your life where you failed to extend grace to someone in need.*

Please use the space below to write down any thoughts or comments you may have.

"May God Bless You,
As you live your Life for Christ,
Empowered by The Holy Spirit."

February 11

John 15:4 NIV.

[4] Remain in me, as I also remain in you. No branch can bear fruit by itself; it must remain in the vine. Neither can you bear fruit unless you remain in me.

Blessed Lord Jesus, your Word says you want to live within me, within my heart and soul. Fill me, Lord, with the gifts of the Holy Spirit so I may be able to magnify your love and grace to the world around me. Father, by your power, through your love and unending grace, you have lifted the clouds of doom and darkness from my life. Thank you for your promises, dear Jesus, that I will not face a hopeless, worthless, or meaningless future as your child. Thank you for your blessings, O Faithful God.

Because I belong to you, O Christ, you have saved me from a fruitless life. You have saved me from a life of meaningless words, empty promises, sinful thoughts, unmet goals, dissatisfying work, and choices that take me down the road of discouragement. Thank you for bringing me the personal fulfillment that can only come from a life of oneness with you.

Father, for all the blessings you have extended to me, I praise you that I will never face a moment where I will not enjoy your gifts when I am in Christ. I pray you will touch my heart and mind with the absolute assurance of my abundant blessings. Praise to you, my Lord. Amen.

REFLECTIONS

How would you describe a fruitless life?

Please use the space below to write down any thoughts or comments you may have.

*"May God Bless You,
As you live your Life for Christ,
Empowered by The Holy Spirit."*

February 12

Ephesians 6:13 NIV.

[13] Therefore put on the full armor of God, so that when the day of evil comes you may be able to stand your ground, and after you have done everything, to stand.

O Lord God, the Alpha, and the Omega bless me with the spirit of wisdom and revelation so I may know the truth of your Word. Give me a thirst and hunger for your Word that creates a desire to draw closer to my Lord Jesus. Fill me with the power of the Holy Spirit so I may have upon my chest the Shield of Armor that will protect me from all adversities born of Satan. Grant me the moral compass to live my life for you. Grant me a heartfelt desire to purge my sinful nature of all the impurities that dishonor your name.

Help me to remember I am your child, created in your image, to reflect the light of your Son, Jesus Christ. Fill me, I pray, with a passion for loving my fellow man and showing compassion for those in need. Most of all, Heavenly Father, let me remember the cost of my Salvation, the life of your precious Son, Jesus Christ. Thank you, Father, for sustaining me in times of weakness. Thank you for the courage to live my life for you. Thank you for your daily blessings. Let me always remember that through your Son, Jesus Christ, I can do all things Amen.

REFLECTIONS

How can a pang of hunger for God's Word help you in your relationship with Christ?

Please use the space below to write down any thoughts or comments you may have.

"May God Bless You,
As you live your Life for Christ,
Empowered by The Holy Spirit."

February 13

Isaiah 51:6 NIV.

[6] Lift up your eyes to the heavens, look at the earth beneath; the heavens will vanish like smoke, the earth will wear out like a garment, and its inhabitants die like flies. But my Salvation will last forever, my righteousness will never fail.

Most Merciful God, thank you for being a God of love. Thank you for being the Great Comforter when I find myself caught up in a tangle of confusion and uncertainty. Without you, O Lord, my life would be meaningless and void of the love that brings happiness and contentment to my life.

Lord, there are many of your children who do not know you as their personal savior. Some of them flat out reject you. Some of them call Christians hypocrites. And some of them wage personal wars against those that believe in your redemptive power. Forgive them, O Christ! Awaken within their souls the truth of your Word. Guide them through the storms of life that pull them further and further away from your love. Let me be a source of comfort and an effective witness of your Gospel to everyone that crosses my path,

O Lord, how I love you. I sing songs of praise and adoration to your Holy Name. I surrender my will and give my life over to you. Sustain me, my Savior, and lift me when the pits of darkness threaten. Be my constant source of light and Truth, so I may always glorify your name. In Christ's precious name, I pray. Amen.

REFLECTIONS

What would you consider a pit of darkness?

Please use the space below to write down any thoughts or comments you may have.

"May God Bless You,
As you live your Life for Christ,
Empowered by The Holy Spirit."

February 14

1 John 1:7 NIV.

[7] But if we walk in the light, as he is in the light, we have fellowship with one another, and the blood of Jesus, his Son, purifies us from all sin.

O Lord, give me the words to express love to my fellow man. Give me the heart to love others as you first loved me. Give me the patience to cope with adversities that threaten my Christian witness before others. Grant me, my Father in Heaven, a devotion to obediently following the teachings of your Word.

Let me be a beacon of light as I go about my day. I want to be bold by proclaiming that I am your child, your warrior, and ambassador of your living grace — poured out upon all those who seek and who need the truth of your Word. Let me be steadfast in my love for you as I strive to fulfill Christ's Great Commission. Lift me, O Lord, when I stumble off the path of righteousness. Grant me the forgiveness paid for by my Savior, Jesus Christ, as I look to my Father in Heaven with a grateful heart. In Jesus's precious name, I pray. Amen.

REFLECTIONS

Say one word that can express God's love to your fellow man.

Please use the space below to write down any thoughts or comments you may have.

"May God Bless You,
As you live your Life for Christ,
Empowered by The Holy Spirit."

February 15

Acts 15:8-9 NIV.

[8] God, who knows the heart, showed that he accepted them by giving the Holy Spirit to them, just as he did to us. [9] He did not discriminate between us and them, for he purified their hearts by faith.

O Father in Heaven, worthy is the Lamb, the Son of God, who sacrificed His life on the Cross of Calvary for the forgiveness of my sins. Thank you for your endless blessings and spiritual gifts. I pray that through the power of the Holy Spirit, they will enable me to live out my life in faithful obedience to your Word.

Take my life, O Lord, and purge from it all impurities that tarnish my witness before your kingdom. Let me be a faithful witness, not only to my brothers and sisters in Christ but to those who are of this world and who have not yet come to know the love of their Savior, Jesus Christ. Help me remember that Christ has paid the price; the cost of my Salvation paid for by the sacrifice of His blood. Let me always walk in the embrace of His love, feeling, and knowing the assurance that in Christ, I can do all things. Amen.

REFLECTIONS

If God loves you, even though you are a sinner, can Satan rob you of God's love and the gift of Salvation?

Please use the space below to write down any thoughts or comments you may have.

"May God Bless You,
As you live your Life for Christ,
Empowered by The Holy Spirit."

February 16

Luke 10:27-28 NIV.

[27] He answered, "'Love the Lord your God with all your heart and with all your soul and with all your strength and with all your mind; and 'love your neighbor as yourself.'" [28] "You have answered correctly," Jesus replied. "Do this and you will live."

O Father, in your Word, you speak of the true nature of love. As Jesus walked this earth, He proclaimed your love for all of humanity. Hear my prayer, dear Lord, that I as your child shall embrace the essence of your love for all those whose paths I cross today. Help me to be willing to reach out to those I do not know so I can shower upon them the same kind of love Christ bestowed upon me. Let me not forget the greatest act of love mankind has ever known, the sacrifice of your Son, Jesus Christ, on the Cross of Calvary.

Thank you for your endless blessing that gives me hope and assurance that all who trust in your Son will spend eternity with Him. Fill me with the power of the Holy Spirit so I may be able to go about your calling to serve others with love, grace, and forgiveness. And may I truly bring forth the fruits of the Holy Spirit as I live my life in faithful devotion to you. Amen.

REFLECTIONS

What scripture verse best describes the true nature of love? What one word describes God's Word for love?

Please use the space below to write down any thoughts or comments you may have.

"May God Bless You,
As you live your Life for Christ,
Empowered by The Holy Spirit."

February 17

Romans 5:9 NIV.

[9] Since we have now been justified by his blood, how much more shall we be saved from God's wrath through him!

Precious Lord Jesus, when you lived your life on earth, you brought joy into the hearts of multitudes who heard your Word. Your Word took the message of comfort and love to those whose hearts were yearning for hope. Praise to you, O Christ, for in and through your name, the wrath of God has been spared. As I go about my day, let me remember the sacrifice of your blood as the only atonement needed to forgive my sins. But also, let me remember the need for repentance from my sinful nature so I can finally strip myself bare of the yoke of Satan that binds me to the ways of this world.

Lord, there are times when I wonder if those who fail to repent from their sins could ever enter the gates of heaven. I know because of my sinful nature; I am doomed to continue to sin. I also know you are a God of love and infinite mercies. You are a God that knows the hearts of your children and whether they are truly sincere in living their lives for you. There are those I know whose salvation and whether I will see them in heaven will come to pass.

This troubles me, O Lord, and so I petition you with an Intercessory Prayer, that if their hearts genuinely love you, you may see fit to allow them to enjoy eternal life with you. Only you know their hearts and if they embrace the truth of your Word. Only you know if they have been living their lives faithfully as a reflection of Christ by following your Word. And so, I ask for your will to be done. In your name, I pray. Amen.

REFLECTIONS

How can you bring joy into the hearts of multitudes?

Please use the space below to write down any thoughts or comments you may have.

"May God Bless You,
As you live your Life for Christ,
Empowered by The Holy Spirit."

February 18

2 Corinthians 12:9 NIV.

[9] But he said to me, "My grace is sufficient for you, for my power is made perfect in weakness." Therefore, I will boast all the more gladly about my weaknesses, so that Christ's power may rest on me.

O Most Gracious God, I come humbly before your Lordship to seek your forgiveness for all my sins. In the name of your Son, Jesus Christ, wipe my slate clean. And through the power of the Holy Spirit, may I rise above the sins of this world so I may live each day of my life consecrated to service in your name. Grant me the spirit of wisdom and revelation so I may continually be aware of this world's demonic spirits. Keep them from tearing me from the hedge of protection your love provides.

Lift me, O Lord, when I am weak and in need of your strength. Bless and anoint me with the power of the Holy Spirit, so I may always find the strength and love in my heart to live my life in faithful obedience to your Word. When I wallow in the despair of this world, awaken me to a new joy found by living my life according to the Truth of your Holy Word. In the precious name of Jesus, I pray. Amen.

REFLECTIONS

What demonic spirits are keeping you from drawing closer to Jesus?

Please use the space below to write down any thoughts or comments you may have.

"May God Bless You,
As you live your Life for Christ,
Empowered by The Holy Spirit."

February 19

Luke 11:34 NIV.

[34] Your eye is the lamp of your body. When your eyes are healthy your whole body also is full of light. But when they are unhealthy your body also is full of darkness.

O Lord, among the names you are known by, you are also known as the Great Comforter. You are the one in whom I can find solace from those things that consume me with worry and create anxiety and fear within me. Free me, Lord, in your name, from all that causes me to be in despair. Free me from all earthly illnesses. Those that are physical, emotional, and mental, that sometimes can cause me to lose faith and bind me to the forces of Satan.

Lord, in your name, I claim freedom from all things of this world that can separate me from unity with you. Let me be strong in spirit, firm in devotion, and confident of the assurance of your Word that all things work together for those that place their trust in you. I ask all this in the name of your Son, Jesus Christ. Amen.

REFLECTIONS

Is there something in your life causing you so much despair that you would like God to help you through?

Please use the space below to write down any thoughts or comments you may have.

"May God Bless You,
As you live your Life for Christ,
Empowered by The Holy Spirit."

February 20

Luke 21:34 NIV.

[34] "Be careful, or your hearts will be weighed down with carousing, drunkenness and the anxieties of life, and that day will close on you suddenly like a trap.

Gracious Lord, you have given me another day to live my life for you. Despite my sinful nature, you see the blood of your Son, Jesus Christ, and still, love me. How incredible is your love! O, God, when my mood is downcast and I struggle to cope with life circumstances, you lift me and wrap your arms around me, and through faith, I find peace and contentment. What a precious gift your love is to me.

Help me, Father, as I share even a small measure of your love for me with my family, neighbors, and strangers. Fill my heart with an earnest desire to always show love, grace, and forgiveness. And when I falter in my witness, grant me forgiveness, and beckon me once again to live out my faith in obedience to your Word. In Christ's name, I pray. Amen.

REFLECTIONS

- *Living for Christ can be a challenge. When the challenge gets tough, what can you do?*

Please use the space below to write down any thoughts or comments you may have.

"May God Bless You,
As you live your Life for Christ,
Empowered by The Holy Spirit."

February 21

Psalm 46:1 NIV.

[1] God is our refuge and strength, an ever-present help in trouble.

Blessed Father, Lord of my Life and Redeemer of my soul, my heart sings songs of praise, joy, and delight as I begin this day in your Word. Thank you for the blessing of Christian brothers and sisters in Christ who live their lives by faith and, through their witness, provide benefits beyond human measure. Grant me the grace and love to be a blessing to others as I go forth this day living my life for you. Let me be offense-proof so my witness may not be compromised or stained by others' actions manipulated by the evil one. Let me be a force of strength, wearing the coat of armor so I may prevail in my walk with Christ.

There is no greater honor in my life than serving you. I struggle at times, I must admit, to contain my frustrations with those that offend me. I know there are times I frustrate others as well. I am not perfect and cannot cover up the facts of my grievous sins. When I am consumed with myself, send your Holy Spirit to guide and redirect me onto the path of righteousness. Restore my heart with love and compassion for my fellow man. In your Son's precious name, I pray. Amen.

REFLECTIONS

- *What does it mean to be offense-proof? How can that help you in your witness to others?*

Please use the space below to write down any thoughts or comments you may have.

"May God Bless You,
As you live your Life for Christ,
Empowered by The Holy Spirit."

February 22

John 8:44 NIV.

[44] You belong to your father, the devil, and you want to carry out your father's desires. He was a murderer from the beginning, not holding to the truth, for there is no truth in him. When he lies, he speaks his native language, for he is a liar and the father of lies.

O Most Merciful Father, hear my plea for spiritual sustenance. Fill me with the power of the Holy Spirit, so I may live my life according to your will. Teach me the ability to hear your voice and whisper so I will have no doubt you are my Creator. Free me from self-talk that is from the devil who uses his wits to confuse and mislead me. Let me be guided by the truth of your Word and the power of the Holy Spirit so I may bear the fruits you desire from me. Give me the peace and assurance of your Word as I go forth in your kingdom to spread the Good News of Jesus Christ.

Lord, you know the plight of your children. There are so many who get caught up in dishonesty and lies that bring dismay to your heart. Father, I want to be honest and truthful, so I may faithfully reflect the life of Christ. Why I let myself succumb to these sins, I do not know. I can blame it on other people who influence me in ways that go contrary to your Word. I can say the Devil made me do it. But the Truth is, while I am constantly bombarded by Satan, I am responsible for my choices. I can choose to either dishonor you or honor you by all I say and do. Help me Father. Let me always embrace Truth and righteousness, so I set an example that brings glory to your name. Bless me now and forever as I do my best to honor you. In the name of the Father, Son, and Holy Spirit. Amen.

REFLECTIONS

Describe self-talk that hinders your relationship with Christ.

Please use the space below to write down any thoughts or comments you may have.

"May God Bless You,
As you live your Life for Christ,
Empowered by The Holy Spirit."

February 23

Luke 16:13 NIV.

[13] "No one can serve two masters. Either you will hate the one and love the other, or you will be devoted to the one and despise the other. You cannot serve both God and money."

Gracious God, please forgive me for my selfish desires in this world of endless materialistic goods. Let me go out among my neighbors and brothers and sisters in Christ and bless them with gifts of food, shelter, and water. Let me learn to live with a loving heart, free of ulterior motives, and with a tendency to have expectations in return for the gifts I give. Let me always remember the Words of Christ to do unto others as I would have them to do unto me.

And Father, let me be faithful in the giving to my local church. Let me provide the financial support so your church on earth will prosper according to your will. Thank you, Lord, for coming into my heart and for blessing me with the gifts of the Holy Spirit. Let me be a blessing each day to those whose lives are in need. Amen.

REFLECTIONS

- *Are there selfish desires of yours that keep you from faithfully living your life for Christ?*

Please use the space below to write down any thoughts or comments you may have.

"May God Bless You,
As you live your Life for Christ,
Empowered by The Holy Spirit."

February 24

1 John 5:4-5 NIV.

[4] for everyone born of God overcomes the world. This is the victory that has overcome the world, even our faith. [5] Who is it that overcomes the world? Only the one who believes that Jesus is the Son of God.

O Christ, my Lord and Savior, you know the condition of my heart, the yearning to serve you and to be obedient to your Word. Father, I ask your blessing upon me this day to accomplish your will for my life. Lord, I do not want to fail in my walk with you. I want to be able to finish my day and rejoice in my victory over Satan. Each day, I look back over the challenges life has put in front of me. I want to be able to say, "Lord, today I have been victorious over sin, and I praise you for being beside me as I faced the temptations of the world."

Only through you, O Lord, and the power of the Holy Spirit, will I have the strength to live my life for you and to be victorious in my walk with you. Grant me the strength each day, so I can be a beacon of hope and light to others who struggle in their walk with you. In Christ's precious name, I pray. Amen.

REFLECTIONS

Why do you think it is so difficult to be obedient to God's Word?

Please use the space below to write down any thoughts or comments you may have.

"May God Bless You,
As you live your Life for Christ,
Empowered by The Holy Spirit."

February 25

Matthew 15:32 NIV.

[32] Jesus called his disciples to him and said, "I have compassion for these people; they have already been with me three days and have nothing to eat. I do not want to send them away hungry, or they may collapse on the way."

O Lamb of God, Father of creation, Lord of the Universe, and the Savior who died for my sins, let the power of your Holy Spirit permeate my heart. Let me go about the task of fulfilling your Great Commission. Let me reach out to my neighbors, family, and strangers in my midst with the good news of your Son, Jesus Christ. Let me always remember I have a sacred duty as a Christian to be a light unto those who are lost and welcome them into the family of believers with love, forgiveness, and mercy so your kingdom on earth may grow.

Grant me the love of Christ as I go about your calling to serve all people. Let me help them regardless of their social status, race, sexual orientation, belief system, relationship with you, or position in life. Let me glorify your name as I exalt it throughout the world. Amen.

REFLECTIONS

How do you love someone whose belief system is contrary or different from yours?

Please use the space below to write down any thoughts or comments you may have.

"May God Bless You,
As you live your Life for Christ,
Empowered by The Holy Spirit."

February 26

Job 2:3 NIV.

[3] Then the Lord said to Satan, "Have you considered my servant Job? There is no one on earth like him; he is blameless and upright, a man who fears God and shuns evil. And he still maintains his integrity, though you incited me against him to ruin him without any reason."

Father in Heaven, in your Word, you call upon me to forgive others as you have forgiven me. Lord, it is often difficult to see beyond my pain and disappointment to show the same love and grace to others that you so freely bestow upon me. Because of my fallen human condition, I often find myself caught up in retribution and anger that consumes and renders me incapable of forgiving those who offended me.

I know that is not how you want me to live my life. I know I am no different from others who are so consumed with anger and frustration that it causes them, and me, to lash out at others with unspeakable words that are demeaning, hurtful, and offensive to your Holy Name. Help me Father. Take control of my foul mouth and despicable acts that are ungodly and downright mean. Cleanse me from all evil spirits that impede my relationship with my Lord and Savior, Jesus Christ.

And, Lord, free me from the forces of Satan that bind me to the ways of the world. And through the power of the Holy Spirit, grant me peace, love, and a forgiving heart so I can be a true reflection of your Son, Jesus Christ. Amen.

REFLECTIONS

Why do we, as children of God, have a fallen and sinful human nature?

Please use the space below to write down any thoughts or comments you may have.

"May God Bless You,
As you live your Life for Christ,
Empowered by The Holy Spirit."

February 27

Matthew 25:35-36 NIV.

[35] For I was hungry, and you gave me something to eat, I was thirsty, and you gave me something to drink, I was a stranger and you invited me in, [36] I needed clothes and you clothed me, I was sick, and you looked after me, I was in prison and you came to visit me.

Loving God, in your infinite compassion, you see the needs of the world you have created. You see the needs of those that are hungry and without shelter and medical care. You see the needs of those suffering from physical and emotional ailments and who cry out to you to restore their health. And you know the heartache and despair of those who are in jails and prisons across our country. Father, these too are your children, children who are lonely and away from those they love. Give those in jails and prisons the peace and assurance they need to find the inner strength and courage to endure their trials and survive their imprisonment.

Praise to you, O God, for giving your children the capacity to fulfill the needs of those who are in need. As your Son, Jesus Christ did during his ministry on earth, let me be the face of Christ so I can minister to those whose hearts are heavy and who feel there is no hope. Move me to live my life in faithful obedience to your Word so, through the power of the Holy Spirit and your love, grace, and forgiveness, I may indeed reflect the life of Christ. Amen.

REFLECTIONS

When you look around the world, what are some of the needs you see?

Please use the space below to write down any thoughts or comments you may have.

"May God Bless You,
As you live your Life for Christ,
Empowered by The Holy Spirit."

February 28

Revelation 2:7 NIV.

[7] Whoever has ears, let them hear what the Spirit says to the churches. To the one who is victorious, I will give the right to eat from the tree of life, which is in the paradise of God.

In your ministry on earth, Precious Jesus, you demonstrated the power of our Almighty God by rising from the dead individuals who died a physical death. Help me remember that you restored life to those who place their trust and faith in you through your crucifixion and resurrection. Praise to you, O Lord, for this gift of Salvation and the gift of eternal life.

Lord, I thank you for my spiritual gifts. I thank you for revealing how I can use them to serve my fellow man and bring glory to your kingdom. Forgive me when I fail to use them to your glory. Forgive me when I allow Satan to use his evil influences to drag me into a pit of hedonistic sexual perversions and self-gratifications. I can do better than that, my Lord.

Let me be mindful that I am a child of God who is responsible for my choices. Guide me back on the path of righteousness so I may once again bring happiness to your heart. Let me show you that I can soar like an eagle, high above any mountain top, and be able to shout out with a heart of fiery passion that I am your child and can conquer all things through Christ Jesus. In the name of your Son, and empowered by the Holy Spirit. Amen.

REFLECTIONS

What does the gift of Salvation mean to you?

Please use the space below to write down any thoughts or comments you may have.

"May God Bless You,
As you live your Life for Christ,
Empowered by The Holy Spirit."

March 1

Matthew 4:23 NIV.

[23] Jesus went throughout Galilee, teaching in their synagogues, proclaiming the good news of the kingdom, and healing every disease and sickness among the people.

My Lord, my God, you alone understand the mysteries of life. You know the afflictions that harm your children and the pain in the hearts of loved ones dealing with loss or sadness they cannot control. Hear my prayer, faithful Jesus. So many of your children are coping with afflictions that compromise their physical and mental health. They often face these calamities with no loved one to support them through their ordeal. They cry out in despair for someone to help them through the darkness so they do not have to do it alone.

Awaken in them, O Christ, with the spirit of wisdom and revelation. Let them hear your soft whisper that can assure them that you are always with them. Let them feel the depth of your love and presence, so hope can once again be restored to their lives.

And through the Holy Spirit, let your grace and divine healing flow through the bodies of all those afflicted with injuries, disease, or other afflictions that harm their health. And may they and their loved ones be healed in your name so they can see and realize the power and grace of the Almighty God. Please give all your children the comfort they need as they wait expectantly for their prayers to be answered. Amen.

REFLECTIONS

What affliction is going on today that is causing distress in the lives of God's children?

Please use the space below to write down any thoughts or comments you may have.

"May God Bless You,
As you live your Life for Christ,
Empowered by The Holy Spirit."

March 2

1 Chronicles 16:9-10 NIV.

[9] Sing to him, sing praise to him; tell of all his wonderful acts. [10] glory in his Holy Name; let the hearts of those who seek the Lord rejoice.

Father God, my heart sings songs of praise, recognizing your blessings are in abundance. Through the power of the Holy Spirit, let me be a blessing to those whose paths I cross today. Let me pray for those that are lost or those that reject your saving grace. In this world, O Christ, so many of your children succumb to depravity and choices that can alter their lives forever.

It does not have to be this way, Lord, because all life can be renewed in you. When darkness surrounds me, I often fall into the deep despair of depression. I cannot see the light of hope because the walls around me are closing in. I am not the only child of yours that faces this despair. We all need your constant presence in our lives. We all need to feel the warmth and comfort of your love. Free all of us from the tyranny of Satan. Free us from the shackles that bind us to the ways of the world. Let us rely on the Holy Spirit to find the strength and courage to persevere under the most challenging trials.

And Father, grant me the serenity to move about my day, free of any distractions that will cause me to lose focus of your calling to bless those around me. You are the one true God. You alone can work through your servants to accomplish miracles and cause the unbelievable to happen. Let me be a dedicated vessel of your love, Truth, and grace as I minister to those that are lost and confused. In Christ Jesus's name, I pray. Amen.

REFLECTIONS

Are there distractions in your life that can cause you to lose focus on God's calling?

Please use the space below to write down any thoughts or comments you may have.

"May God Bless You,
As you live your Life for Christ,
Empowered by The Holy Spirit."

March 3

Romans 6:23 NIV.

[23] For the wages of sin is death, but the gift of God is eternal life in Christ Jesus our Lord.

Gracious Father, thank you for the precious gift of life, the time I have on this earth to prepare my heart and mind for the day you welcome me into your heavenly kingdom. Lord, you know my failures, the scope of my sinful nature, and how often I have grieved your heart. Praise to you, O Lord, for your precious gift of grace that has shielded me from tragedies and heartaches beyond my ability to bear. I give glory to you, my God, for your endless love and the gift of Eternal Life, through your Son, Jesus Christ, my Lord, and Savior. Amen.

REFLECTIONS

Describe the scope of your sinful nature. Be honest with yourself.

Please use the space below to write down any thoughts or comments you may have.

March 4

2 Corinthians 1:6 NIV.

[6] If we are distressed, it is for your comfort and Salvation; if we are comforted, it is for your comfort, which produces in you patient endurance of the same sufferings we suffer.

Lord, My God, you are the Great Comforter, the one whom I should turn to when I find myself in distress. Thank you, Lord, for wiping away my tears, for bringing joy into situations that seem hopeless. There are days, my Lord Jesus, where I find myself held hostage by sins that permeate my life and cling to me until I once again recognize the power of your redeeming blood. Forgive me for being weak in spirit. Forgive me of all my transgressions. While enslaved to the world, I was hoping you could grant me the courage to look to you as my refuge, my rock, and my strength until I reflect the likeness of your Son, Jesus Christ. I sing praises to your name and rejoice in your Son, Jesus Christ, as my Savior. Amen.

REFLECTIONS

When you are weak in spirit, is God still with you?

Please use the space below to write down any thoughts or comments you may have.

*"May God Bless You,
As you live your Life for Christ,
Empowered by The Holy Spirit."*

March 5

Psalm 96:13 NIV.

[13] Let all creation rejoice before the Lord, for he comes, he comes to judge the earth. He will judge the world in righteousness and the peoples in his faithfulness.

Most merciful God, your glory and the magnitude of your creation unfold each day of my life. Thank you for your endless mercies, unconditional grace, and precious love that sustains me in times of joy and in times of despair. Father, when the day of my judgment comes, please remember that although my sinful nature often reared its ugly side, I was still perfect in your sight. Please remember that I tried my best to be faithful in my walk as a disciple of Jesus Christ. And please remember that despite all my failings, my love for you could never be more sincere.

You are the Lord of the Universe, the Alpha and Omega, and the Lord of my heart and mind. I bow before you and submit my stubborn will to be shaped by the power of the Holy Spirit. Help me be a faithful and loving servant, obedient to your plans for my life, and a true disciple of my Lord and Savior, Jesus Christ. Amen.

REFLECTIONS

Can your stubborn will be shaped for something good by the Holy Spirit?

Please use the space below to write down any thoughts or comments you may have.

"May God Bless You,
As you live your Life for Christ,
Empowered by The Holy Spirit."

March 6

Psalm 86:2-3 NIV.

[2] Guard my life, for I am faithful to you; save your servant who trusts in you. You are my God; [3] have mercy on me, Lord, for I call to you all day long.

Gracious Father, in faith, will I walk through the dark valleys of my life, secure in the knowledge of your Word that I will receive the grace to sustain me in my darkest days through faith. My heart is encouraged to serve you and to resist Satan in all his earthly forms. No longer will I suffer needlessly because now, as a believer in Christ, I can do all things. Praise to you, O Lord, as I magnify your name and give daily praises of thanksgiving for all the love you have bestowed upon me. Grant me the insight and love of your Word to guide me as I place my trust in you. In Christ Jesus's name, I pray. Amen.

REFLECTIONS

- *Describe one of the darkest days in your life and how God helped you through it.*

Please use the space below to write down any thoughts or comments you may have.

March 7

Psalm 92:4 NIV.

[4] For you make me glad by your deeds, Lord; I sing for joy at what your hands have done.

O Holy Father, as a new day begins, instill in me the gifts of the Holy Spirit. Allow them to empower me to show the love and grace I need to be a loving ambassador of your Word. Let me renew my spiritual strength so through the power of the Holy Spirit, I can touch the hearts of all those in need of your grace and forgiveness. Let me not get caught up in vindictiveness or hatred where I tarnish my witness and effectiveness as a witness of your Son, Jesus Christ.

Praise to you, dear Jesus, for the power of your love and the awesomeness of your grace that empowers me to live my life in faithful obedience to you. I ask for your constant blessings as I look to you for all the joy in my life. In Jesus's name, I pray. Amen.

REFLECTIONS

As your new day begins, what are the biggest challenges you face, and how can God help?

Please use the space below to write down any thoughts or comments you may have.

"May God Bless You,
As you live your Life for Christ,
Empowered by The Holy Spirit."

March 8

1 John 1:9 NIV.

If we confess our sins, he is faithful and just and will forgive us our sins and purify us from all unrighteousness.

Most Gracious God, I come before you on bended knees with a humble heart. I confess my sins and ask for your help in bringing my heart and soul into submission to your will for my life. When I stumble in my walk with Christ, awaken in me the discernment and spiritual wisdom to cry out to you the troubles I have been facing. Help me to walk on the path of righteousness once again. Purge me, Lord Jesus, of all my sins so I may be as clean as snow and able to bear the fruits of the Holy Spirit. Forgive me of all my transgressions so that I may be acceptable in your eyes. Grant these things, my Lord, in the name of the Father, Son, and Holy Spirit. Amen.

REFLECTIONS

Share with God a sin that has been wreaking havoc in your life.

Please use the space below to write down any thoughts or comments you may have.

"May God Bless You,
As you live your Life for Christ,
Empowered by The Holy Spirit."

March 9

1 John 4:18 NIV.

There is no fear in love. But perfect love drives out fear because fear has to do with punishment. The one who fears is not made perfect in love.

Gracious Lord Jesus, I come to you on bended knees and with a contrite heart, crying out for your forgiveness and your comforting love. Lord, you know the concerns of my heart, and you know the difficulties I not only face but my loved one's face. Shower your blessings upon me so I may rise victorious in my faith. If I am physically and mentally healthy, no matter what challenges I face this day, I can conquer my fears. Praise to you, O Christ, for you alone are the Great Physician, and in you alone do I place my trust for all my needs. I ask all this in your precious name. Amen.

REFLECTIONS

When you pray to God, do you remember the difficulties your loved ones are going through?

Please use the space below to write down any thoughts or comments you may have.

"May God Bless You,
As you live your Life for Christ,
Empowered by The Holy Spirit."

March 10

Psalm 108:3 NIV.

[3] I will praise you, Lord, among the nations; I will sing of you among the peoples.

Glory to you, O Lord. Let the earth sing praises to your name as I once again enter a new day, full of promise and hope. Praise to you, O God. Father in Heaven, the gift of your Son, Jesus Christ, and the power of the Holy Spirit enable your children to rise above their sinful natures and to glorify your name by embracing the fruits of the Holy Spirit. Help me, Lord, as I live my life in faithful obedience to your Word. Thank you for the ceaseless gifts of forgiveness, love, and mercy you continuously shower upon me. Into your hands, I surrender my will. Through the power of the Holy Spirit. Amen.

REFLECTIONS

What fruits of the Holy Spirit can you use to glorify God?

Please use the space below to write down any thoughts or comments you may have.

March 11

1 Corinthians 15:56-57 NIV.

[56] The sting of death is sin, and the power of sin is the law. [57] But thanks be to God! He gives us the victory through our Lord Jesus Christ.

Great Jehovah, Father of Abraham and Father of my Lord and Savior, Jesus Christ, I exalt your name. I cling to your promises that as your child, loved by the one true God, I am redeemed from my transgressions. Through the blood of your Son, Jesus Christ, I will always be loyal and passionate in my desire for true repentance. Claim me as your child, so I can receive your blessings as I live my life for you.

I look forward with certainty to my eternal home with you in Heaven. Shower your grace upon me when I am weak, lost, and have walked off the path of righteousness. Restore me through your mercy and the power of the Holy Spirit so by my love for you, I can break the shackles of Satan and claim victory in Christ. Praise to you, O Lord, for the assurance of my Salvation through Christ Jesus. Amen.

REFLECTIONS

Describe what it means to be a child of the almighty God?

Please use the space below to write down any thoughts or comments you may have.

"May God Bless You,
As you live your Life for Christ,
Empowered by The Holy Spirit."

March 12

Matthew 26:35 NIV.

[35] But Peter declared, "Even if I have to die with you, I will never disown you." And all the other disciples said the same.

O Lord, my Creator, my Fortress of Strength, guide my thoughts and actions today, so I may be an effective disciple of your kingdom on earth. Lord, you know the turmoil that sometimes consumes my heart and weakens my resolve to live my life for you faithfully. You know the depths of despair that tear me from the comfort of your love. Father forgive me and restore me unto the path of righteousness so I may be a faithful child of yours who is worthy of your grace and forgiveness.

I praise you, Lord, for your enduring presence in my life even when I feel alone and lost in this world. You are my rock, my constant source of love, my constant source of strength, and my constant source of Truth. Loved by you and your Son, Jesus Christ, I implore the Holy Spirit to guide my thoughts and actions so I may face down the enemies of your kingdom and rejoice in the wonders of faith in Christ. In the name of the Father, Son, and Holy Spirit. Amen.

REFLECTIONS

- *When you fall off the path of righteousness, do you give up or cry out for God's help?*

Please use the space below to write down any thoughts or comments you may have.

"May God Bless You,
As you live your Life for Christ,
Empowered by The Holy Spirit."

March 13

Matthew 10:29-31 NIV.

[29] Are not two sparrows sold for a penny? Yet not one of them will fall to the ground outside your Father's care. b [30] And even the very hairs of your head are all numbered. [31] So do not be afraid; you are worth more than many sparrows.

Gracious Father, praise to you for your steadfast love and unending grace. Help me, Father, to always feel and know the depth of your love for me. Help me to always look upon my fellow man with the same love and compassion you have for me. Purge from me evil thoughts and actions that are contrary to your Holy Word. Lift me when I fall so I may soar like an eagle, confident in myself and secure in the knowledge that your Word is the same today as it was yesterday. Grant me the spirit of understanding and the desire to fulfill my calling as a child of God. And, when I come across someone troubled, lonely, and unable to care for himself, give me the desire to look to you for the spiritual guidance to bring hope and joy into this person's life. Encourage me to share your Word with all those who are lost and searching for answers to life's difficulties. In the name of the One who laid down His life for all of us, Jesus Christ. Amen.

REFLECTIONS

How do you know God's Word is the same today as it was yesterday?

Please use the space below to write down any thoughts or comments you may have.

"May God Bless You,
As you live your Life for Christ,
Empowered by The Holy Spirit."

March 14

Hebrews 3:5-6 NIV.

[5] "Moses was faithful as a servant in all God's house," a bearing witness to what would be spoken by God in the future.

Lord, comforter of my heart and Redeemer of my soul, guide my thoughts and actions as I embark on a new day, full of trepidation and fear of the unknown. Ease the concerns and frustrations I face as I attempt to live a life of faithfulness to your Word.

O Lord, ban from my heart and thoughts all attempts by Satan to undermine the faith I have in your Word. Place a hedge of protection around me that will fend off all the evil plans to destroy the devotion and faithfulness to live my life for you. Let me be ever so diligent in keeping on the armor of the Lord as a faithful shield that will protect me from the insidious nature of sin. Let me be victorious in all I do so the world will see me as a faithful servant and true disciple of your Word. May I be pleasing in your sight, O Lord, so at the end of the day, you can say of me, "Well done, my child, well done." Amen.

REFLECTIONS

As you begin this new day, what fears, or anxieties concern you the most?

Please use the space below to write down any thoughts or comments you may have.

"May God Bless You,
As you live your Life for Christ,
Empowered by The Holy Spirit."

March 15

2 Kings 20:3 NIV.

[3] "Remember, Lord, how I have walked before you faithfully and with wholehearted devotion and have done what is good in your eyes." And Hezekiah wept bitterly.

Gracious Father, Lord of my heart, preserve and protect me today as I go forth proclaiming my love for you. Guide my thoughts and actions as I strive to live my life in faithful devotion to your Word. Grant me the peace and serenity I need so I may be a source of comfort to those in need of your grace. Lift me when I falter and restore me on the path of righteousness so I may be a faithful beacon of light and hope to all those around me. Cast off all evil influences, so your Word and my witness are not tarnished. Grant me the assurance of my Salvation so I will never doubt the forgiveness of my sins paid for by my Lord and Savior, Jesus Christ. In the name of the Father, Son, and Holy Spirit, hear my prayer. Amen.

REFLECTIONS

If you come across someone you feel needs grace, what should you do?

Please use the space below to write down any thoughts or comments you may have.

"May God Bless You,
As you live your Life for Christ,
Empowered by The Holy Spirit."

March 16

Psalm 119:108 NIV.

[108] Accept, Lord, the willing praise of my mouth, and teach me your laws.

Merciful Father, how I adore you. My heart sings songs of praise and adoration because, in you, my life is complete. When I am of this world, lost in the turmoil and confusion that threatens my happiness and contentment found in your Word, your voice beckons me. It draws me once again into the warm embrace of your love. How can I not rejoice in knowing you have not and will never forsake me? I am your child; no matter how much I sin, you still love me and claim me because of the redemptive sacrifice of your Son, Jesus Christ.

Father put in me a deep desire to always be faithful to your Word and to be full of love, mercy, and forgiveness for all those who grieve my heart. Let me always be a strong warrior willing and ready to forsake my life, knowing that in your Son, I will have eternal life in your kingdom. Praise to you, O Lord! All glory to your name. Amen.

REFLECTIONS

Describe a time in your life when you were of this world and not a faithful child of God?

Please use the space below to write down any thoughts or comments you may have.

"May God Bless You,
As you live your Life for Christ,
Empowered by The Holy Spirit."

March 17

Proverbs 22:9 NIV.

[9] The generous will themselves be blessed, for they share their food with the poor.

Lord, of mercy, blessed be your name. As I awaken this morning, let me shout words of adoration to you. When I face a day full of anxiety and stress, blessed be your name, for you will comfort me. When I am confronted by Satan in my darkest hours, blessed be your name because I find my refuge in you. When I struggle to stay on the path of righteousness, blessed be your name, for thy rod and thy staff, they shield me. When I see the beauty in your creation, blessed is your name, for I know that you created it for me to love and protect.

Blessed is your name, for, through your Son, I will find my eternal home. When I see the poor and the homeless, blessed be your name, for, through the gifts of love and compassion, there are opportunities to bless your children. When I lay my head down to sleep, blessed be your name for by your grace, you have sustained me so I may begin a new day full of joy as I live my life in service to you. Blessed be your name, O God, my Rock, and my Redeemer. Send now your Holy Spirit, so through the truth of your Word, I can bless those in need as you have blessed me. Amen.

REFLECTIONS

Is there something or someone in your life that you would like God to bless?

Please use the space below to write down any thoughts or comments you may have.

"May God Bless You,
As you live your Life for Christ,
Empowered by The Holy Spirit."

March 18

Mark 3:29 NIV.

[29] but whoever blasphemes against the holy spirit will never be forgiven; they are guilty of an eternal sin."

Lord, my God, my Savior, there is none like you. From your death on the Cross of Calvary until this very moment, you claimed me as your own. From the beginning, the heavens and the earth were brought into existence by you. You were there from the start preparing a place for all your children to live in your kingdom.

My God, my heart is complete with gratitude and love for your precious gift of Salvation and your gifts of mercy, love, and forgiveness. Why you chose me, a sinner consumed with a sinful nature, not worthy of your love and compassion, is beyond human understanding. But you did choose me, to love, and to wrap in the bosom of your arms. You comfort me when I am in distress and shield me from the claws of Satan. Prune my branches so I may be Holy in your sight.

What greater love is there than what you bestow on me each day of my life. In what ways can I repay you, O Lord? There are none, for my works pale in comparison to the grace you freely give. Know this, O Christ my King, with every fiber of my being, I will strive to serve you faithfully, to trust your Word, and to live my life following your will. And if I fail, remember me as your child, guilty of a sinful nature, but pure as snow through the blood you shed on the Cross of Calvary. All glory to you, my Lord, and my King. Amen.

REFLECTIONS

Why do you think God chose you, a sinner, to be worthy of His great love?

Please use the space below to write down any thoughts or comments you may have.

"May God Bless You,
As you live your Life for Christ,
Empowered by The Holy Spirit."

March 19

Nahum 1:2 NIV.

[2] The Lord is a jealous and avenging God; the Lord takes vengeance and is filled with wrath. The Lord takes vengeance on his foes and vents his wrath against his enemies.

Father in Heaven, my risen King, cleanse my heart through the power of the Holy Spirit and renew my soul so I may faithfully live my life for you. I struggle with my sinful nature because of Satan's relentless pursuit and my failure to call on you when I need help. Father, our nation is spinning out of control. Your Word is under attack by our political leaders and the people they serve. We have become a nation so engrossed in seeking our own will that we have lost sight of what it means to be one nation under God.

Forgive me, Lord. Let your spirit spring forth to remind your children that your love is not a one-way street. Let me realize you are a jealous God and desire not only my obedience to your Word but my steadfast love. Strengthen my moral character, as well as that of our political leaders. Let the words uttered from their mouths bring honor and glory to your name. Pour out your grace upon our nation so I can remain on the path of righteousness. Let our country be a true beacon of light and hope to the rest of the world.

Father, we are a nation of fallen children struggling to make sense of the chaos in this world. Let us go forth this day, renewed in a spirit of righteousness. Give us the integrity and moral fiber we need to restore our country to the greatness it once had. Bless our nation as we discern your will for our lives and the future of our country. In Christ's name, I pray. Amen.

REFLECTIONS

What concerns you most about the decline of God's Word by our world leaders and us?

Please use the space below to write down any thoughts or comments you may have.

"May God Bless You,
As you live your Life for Christ,
Empowered by The Holy Spirit."

March 20

Romans 1:9 NIV.

[9] God, whom I serve in my spirit in preaching the Gospel of his Son, is my witness how constantly I remember you.

O Jesus, my Lord, and my Shepherd guide my footsteps today as I navigate the obstacles in this world. Let me not wander from the protective fold of your love. Through all the dangers and trappings of sin, let me be strong and resourceful as I battle Satan. Purge my heart from all impurities so I may be a faithful champion of your Word, committed to proclaiming your Gospel to the lost. Let me be a source of strength and rock of steadfast faith that is unwavering in my witness to all believers and non-believers in Christ.

Hear my plea for spiritual sustenance so I, through the Holy Spirit, may receive Living Water to preserve me in the unity of the Father, Son, and Holy Spirit. Forgive me of my trespasses and fill me with a heart of true repentance. Let me be worthy of your grace, full of your love for others, and a devoted disciple of your Word. Bless me, Father, as I go forth this day proclaiming the glory of your kingdom. Amen.

REFLECTIONS

How can you be a rock of steadfast faith in your witness to others?

Please use the space below to write down any thoughts or comments you may have.

"May God Bless You,
As you live your Life for Christ,
Empowered by The Holy Spirit."

March 21

Proverbs 28:13 NIV.

[13] Whoever conceals their sins does not prosper, but the one who confesses and renounces them finds mercy.

Lord, hear the words of my heart and the cry of my aching soul. Free me of all unrighteousness and the guilt that plagues my walk with Christ. I look upon my Savior and rejoice in the saving grace of His death on the Cross of Calvary. But in my daily walk, I am constantly reminded of how much I fail to return the same love, grace, and forgiveness to those whose lives I come upon.

Look upon me, O Christ, and see the person I am, scarred, torn, and weary from my battles with the forces of Satan. I am a wretched sinner, O God of hope and forgiveness. I need to feel the warm embrace of your love and the sweet whisper of your voice bringing me back into the assurance of faith.

Praise to you, my God, for into your hands I rest all my faults. I rejoice at the endless compassion and forgiveness for my transgressions. I pray for true repentance of my heart so I may be fruitful by following your Word. Please, Lord, as a child of yours, let my witness shine brightly before those in need of your grace. Amen.

REFLECTIONS

As a wretched sinner, what concerns you most when you cry out to God through prayer?

Please use the space below to write down any thoughts or comments you may have.

"May God Bless You,
As you live your Life for Christ,
Empowered by The Holy Spirit."

March 22

2 Corinthians 1:12 NIV.

[12] Now this is our boast: Our conscience testifies that we have conducted ourselves in the world, and especially in our relations with you, with integrity and godly sincerity. We have done so, relying not on worldly wisdom but on God's grace.

Lord Jesus, it is with a joyful heart that I reflect on the countless blessings I have received from you. Your gifts have lifted me from the depths of despair. Prayers have healed my body and have restored my emotional and mental health. How grateful I am, O Lord, for you love me, and you bless me even though I am still a sinner lost in the confusion and mayhem of this world. Yet, when night falls, and I reflect on how well I lived up to being a child of God, I am saddened by my shortcomings and failure to keep my simple promise of faithfulness to you.

Lord, my heart seeks to live out the truth of your Word. My heart desires to reflect the love and grace you have asked me to share with my fellow man. It seeks to proclaim to the world your great love for me. I want to let them know you are the Living God, the one true God, the God who sacrificed the life of his Son, Jesus Christ, on the Cross of Calvary. Father, I am unworthy of such great love. When it has all been said and done, when you call me home to your kingdom, and my life is before you, I pray, dear Father, that you will know, despite my failings, that my love for you is sincere.

You are the source of all my hope and Salvation. And, through faith, I ask for your unending mercies. Let me unyielding in my will and desire to always live my life for you. All glory to you, O Lord. Amen.

REFLECTIONS

When God calls you home, what do you want others to remember about you?

Please use the space below to write down any thoughts or comments you may have.

"May God Bless You,
As you live your Life for Christ,
Empowered by The Holy Spirit."

March 23

Ephesians 5:1-2 NIV.

[1] Follow God's example, therefore, as dearly loved children [2] and walk in the way of love, just as Christ loved us and gave himself up for us as a fragrant offering and sacrifice to God.

O Christ, my Redeemer, what a joy it is to wake up this morning to a day of your making and what promises to be a day full of hope. As my day progresses, Lord, let me reflect your light so someone who does not know you as Lord and Savior may come to know you. Father, the gift of Salvation is offered to all who believe in you. It is a gift where we can enjoy eternal life with you in Heaven. It is through you that I have power over sin. It is through you that true love can radiate from my life. And Lord, it is through you that no matter what difficulty I may be facing, I can find the peace and comfort to face the storms of life.

Father, so many people, need this precious gift of love that can only come from having a personal relationship with you. Let me not falter in my witness to others less I lead them astray. Let me be a shining example of your love so I may be an effective instrument in leading others to know you. Keep me ever aware of my responsibility as a Christian to follow in your footsteps. And when I stumble, summon your guardian angels to place me once again on the path of righteousness. Keep me united with you, so as this day draws to a close, I can honestly say my strength has come from Heaven above.

Thank you, Jesus, for this precious gift of love and Salvation. Bless me today with opportunities to live out my faith. In your holy and beloved name, I give my life to you. Amen.

REFLECTIONS

How can you be a shining example of God's love to others?

Please use the space below to write down any thoughts or comments you may have.

"May God Bless You,
As you live your Life for Christ,
Empowered by The Holy Spirit."

March 24

Luke 8:13 NIV.

[13] Those on the rocky ground are the ones who receive the word with joy when they hear it, but they have no root. They believe for a while, but in times of testing they fall away.

O Christ, my Rock and my dependable source of strength and inspiration, fill me with the power of the Holy Spirit so I might be a faithful witness of your love. Bind me with the truth of your Word. Encourage me to proclaim to the world that you are the Almighty God, ruler of all principalities in Heaven and on earth. Reveal to them that you are the Savior that died on the Cross of Calvary for our sins.

Lord, let me be faithful in times of duress or adversities that can test my resolve as a child of God. Fortify me with a hedge of protection, strengthened by your Holy Word, that will see me through days of calamity to days where I can rest in the peace and comfort of your arms. Let me not waver from my love for you after times of crisis. Let me be at peace with the world. Give me the security and wisdom to know when my emotions are born out of fear and when they are taken from the strength I find rooted in your Word. Grant me these things, I pray, in the name of the Father, Son, and Holy Spirit. Amen.

REFLECTIONS

- *What fruit of the Holy Spirit can help you to not waver from God's love in a time of crisis?*

Please use the space below to write down any thoughts or comments you may have.

"May God Bless You,
As you live your Life for Christ,
Empowered by The Holy Spirit."

March 25

1 Corinthians 9:23 NIV.

[23] I do all this for the sake of the gospel, that I may share in its blessings.

Good Morning, Jesus! How I love to talk to you. When I wake up, I remember the joy I have in my heart when I serve you. There is pleasure in loving and devoting my life to you, but especially to be loved by you. The warmth, the security of knowing that no matter what happens to me during the day, you are always there as my Great Comforter.

How do I thank you for all your blessings? How do I explain to my family, friends, and strangers the tremendous joy there is in having you as my Savior? Lord, allow me to a vessel of your Truth. Allow me to be a faithful witness of your Word. Allow me to be an authentic reflection of your grace by sharing the same blessings of love you shower upon me.

Bless me with the words to say to others that you are the Christ, the Son of the Living God. Bless me with Divine Opportunities to reflect in faithful obedience one who walks in the path of righteousness. And, Lord, when I falter, forgive me of my transgressions and wipe my slate clean so, in your eyes, I am pure and white as snow. Praise to you, O Christ! Amen.

REFLECTIONS

How would you explain to your family, friends, or strangers the wonder of God's love?

Please use the space below to write down any thoughts or comments you may have.

"May God Bless You,
As you live your Life for Christ,
Empowered by The Holy Spirit."

March 26

James 1:6 NIV.

[6] But when you ask you must believe and not doubt, because the one who doubts is like a wave of the sea, blown and tossed by the wind.

Gracious Father, you have chosen me to be worthy of your love and sacrifice on the Cross of Calvary. You have taken me from the clutches of Satan and, through baptism into the Holy Spirit, brought me into your kingdom of believers. Father, I thank you for the gift of Salvation, your redeeming blood, and the joy of being in your presence through the gifts of grace and faith.

Lord, although I am a sinner caught up in the sins of this world, your love is so great, so faithful, that no matter what my sinful state, you are loyal and devoted to your Word. Let me always be grateful for the love and grace you continuously bestow upon me. Grant me the peace, assurance, and security in your Word when my actions may cause me to doubt the gift of Salvation. I dedicate my life with a grateful heart and offer my heart as a faithful creation of love and obedience to your Word. Amen.

REFLECTIONS

Have you ever doubted your Salvation, and if so, do you now feel secure in God's love?

Please use the space below to write down any thoughts or comments you may have.

"May God Bless You,
As you live your Life for Christ,
Empowered by The Holy Spirit."

March 27

Isaiah 56:1 NIV.

[1] This is what the Lord says: "Maintain justice and do what is right, for my Salvation is close at hand and my righteousness will soon be revealed.

Most merciful Father, Lord of the earth and the Great Mediator, you are the source of all righteousness on this earth. You alone are the Father of all Truth. In your infinite wisdom, you decided to let mankind have the freedom of choice and the freedom to choose whether to base their laws over your children on biblical scripture or society's changing mores.

Father, our nation is caught up in a downward spiral where it drifts further from the truth of your Word. Forgive your children, O Christ! Restore our country on the path of justice and Truth that embodies your Holy Word. Bring our leaders to their knees so they may know you are the real source of Truth and justice in this world. Instill in them an earnest desire to rid our nation of corruption, deceit, and moral weakness so we can once again be one nation under God. Bless our country, O Lord, and keep its feet firmly planted on the truth of your Word. Amen.

REFLECTIONS

When there is social unrest in our country, is it part of God's plan?

Please use the space below to write down any thoughts or comments you may have.

"May God Bless You,
As you live your Life for Christ,
Empowered by The Holy Spirit."

March 28

Matthew 17:20 NIV.

[20] He replied, "Because you have so little faith. Truly I tell you, if you have faith as small as a mustard seed you can say to this mountain, 'Move from here to there,' and it will move. Nothing will be impossible for you."

O Christ, my Lord, and my Savior, nothing is impossible with you. I can do all things when guided by the truth of your Word and the power of the Holy Spirit. Father, I am a fallen creature, riddled with the sins of this world. Through the redemptive power of your bloodshed on the Cross of Calvary, I can rise above the evils that torment me and shake off the shackles of Satan. I am your child, and because you love me, nothing will stop me from striving to live my life for you. I am yours, and you are mine. I love you, my Lord!

Bless me through the power of the Holy Spirit to be a faithful witness of your Word and your Truths. Guide me along the path of righteousness so I may not waver in my witness to the world around me. And, when I falter in my walk, lovingly rebuke me, and set me once again on a straight path committed to living my life for you. In the name of the Father, Son, and Holy Spirit. Amen.

REFLECTIONS

If Satan has you bound with shackles, what can you do to break free of them?

Please use the space below to write down any thoughts or comments you may have.

"May God Bless You,
As you live your Life for Christ,
Empowered by The Holy Spirit."

March 29

Psalm 108:13 NIV.

[13] With God we will gain the victory, and he will trample down our enemies.

Precious Father, how I exalt you for all your love and mercies you generously bestow on me. You know the condition of my heart and soul, Lord, yet you still love me. Praise to you, O Christ, for it is through my proclaiming and living out the truth of your Word that I can rise and proudly say I have real victory in Christ Jesus. When Satan knocks at my door, I put on the armor of your Word and rebuke him. When Satan tempts me with sordid thoughts of lust, pride, and other ungodly thoughts, I hear your sweet whisper gently pulling me back into your fold.

There is nothing in my life that Satan can have unless I submit to his desires. I am building my character on the truth of your Word and on the solid rock that will sustain me through his demonic ploys. Through my faith and trust in you, I can have real victory in my battle against all evil perpetrated by Satan. I am yours, my Lord, and through you, I claim victory in Christ. Amen.

REFLECTIONS

When thoughts of lust fill your heart, who is the perpetrator of those thoughts?

Please use the space below to write down any thoughts or comments you may have.

"May God Bless You,
As you live your Life for Christ,
Empowered by The Holy Spirit."

March 30

Ephesians 3:17-18 NIV.

[17] so that Christ may dwell in your hearts through faith. And I pray that you, being rooted and established in love, [18] may have power, together with all the Lord's holy people, to grasp how wide and long and high and deep is the love of Christ,

Most Gracious Heavenly Father, it is through the power of the Holy Spirit and the promises in your Word that I know you are the Living God. You are the Father of a Son you sent to die on the Cross of Calvary for my sins. Praise to you for this priceless sacrifice that has redeemed my sins.

Lord, it is difficult to comprehend the depth of your love. No matter how many times I have failed you, you have remained faithful and true to forgive me of my sins because of your great love for me. You have surrounded me with blessing after blessing that has enriched my life beyond measure. You do this because of your infinite love for me.

I am so grateful, my Father, for, without you, I would be eternally lost. Let me always recognize the power of your love and how it transcends any earthly passion of mine. Continue to bless me, I pray, as I live my life for you and faithfully reflect the love of Jesus Christ. Amen.

REFLECTIONS

How can you know in your heart that God is real?

Please use the space below to write down any thoughts or comments you may have.

"May God Bless You,
As you live your Life for Christ,
Empowered by The Holy Spirit."

March 31

Proverbs 14:26 NIV.

[26] Whoever fears the Lord has a secure fortress, and for their children it will be a refuge.

Glory to you, O Lord, for you are the Almighty God, the God in whom I place my trust, hope, and faith to sustain me during times of uncertainty. When faced with health concerns, you are the Great Physician and the Great Comforter. When I am depressed and full of anxiety, you calm my soul. You provide a haven of warmth to soothe my fears. When financial worries consume my thoughts, you always provide for my needs.

How great thou art, my Lord! You have not only been with me during times of uncertainty, but you continually forgive me of my sins and restore my heart and soul on the path of righteousness. How can I not love you? Praise to you, O Christ, for you are the Great I Am. And in and through you, I can do all things. Thank you, Father, for all your gifts of love, mercy, and forgiveness. Amen.

REFLECTIONS

- *When you are depressed or facing health concerns, how do you know God is in control?*

Please use the space below to write down any thoughts or comments you may have.

April 1

John 3:21 NIV.

[21] But whoever lives by the truth comes into the light, so that it may be seen plainly that what they have done has been done in the sight of God.

Glory to you, O Christ! In your name, the pillars of the earth bow. In your name, the majesty of your kingdom shines above the rising sun. In your name, the truth of your Word brings a reflection for love and Truth in my life. Praise to you, my Lord! Your grace and forgiveness are the greatest gifts of love and sacrifice the world has ever known. I love you, my God, and I long to be a faithful servant of you to my fellow man.

Help me when I stumble and fall short of your will for my life. And when I fall short, awaken in me the fire that breathes a passion and love for the truth of your Word. Grant me the spiritual countenance to withstand the temptations of the world. Grant me, I pray, the faithfulness to be steadfast in my belief so I may faithfully lead others to a loving relationship with you. You are my Rock, O Christ, and I offer these petitions so I may always stand firm in your Truth. Amen.

REFLECTIONS

In your daily walk with Christ, if you stumble and take God's name in vain, what can you do?

Please use the space below to write down any thoughts or comments you may have.

"May God Bless You,
As you live your Life for Christ,
Empowered by The Holy Spirit."

April 2

Romans 8:20-21 NIV.

[20] For the creation was subjected to frustration, not by its own choice, but by the will of the one who subjected it, in hope [21] that the creation itself will be liberated from its bondage to decay and brought into the freedom and glory of the children of God.

O Lord, I come to you this morning with a burden of frustration. In my human frailty, I often have difficulty coping with many of the stresses of daily life. At times I am weak in spiritual maturity and seek my own will instead of yours. I succumb to temptations and react to situations that require grace, love, and forgiveness. I fail to look to you for the strength and wisdom to overcome these adversities.

O Lord, you are my refuge and my source of power. I release this burden of frustration to you and ask that you give me the strength to always prevail in my efforts to overcome sin. You are my Great Redeemer, and through you, I can do all things. Praise to you, Lord, for your loving grace and spiritual strength that can overcome the forces of darkness. I surrender my will to you and offer my contrite heart to prune and shape into a faithful servant. Through your Son, Jesus Christ, I pray. Amen.

REFLECTIONS

Has the wisdom or truth of God's Word helped you overcome your spiritual weakness?

Please use the space below to write down any thoughts or comments you may have.

"May God Bless You,
As you live your Life for Christ,
Empowered by The Holy Spirit."

April 3

Revelation 3:20 NIV.

[20] Here I am! I stand at the door and knock. If anyone hears my voice and opens the door, I will come in and eat with that person, and they with me.

Precious Father, Lord of my life, hear my heartfelt pleas. I often hear you knocking on the door of my heart and fail to let you in. So often, I know the path of Truth and righteousness and walk in the wrong direction. So often, I see the beauty of your creation and dismiss it to the efforts of man. Forgive me, O Lord, for these sins. Forgive me for not letting you always be the guiding light of my life.

When I succumb to temptations, looking for gratification in the world, rather than from your Holy Word, please remember I am a work in progress and need your patience. I am weak, O Christ, and long to be pleasing in your sight. Grant me the continuing knowledge that I can do all things because you love me and because of your forgiveness. Grant me the spirit of wisdom and revelation not only to know when I am off the path of righteousness but the courage to step back on it. In your Son's precious name, I pray. Amen.

REFLECTIONS

When you hear God knocking on the door of your heart, why is it difficult to let Him enter your heart?

Please use the space below to write down any thoughts or comments you may have.

"May God Bless You,
As you live your Life for Christ,
Empowered by The Holy Spirit."

April 4

Psalm 145:18-19 NIV.

[18] The Lord is near to all who call on him, to all who call on him in truth. [19] He fulfills the desires of those who fear him; he hears their cry and saves them.

O Christ, my Lord, and my Redeemer. Praise to you for your precious gift of Salvation. Praise to you for hearing my voice when I call upon your name. You are the Almighty God in whom I fear out of love and respect. Break free, my Lord, the shackles of my burdens.

Lord, there are sins I have not confessed. Evils that cause me anxiety and remorse, and sins that plague me with guilt. Lord, these sins hinder my relationship with you. Free me, O Christ, and ease my conscious from these burdens so I may come before you with a pure heart and declare with reverence and awe that you are indeed the Son of the Living God!

O how I love you, my God, and I bow down in humble submission to your will. Beckon me, as a child of God, into your loving embrace. In your Son's name, I pray. Amen.

REFLECTIONS

What sins in your life have you not confessed before God?

Please use the space below to write down any thoughts or comments you may have.

"May God Bless You,
As you live your Life for Christ,
Empowered by The Holy Spirit."

April 5

Deuteronomy 31:8 NIV.

[8] The Lord himself goes before you and will be with you; he will never leave you nor forsake you. Do not be afraid; do not be discouraged.

Lord, my most Merciful God, today I am full of fear and trepidation. I do not know what this day may bring with the doubt and fears that consume me. I find myself lost in a sea of rolling waves that toss my emotions back and forth. I know I should not fear because you are with me. Yet, I am still discouraged and consumed with the unknown. Purge me, my God, from these doubts and fears. Pull me out of the stormy sea and quiet my heart. Reassure me you are in control, and you will not forsake me.

Grant me the peace of understanding that can only come from true faith in your Word. Keep me safe and secure in your arms. O God, restore my soul and let me bask in the light of your Son, Jesus Christ. Let me be renewed by the Holy Spirit, so I can go forth and proclaim you are the Great Comforter. Praise to you, O Christ. Amen.

REFLECTIONS

When you are facing the unknown, how do you know God is with you?

Please use the space below to write down any thoughts or comments you may have.

"May God Bless You,
As you live your Life for Christ,
Empowered by The Holy Spirit."

April 6

1 John 5:14-15 NIV.

[14] This is the confidence we have in approaching God: that if we ask anything according to his will, he hears us. [15] And if we know that he hears us—whatever we ask—we know that we have what we asked of him.

Father, God of all mercy and Lord of my life, I exalt you with ovations of praise to your Holy Name. How thankful I am, O Christ, for the opportunity to come before you with the certainty you will hear my prayers. You have assured me you will listen to me if I ask anything according to your will. How precious is this gift of yours that never stops overflowing? Children worldwide cry out for prayers to be answered, yet you still find time to answer mine. The blessing of Salvation. The joy of love, hope, and forgiveness. All these gifts and many more you bestow on me out of your precious grace.

Thank you, Lord! Thank you for loving me. Thank you for forgiving me of my sins. Bless me when I falter in my walk with the gift of restoration to guide me back onto the path of righteousness. And may I be a faithful witness every day to your Truth and the power of your Word. In Christ's name, I pray. Amen.

REFLECTIONS

Finding the patience to be a faithful child of God can sometimes be challenging. Why?

Please use the space below to write down any thoughts or comments you may have.

"May God Bless You,
As you live your Life for Christ,
Empowered by The Holy Spirit."

April 7

Ephesians 3:12 NIV.

[12] In him and through faith in him we may approach God with freedom and confidence.

Precious Savior, in whom I place my faith. I come before you with a heart full of joy, knowing that because of your love for me, I will spend eternity with you. You are my refuge. You are my strength, and you are the foundation of my life. I could not be more grateful for the gifts you continuously bestow upon me. Praise to you, O Christ. All glory and honor are yours. When the garden of my life needs pruning, you send me opportunities to grow and to have the scarred branches in my life healed. You send me trials from which to learn and tests of faith to help me to rely on you and not my own devices.

Praise to you, O Lord. You are the glorious Son of my Father in Heaven. Redeem me from my transgressions and embrace me with your sweet whisper of love when I may be in doubt. Look upon me with favor so I may one day be welcomed into your kingdom to sing eternal praises to your name. Glory to you, O Christ. Amen.

REFLECTIONS

Is there something in your Garden of Life that needs pruning? If so, what is it?

Please use the space below to write down any thoughts or comments you may have.

"May God Bless You,
As you live your Life for Christ,
Empowered by The Holy Spirit."

April 8

Isaiah 40:8 NIV.

[8] The grass withers and the flowers fall, but the word of our God endures forever.

Glorious King and my God of love, hear the joy in my voice as I proclaim the Truth of your Word. Jesus Christ, my Redeemer, is Lord of my life. Your Word endures forever and will never wither away. In this time of uncertainty, so much of the world is lost and caught up in turmoil and conflict. People who intend to destroy the truth of your Word will one day realize you are the Almighty God and that the reality of your Word will stand forever. Praise to you, O Christ! No matter the adversities or tragedies that may befall me, I am yours, my Lord, to shape into the child of God you destined me to be. I thank you. I love you. I give all glory to you, and through the power of the Holy Spirit, I will forever live my life in faithful obedience to your Word. Amen.

REFLECTIONS

When God's truth conflicts with the worldview of man, what should you do?

Please use the space below to write down any thoughts or comments you may have.

"May God Bless You,
As you live your Life for Christ,
Empowered by The Holy Spirit."

April 9

2 Timothy 1:9 NIV.

[9] He has saved us and called us to a holy life---not because of anything we have done but because of his own purpose and grace. This grace was given us in Christ Jesus before the beginning of time.

All glory to your name, Holy Father. All praise shall be sung from my lips, for you are a God of love and grace. You have called me to live a Holy life. You have called me to live a life of righteousness and love that is reflective of the same passion my Lord and Savior, Jesus Christ, has graciously bestowed on me.

Lord, there is nothing I can do on my own to justify the love and grace you have extended to me. From the beginning of time, you had a purpose for your children, and you had a purpose for my life. I lift my broken and sinful spirit and ask that you free me of all the trappings of Satan so I can fulfill my purpose in life to you. Forgive me of my sins, and through the power of the Holy Spirit, I humbly submit my stubborn will for your pruning. Praise to you, O Christ! Amen.

REFLECTIONS

How can you praise God today, and why should you proclaim your love for Him?

Please use the space below to write down any thoughts or comments you may have.

"May God Bless You,
As you live your Life for Christ,
Empowered by The Holy Spirit."

April 10

Psalm 28:7 NIV.

[7] The Lord is my strength and my shield; my heart trusts in him, and he helps me. My heart leaps for joy, and with my song I praise him.

O Christ, my Savior, it is in you whom I place my trust. My heart is full of gratitude for your love and jumps with joy and songs of rejoicing as I face this coming day. With you as my strength and shield, there is no adversity I cannot meet. When Satan beckons me with temptations of the flesh, I stomp him into the ground and claim victory over sin. When he creates doubt and fear in me, I cling to you, O Lord, and rest in the comfort and assurance of your loving embrace. When my heart is full of grief, I come to you, the Great Physician, for your healing power. When I seek to hear your whisper to guide me down the path of righteousness, I call on your Holy Spirit to reveal to me the spirit of wisdom and revelation. You are the Great "I Am," the God of my heart and the God of all creation. Through you, I claim victory in Christ and praise you for your enduring love and grace. Amen.

REFLECTIONS

How does it feel when you find victory in Christ over Satan?

Please use the space below to write down any thoughts or comments you may have.

"May God Bless You,
As you live your Life for Christ,
Empowered by The Holy Spirit."

April 11

Psalm 25:4-5 NIV.

[4] Show me your ways, Lord, teach me your paths. [5] Guide me in your truth and teach me, for you are God my Savior, and my hope is in you all day long.

Praise to you, O Christ, for you are Lord of my life, my Rock, my Deliverer, and the source of all my strength. In you, I find the spirit of wisdom and revelation from which I discern the righteousness of my walk with you. How great thou art, my God. How great thou art! I praise you for your unending love, my passion for your Truth, and the wisdom to know how to embrace it in times of uncertainty. Through your Holy Name, I can fend off the forces of confusion that threaten to destroy relationships with your children. Through your Holy Spirit, I gain the strength and wisdom to pursue the truth of your Word. Through my faith, hope, and trust in you, I know your Word endures despite my human condition. O Lord, you are so gracious. Praise to you, my Savior. Amen.

REFLECTIONS

What does having the spirit of wisdom and revelation mean to you?

Please use the space below to write down any thoughts or comments you may have.

"May God Bless You,
As you live your Life for Christ,
Empowered by The Holy Spirit."

April 12

Romans 8:26 NIV.

[26] In the same way, the Spirit helps us in our weakness. We do not know what we ought to pray for, but the Spirit himself intercedes for us through wordless groans.

O Christ, for whom I live my life, sometimes I fail to give you thanks for all the blessings you have so generously bestowed upon me. In moments when I am weak, you send your Holy Spirit to intercede on my behalf, chastising me for my sinful thoughts and behavior. Yet, you still love me despite my sinful nature. When Satan challenges me with temptations, I call upon the Holy Spirit so I can gain freedom over sin by demonstrating my faithfulness to you. You shower your grace upon me, and in the process, you teach me how to show acts of kindness to my fellow man. What a glorious God you are! With a heart full of gratitude, I thank you for your steadfast love, grace, and forgiveness. Praise to you, O Christ. All praise to you! Amen.

REFLECTIONS

What are some ways you can demonstrate grace to others?

Please use the space below to write down any thoughts or comments you may have.

"May God Bless You,
As you live your Life for Christ,
Empowered by The Holy Spirit."

April 13

Psalm 32:2 NIV.

[2] Blessed is the one whose sin the Lord does not count against them and in whose spirit is no deceit.

Father, fill me with the power of the Holy Spirit, a spirit of honesty, and a heart free of deceit so I may glorify you by all my thoughts and actions. Renew my spirit, gracious Lord, so through the power of your redeeming blood, I may continue to be seen blameless in your sight. And when my walk with you is tainted with sin, admonish me, correct me, and steer me back on the path of righteousness so I may once again be pleasing in your sight.

Praise to you, O Christ, for your precious gift of Salvation. Let me be a true disciple of your Word as I share the good news of your Gospel. In the name of the Father, Son, and Holy Spirit. Amen.

REFLECTIONS

- *Have you been able to feel the presence of the Holy Spirit in your life? If not, what could you do to let Him speak to you?*

Please use the space below to write down any thoughts or comments you may have.

"May God Bless You,
As you live your Life for Christ,
Empowered by The Holy Spirit."

April 14

Isaiah 40:31 NIV.

[31] but those who hope in the Lord will renew their strength. They will soar on wings like eagles; they will run and not grow weary they will walk and not be faint.

Father God, thank you for the power of your Son's redeeming blood. Thank you for carrying me through the dark days that cross my path. Thank you for giving me the strength to weather any storm in life so I may rise above it like a soaring eagle with wings spread wide over the beauty of your creation.

Lord, see how grateful my heart is. See how deep my love is for your Word and the Truth of your Holy Scripture. How great thou art, my God. Although I am a worthless sinner lost in a pit of shame, you still love me and extend your forgiveness when I call upon your name. Praise to you, O Christ, for you are my loving Father. Amen.

REFLECTIONS

What does it mean to you to be covered by Christ's redeeming blood?

Please use the space below to write down any thoughts or comments you may have.

"May God Bless You,
As you live your Life for Christ,
Empowered by The Holy Spirit."

April 15

1 Peter 5:6 NIV.

[6] Humble yourselves, therefore, under God's mighty hand, that he may lift you up in due time.

Precious Lord, my Savior, and Redeemer, I bow before you in humble submission to your will for my life. Purge my heart and mind of all evil thoughts that hinder my relationship with you. Cleanse me with a spiritual soap that will wipe me clean of all iniquities that cause my witness of you to falter. You are my God, the shepherd of my life. Lead me down the path of righteousness so I may be pleasing in your sight. Lift me into the bosom of your arms when I cry out in distress. Comfort me, O Lord, and grant me the grace to love others as you first loved me. Praise to you, O Christ, for you are the Great Redeemer, the Shepherd of my Life, now and forever. In Christ's name, I pray. Amen.

REFLECTIONS

- *Do you find it difficult to humble yourself so you can accomplish God's will for your life?*

Please use the space below to write down any thoughts or comments you may have.

"May God Bless You,
As you live your Life for Christ,
Empowered by The Holy Spirit."

April 16

Matthew 28:5-6 NIV.

[5] The angel said to the women, "Do not be afraid, for I know that you are looking for Jesus, who was crucified. [6] He is not here; he has risen, just as he said. Come and see the place where he lay.

O Lamb of God, the Christ, you have risen from the dead to fulfill scripture's prophecies. Still, more than that, O Lord, you are the Son of the Living God who saved His children from the penalty of sin by dying on the Cross of Calvary. I am so profoundly grateful for the price you paid.

I am looking forward to spending eternal life with you in Heaven. I am so deeply thankful that you find me worthy of your love, grace, and forgiveness despite my grievous sins.

Praise to you, O Lord, My King, and my Redeemer. Fill me now with the power of your Holy Spirit, so I may lift my voice and rejoice to all those around me, "He is Risen, He is Risen indeed." Praise to God on the Highest! May your angels sing songs of joy and triumph as I proclaim my love for you. In Christ's name, I pray. Amen.

REFLECTIONS

What does the "Lamb of God" mean to you in your Christian faith?

Please use the space below to write down any thoughts or comments you may have.

"May God Bless You,
As you live your Life for Christ,
Empowered by The Holy Spirit."

April 17

John 11:25-26 NIV.

[25] Jesus said to her, "I am the resurrection and the life. The one who believes in me will live, even though they die; [26] and whoever lives by believing in me will never die. Do you believe this?"

Lord Jesus, in this sweet hour of prayer, I come before you on bended knees. I rejoice in your resurrection and your ascension into Heaven to sit at the right hand of the Almighty God. Praise to your Holy Name, O Christ. May the earth and all its rulers bow down in humble submission to your Lordship.

Let your Word go forth from all your disciples that you are the King of all creation, the Master Carpenter, the Great Physician, Alpha, and the Omega. You are my God! I love you. I praise you. I sing songs of praise to your Holy Name.

On the Cross of Calvary, Christ bore the suffering of all humanity so I could be free of Satan's dominion over my life. Through the Holy Spirit, you give me the power to squash the ravages of sin over my life. Praise to you, O Christ. Glory to you, All-Mighty Redeemer! Amen.

REFLECTIONS

- *Do you think the rulers of the earth will ever accept Christ's Lordship over the world?*

Please use the space below to write down any thoughts or comments you may have.

"May God Bless You,
As you live your Life for Christ,
Empowered by The Holy Spirit."

April 18

Hebrews 7:25 NIV.

[25] Therefore he is able to save completely those who come to God through him, because he always lives to intercede for them.

O Christ my Lord, when I reflect on the pain you suffered on the Cross of Calvary, my heart swells up with grief. Tears come to my eyes because I know the hurt you suffered was for my sins; sins so grievous to your Holy Name that I withdraw into a pit of shame. Praise to you, my Christ. You are always there to intercede on my behalf before the Almighty God. I am lost without you and cannot save myself. I wallow in a sea of tears because of my transgressions.

Praise to you for your redeeming love, grace, and forgiveness. Praise to you that I, as a sinner, can find refuge and comfort in the truth of your Word. Tear me from the shackles of sin so I may always be free from the torment of Satan. Praise to your name, O Christ! Amen.

REFLECTIONS

Are there problems in your life where you would like Christ to intercede?

Please use the space below to write down any thoughts or comments you may have.

"May God Bless You,
As you live your Life for Christ,
Empowered by The Holy Spirit."

April 19

Psalm 106:3 NIV.

[3] Blessed are those who act justly, who always do what is right.

Blessed Father, through the power of the Holy Spirit, I am given the ability to rise above my sinful state and to live a life of righteousness for you. While I often fail, my Lord, I know the strength I gain from your Word will sustain me and lift me in moments of darkness. As often as I sin, you cleanse me through the blood of my Redeemer, Jesus Christ. How can I not rejoice in a Savior that loves me and forgives me as you do? Thanks be to God, O Christ. For I know if I strive to do right in your eyes, you will be faithful to me and love me despite myself. What a Glorious Savior you are, my Lord, what a Glorious Savior you are. Amen!

REFLECTIONS

Describe the strength you gain from God's Word that can help you in moments of darkness.

Please use the space below to write down any thoughts or comments you may have.

"May God Bless You,
As you live your Life for Christ,
Empowered by The Holy Spirit."

April 20

Ephesians 2:8-9 NIV.

[8] For it is by grace you have been saved, through faith --- and this is not from yourselves, it is the gift of God --- [9] not by works, so that no one can boast.

Heavenly Father, I come before you today filled with a heart of gratitude for the grace you have extended to me. I do not come by this grace because of some work I have done. I do not come by this grace as a reward for doing something right in my life. I come by this grace because I accepted your Son, Jesus Christ, as my Savior. I come by this grace because of your unfailing love for me, despite my shortcomings and sinful nature. I come by this grace when I acknowledge my sins and turn from them. I come by this grace because you are a forgiving God, a God of hope, love, and forgiveness. You are the Almighty God, and I seek refuge in your arms when I am wandering in a storm of darkness. Glory to you, O Lord. Praise to you, O Christ. Glory to you, my Savior. Into your hands, I deliver myself. Amen.

REFLECTIONS

If you do good works, will it earn you anymore grace from God?

Please use the space below to write down any thoughts or comments you may have.

"May God Bless You,
As you live your Life for Christ,
Empowered by The Holy Spirit."

April 21

Romans 8:38-39 NIV.

[38] For I am convinced that neither death nor life, neither angels nor demons, neither the present nor the future, nor any powers, [39] neither height nor depth, nor anything else in all creation, will be able to separate us from the love of God that is in Christ Jesus our Lord.

Most Merciful Lord, the Redeemer of my heart and soul, nothing can separate me from your love if I remain in Christ. When love fails in my earthly relationships or when a calamity hits and I am flailing in a frenzy of lies and deception by Satan, you remain steadfast in your love for me. Despite my human failings and tendency to withdraw into myself, you claim me as your child and pull me close to your bosom. Thank you, my Lord, for your faithfulness to me. Let me always honor your name by showing the same dedication to your Word. Praise to your name, O Christ. Bless me this day, as I live my life for you. Amen.

REFLECTIONS

Think of your human nature. Why would God draw you close to His bosom if you sin?

Please use the space below to write down any thoughts or comments you may have.

"May God Bless You,
As you live your Life for Christ,
Empowered by The Holy Spirit."

April 22

Matthew 11:28-30 NIV.

[28] "Come to me, all you who are weary and burdened, and I will give you rest. [29] Take my yoke upon you and learn from me, for I am gentle and humble in heart, and you will find rest for your souls. [30] For my yoke is easy and my burden is light."

O Lord, hear the pleas from my weary heart. Hear the prayers I offer when I am in despair. Hear the prayers of comfort I seek from your Word. My heart is laden with sadness from the turmoil in this world. A world that has lost its way has strayed into chaos, confusion, and self-righteous behavior that has pitted man against man. Where am I to turn, my Father? When the thundering noise of war deafens your people to your Word, you alone can break through these storms of conflict and beckon your children to peace.

Hear my plea, O Lord! Calm these waters and let the truth of your Word reconcile your children to peace, love, and harmony. Quell any discord that threatens to disrupt your plans for peace and give the leaders of our world the wisdom, character, and perseverance to bring peace among the nations of the earth. In your Son's Holy Name, I pray. Amen.

REFLECTIONS

- *If our world has drifted into chaos and confusion, is there still hope for us? If so, why?*

Please use the space below to write down any thoughts or comments you may have.

"May God Bless You,
As you live your Life for Christ,
Empowered by The Holy Spirit."

April 23

Romans 5:6-8 NIV.

[6] You see, at just the right time, when we were still powerless, Christ died for the ungodly. [7] Very rarely will anyone die for a righteous person, though for a good person someone might possibly dare to die. [8] But God demonstrates his own love for us in this: While we were still sinners, Christ died for us.

O Lamb of God, my Great Redeemer, thank you for the eternal mercies you have given to me, a wretched sinner caught up among the unrighteous in the world. Free me from the ungodly behavior and thoughts that dishonor your Holy Word. Dear Jesus, because of your great love for my Father in Heaven, you obeyed His will and sacrificed your life on the Cross of Calvary.

Praise to you, O Christ! Your character and love are what I seek to emulate. But because I am sinful and unclean, my struggle continues as I strive to be faithful in my Christian walk. When faced with choosing you or denying you, O Lord, let me be strong in my Christian character. Because of your great love for me, I resoundingly proclaim, you are the Christ, the Son of the Living God, and my life belongs to you. Amen.

REFLECTIONS

- *If faced with the choice of choosing Christ or denying Him, what would you do?*

Please use the space below to write down any thoughts or comments you may have.

"May God Bless You,
As you live your Life for Christ,
Empowered by The Holy Spirit."

April 24

1 Peter 3:12 NIV.

[12] For the eyes of the Lord are on the righteous and his ears are attentive to their prayer, but the face of the Lord is against those who do evil."

Hear my prayer, O God, the creator of Heaven and earth. You alone are omnipotent. You know my heart and what it feels like to be lonely, confused, and unsure of my purpose. You know my thoughts before I speak them. You know my fears before I encounter them. You indeed are an all-knowing God.

Because you know me so well, I can assure you that I feel safe in your arms. When the rain falls from storm clouds, I know you are in control. I am free from fear because I know that you will rescue me through Divine Intervention. After all, you are my God. Help me to remain faithful and strong in times of weariness so I can be seen righteous in your eyes.

Lead me in the face of danger as a warrior for the truth of your Word. And when my day of judgment shall come, let it be said, all is well with my soul. Amen.

REFLECTIONS

Would you recognize the presence of Divine Intervention in your life? If so, how?

Please use the space below to write down any thoughts or comments you may have.

"May God Bless You,
As you live your Life for Christ,
Empowered by The Holy Spirit."

April 25

John 7:38 NIV.

[38] Whoever believes in me, as scripture has said, rivers of living water will flow from within them."

O Christ, the Living Water that flows within me, cleanse all impurities that undermine and corrupt the truth of your Word. Lord, you know I have not been entirely faithful in my walk with you. Spare me thy rod yet correct me, so I am convicted of my sins and turn from them in true repentance. I praise you, my King, and bow down before you in humble reverence to your Lordship. My heart sings songs of joy and adoration, for you are the Prince of Peace for whom, in the presence of your angels, covers me with the sacrificial blood of Christ. In Christ's Holy Name, I pray. Amen.

REFLECTIONS

What does it mean to bow down in humble reverence to God?

Please use the space below to write down any thoughts or comments you may have.

"May God Bless You,
As you live your Life for Christ,
Empowered by The Holy Spirit."

April 26

1 Peter 2:12 NIV.

[12] Live such good lives among the pagans that, though they accuse you of doing wrong, they may see your good deeds and glorify God on the day he visits us.

My Beloved Lord Jesus, through your crucifixion and resurrection, you have broken the shackles of sin that has entrapped mankind. My sinful nature has tried to hold me hostage, through the ploys and trappings of an ungodly life. Despite the evil of Satan, because of your strength, and grace, I have been able to break the shackles of his dominion over me. I fear not, O Christ, for when I sin, you are always there through the power of the Holy Spirit to convict my heart and turn me from the evil that displeases you.

What a loving and gracious God you are! Lord, you are the Great Physician, the one who bore the horrible, brutal lashings of the whip before your crucifixion. Because of your sacrifice, I reject any affliction, physical, mental, emotional, and spiritual, that threatens to turn me from your love and redeeming grace.

Praise to you, my faithful Lord! I exalt you for the tenderness of your heart when I need your comfort. In your precious name, I pray. Amen.

REFLECTIONS

How can you be healed of your afflictions through the crucifixion of Christ?

Please use the space below to write down any thoughts or comments you may have.

*"May God Bless You,
As you live your Life for Christ,
Empowered by The Holy Spirit."*

April 27

Psalm 55:22 NIV.

[22] Cast your cares on the Lord and he will sustain you; he will never let the righteous be shaken.

O Christ, the light of the world, you have blessed me with the spirit of wisdom and revelation. Through your Holy Spirit, I hear your whisper and heed the words you speak to my heart. Because of your great love for me, I know you will walk beside me as I travel down the path of righteousness. Moreover, I can cast my cares upon you and know that you will sustain me through faith.

O Lord, you are the rock upon which my faith was born. Satan or worldly influences will not shake me. I delight in you, O Christ, and praise you for lifting me from despair when my heart is heavy laden. All glory is yours, O Faithful Lord. For through the power of the Holy Spirit, I can rise above my sinful nature and soar like an eagle. In Christ's name, I pray. Amen.

REFLECTIONS

- *When you cast your cares upon the Lord, how do you know Christ will help you?*

Please use the space below to write down any thoughts or comments you may have.

"May God Bless You,
As you live your Life for Christ,
Empowered by The Holy Spirit."

April 28

2 Corinthians 5:17-18 NIV.

[17] Therefore, if anyone is in Christ, the new creation has come: The old has gone, the new is here! [18] All this is from God, who reconciled us to himself through Christ and gave us the ministry of reconciliation.

O Father in Heaven, my wonderful counselor, I come before you with a repentant heart as a child of God. I know my sins are grievous and dishonoring to the truth of your Word. But because I am a new creation in Christ, I am committed to living my life in faithful obedience to your Word.

Now, I can rest with the assurance that your love will sustain me in my darkest hours. It is a great comfort to my soul to have the confidence and security that you are the only true God. You are the Alpha, the Omega, the Truth above all falsehoods, and the Living Water that floods my heart with happiness.

Bless you, my God! Strengthen and encourage me when Satan tries to disrupt my life. Give me the wisdom to turn from the evil one as he plots against me. Let me demonstrate my faithfulness to you so I may be a light of yours unto the world. Through Christ Jesus, I pray. Amen.

REFLECTIONS

What does it mean to be a new creation in Christ?

Please use the space below to write down any thoughts or comments you may have.

"May God Bless You,
As you live your Life for Christ,
Empowered by The Holy Spirit."

April 29

2 Corinthians 13:8 NIV.

[8] For we cannot do anything against the truth, but only for the truth.

O King of Kings, the Master of the Universe, thank you for sending your Son, Jesus Christ, as the substitute on the Cross of Calvary for the sins of humanity. I bow before you. I am held captive to Christ as a slave that does not want to be apart from my savior. I willingly give my life for you and submit my unclean thoughts, my shameful behavior, and every sin Satan lures me with for you to cleanse and purge from my heart. I live for your Truth, the Truth of your Holy Word, to sustain me when I am stricken with a weak heart. I am your child, a child of God, and I rejoice that because of your love, grace, and forgiveness, I can live in the righteousness of your Truths and glow as a beacon of hope to your life. Amen.

REFLECTIONS

If you are a slave to Christ, do you still have free choice?

Please use the space below to write down any thoughts or comments you may have.

"May God Bless You,
As you live your Life for Christ,
Empowered by The Holy Spirit."

April 30

Revelation 6:9 NIV.

[9] When he opened the fifth seal, I saw under the altar the souls of those who had been slain because of the word of God and the testimony they had maintained.

Bless the Lord, O my soul, for you have given me the power of the Holy Spirit from which to draw my strength. From my heart, bless the Lord, for my soul is full of gratitude and love for the mercies I have received. But, because of you, O Christ, I have been lifted from the depths of despair to the mountain tops where I can look out upon your creation and proudly proclaim, it is indeed well with my soul.

Praise to you, my Lord, for I am your child, a child of God, and no matter what tragedy may befall me and no matter what despair may grip my heart, my life belongs to you. I am yours entirely and pray I may indeed reflect the love of Christ to all people whose paths I cross. In Christ's Holy Name, I pray. Amen.

REFLECTIONS

Describe the depth of your gratitude for all Christ has done for you.

Please use the space below to write down any thoughts or comments you may have.

"May God Bless You,
As you live your Life for Christ,
Empowered by The Holy Spirit."

May 1

Isaiah 41:10 NIV.

[10] So do not fear, for I am with you; do not be dismayed, for I am your God. I will strengthen you and help you; I will uphold you with my righteous right hand.

O Christ, my redeeming Savior, in times of weakness and uncertainty, I give in to the temptations Satan places before me. He knows in his cunning ways what sins I am more likely to indulge. He knows my carnal nature and the lustful ways that sway my thoughts and behavior.

Praise to you, My God, that through your love, grace, and forgiveness, Satan's dominion over me is short-lived. For you are the Almighty God. You are the Great Redeemer. You are the Way, the Truth, and the Life. And because of my faith and trust in you, I can overcome and break free of the shackles of Satan that attempts to destroy my relationship with you.

O Lord, let me be forever righteous in your sight, but when I do fall, gather me quickly into your arms and pull me from the claws of Satan. In the name of the Father, Son, and the Holy Spirit. Amen.

REFLECTIONS

How can you stay righteous in God's sight?

Please use the space below to write down any thoughts or comments you may have.

"May God Bless You,
As you live your Life for Christ,
Empowered by The Holy Spirit."

May 2

Proverbs 3:5-6 NIV.

[5] Trust in the Lord with all your heart and lean not on your own understanding; [6] in all your ways submit to him, and he will make your paths straight.

O Son of God, the Christ, and the Redeemer of my sinful life, so often, I live my life and follow the path the world has instilled in me. Forgive me, my Lord, for I am a sinner lost in the ways of the world and put my understanding and faith into things I can see, touch, and feel. O Father, how it must grieve you when I fail to place my trust, confidence, and understanding in your Holy Word. Correct me, my God, with a firm, loving hand so I may be held accountable for my sinful ways and failure to love you as a faithful child of God.

You are my God, and it is in you that I place my trust and faith. Build me up with the spiritual guidance and mentoring that will shield me from myself and my headstrong ways. Preserve me through the body and blood of my Savior, Jesus Christ, so when I walk down the path of righteousness, you will say, "I am pleased with my child." Amen.

REFLECTIONS

When you fail to place your trust in God, will He still love you?

Please use the space below to write down any thoughts or comments you may have.

"May God Bless You,
As you live your Life for Christ,
Empowered by The Holy Spirit."

May 3

Psalm 22:24 NIV.

[24] For he has not despised or scorned the suffering of the afflicted one; he has not hidden his face from him but has listened to his cry for help.

O Lord, as this day begins, my heart is heavy for the children of this world. There are children in neighborhoods across America, and faraway lands who suffer from malnutrition and are on the brink of dying from starvation. Hear my plea for them, O Christ, that you may move the hearts of your people throughout the world to respond with love and compassion to help feed the mouths of those less fortunate.

Preserve these children in your loving and tender care. Comfort them, ease their anguish, and bless them through the power of the Holy Spirit with a spiritual anointing that will seal them with the blood of Christ. You are the Almighty God, the Great Provider, the source of all strength capable of easing the suffering of these children. Through your Son, Jesus Christ, may my petition, nurtured through the truth of your Word, move all people to care and provide for these children of God. In your Holy Name, I pray. Amen.

REFLECTIONS

How does it make you feel when you help those that are less fortunate than you?

Please use the space below to write down any thoughts or comments you may have.

*"May God Bless You,
As you live your Life for Christ,
Empowered by The Holy Spirit."*

May 4

Romans 12:9 NIV.

[9] Love must be sincere. Hate what is evil; cling to what is good.

Precious Father in Heaven, through your Son, Jesus Christ, you have set the standard for the essence of beauty and love. Nothing can compare to your incredible display of love than when your Son died at the Cross of Calvary.

I pray, Lord, that through my faithfulness to your Word, I may in some small measure demonstrate the love I have for my Savior. Let me be sincere in all my love efforts so the people whose lives I touch may come to have a closer relationship with you. Let me be honorable, truthful and maintain the values that are reflective of one in Christ.

Preserve me, through your mercies, so I will have the strength and courage to follow you without faltering and falling prey to Satan. Bless me, Lord, and keep me in your tender care. In Jesus' name, I pray. Amen.

REFLECTIONS

In what small measure can you demonstrate your love for Christ?

Please use the space below to write down any thoughts or comments you may have.

May 5

Daniel 12:3 NIV.

[3] Those who are wise will shine like the brightness of the heavens, and those who lead many to righteousness, like the stars for ever and ever.

Bless the Lord, O my soul, and all my being. Bless his Holy Name. Father, in your divine wisdom, you have seen fit to shower your graces upon me. You have taken me, a wretched sinner, and redeemed me through the blood of your Son, Jesus Christ.

Through the power of the Holy Spirit, you have given me a choice to exercise wisdom when confronted with complex life issues. I have come to learn, my Lord, that by myself, I am weak and without the moral fortitude to seek your help. But with you, and through your grace, I can accomplish all things. No mountain is too high for me to climb. No tragedy is too overwhelming to live through. No temptation by Satan can turn my love from you if I remain in Christ.

Let me be strong in my witness so I may lead others, through the righteousness of your Word, to an enduring and loving relationship with you. In Christ's name, I pray. Amen.

REFLECTIONS

Describe what you can accomplish when you live your life for Christ.

Please use the space below to write down any thoughts or comments you may have.

"May God Bless You,
As you live your Life for Christ,
Empowered by The Holy Spirit."

May 6

James 1:2-4 NIV.

[2] Consider it pure joy, my brothers and sisters, whenever you face trials of many kinds, [3] because you know that the testing of your faith produces perseverance. [4] Let perseverance finish its work so that you may be mature and complete, not lacking anything.

Gracious God, thank you for being the Lord of my life. Thank you for sending your Son, Jesus Christ, as the substitute for my sinful nature. Thank you for being with me when confronted with adversities in life. Lord, you know the trials I have encountered in the past. You know the difficulties that have caused me to wander off the path of righteousness. If not for your grace, my God, I would be forever lost and vulnerable to the influences of Satan. Yet, while Satan still attempts to undermine my love and faith in you, he will gain no foothold if I remain in Christ.

I am yours, my God, to chisel and shape into a faithful follower of Christ. You are my light. You are my refuge. You are the source of my strength. Bless me now, my Lord, as I persevere and bring to maturity my faith in you. In Christ's name, I pray. Amen.

REFLECTIONS

What are some of the satanic influences you may face today?

Please use the space below to write down any thoughts or comments you may have.

"May God Bless You,
As you live your Life for Christ,
Empowered by The Holy Spirit."

May 7

Galatians 5:25 NIV.

[25] Since we live by the spirit, let us keep in step with the spirit.

O Christ, by your cross and resurrection, you have set me free. No longer am I bound hopelessly to this world of decadent behavior and insidious attacks on my faith. Through your Word and promises, I am open to choosing who my God is and where I shall place my trust. I bow before you, Lord, and ask that you prune the withering branches in my life and restore me on the path of righteousness so I may always bring glory to your name.

Lord, I am lost without you and know apart from you, I can do nothing. For through the Word of God, I have the strength and moral fortitude to conquer any adversity Satan places in my path. I am your creation. I belong to you. I love you and promise my faithfulness and love as I worship you each day. Glory to you, my Lord. Praise to you, my God! Amen.

REFLECTIONS

What truth of God's Word can you share with someone who may need God's love?

Please use the space below to write down any thoughts or comments you may have.

"May God Bless You,
As you live your Life for Christ,
Empowered by The Holy Spirit."

May 8

John 5:24 NIV.

[24] "Very truly I tell you, whoever hears my word and believes him who sent me has eternal life and will not be judged but has crossed over from death to life.

Come Holy Spirit and be with me as I embark upon this day of certainty. Despite Satan's attempts to worm himself into my thoughts and actions, I can be confident of your love and the presence of your redeeming blood for the atonement of my sins. Because I am your child, I can be sure that whatever adversity crosses my path this day, I can call upon your name for the help I need. And with your help, I can break free of the shackles Satan tries to use to destroy my relationship with you.

You are my God, the Great Redeemer. Through your Son, Jesus Christ, I have the assurance I shall spend eternity with you in Heaven. Bless me with divine encounters today, so I may be a faithful witness of your love, grace, and forgiveness. Grant me the opportunity to be a blessing to someone who is a stranger to your Word. May they find eternal peace and assurance that you are their God, ready to ease their burdens and heartaches. Praise to you, O Christ, for you are the Great One, the Almighty God, the Alpha, and the Omega, and in you do I place my trust. Amen.

REFLECTIONS

Is there someplace you may be going to today where you can be a faithful witness of Christ?

Please use the space below to write down any thoughts or comments you may have.

"May God Bless You,
As you live your Life for Christ,
Empowered by The Holy Spirit."

May 9

John 14:21 NIV.

[21] Whoever has my commands and keeps them is the one who loves me. The one who loves me will be loved by my Father, and I too will love them and show myself to them."

Most Merciful Father, who am I that you shower your love upon me? Who am I that no matter what my sinful state, you only see your love for me? Who am I, dear Lord, that you would send your Son, Jesus Christ, to die on the Cross of Calvary for my sins? Lord, your Word is embedded in my soul. Because of that, I hold your commands close to my heart. I am your child, a child of God, devoted to living out my faith as a dedicated disciple of your Word. I am no longer of this world. Satan no longer has control over me if I remain in you. I am your creation, your faithful warrior to battle the forces of evil and to shatter the strongholds of rebellion in my heart.

Praise to you, O Christ! Hallelujah to your Holy Name. Let my light be bright as I reflect the love of Christ to my fellow man. I bow before you. I love you. I am your faithful servant to shape with the fruits of the Holy Spirit into the person you mean for me to be. Praise to you, O Lord. Amen.

REFLECTIONS

Describe the person you believe God means for you to be.

Please use the space below to write down any thoughts or comments you may have.

"May God Bless You,
As you live your Life for Christ,
Empowered by The Holy Spirit."

May 10

James 1:12 NIV.

[12] Blessed is the one who perseveres under trial because, having stood the test, that person will receive the crown of life that the Lord has promised to those who love him.

O Prince of Peace, Lord of all creation, I come to you with gratitude in my heart for the trials you have seen me through. You have been my source of strength, even when I was pulling away from your love. No matter what tests of adversity I had to face, because of your grace, I have been able to persevere. Not only that, but I have also had the peace and assurance you would forgive me of my sins.

Glory to you, O Christ, for you have promised me the crown of life because of my love and faith in you. You have pledged to me eternal life if I repent from my sins and trust in you as my Lord and Savior. I am not worthy of the crown of life, except by the blood of Jesus Christ. Spare me, my Lord, from any condemnation so I may be found worthy of eternal life with you. Grant now, my petitions, in the name of the Father, the Son, and the Holy Spirit. Amen.

REFLECTIONS

What does the "Crown of Life" mean to you?

Please use the space below to write down any thoughts or comments you may have.

"May God Bless You,
As you live your Life for Christ,
Empowered by The Holy Spirit."

May 11

2 Corinthians 3:3 NIV.

[3] You show that you are a letter from Christ, the result of our ministry, written not with ink but with the spirit of the living God, not on tablets of stone but on tablets of human hearts.

O Father, how I long to be a minister of your Word. Reveal to me the truth of your Word, so, I may be a faithful servant in proclaiming you are the Almighty God, the Alpha, and the Omega. Lord, I can do nothing unless I prostrate myself before you and look beyond myself to the revelation of the Holy Spirit. Engrave your Words upon my heart so what I speak is not of me but the spirit of wisdom and revelation.

Please grant me the understanding, the spiritual discernment, and the passion needed for living out my faith in steadfast obedience to your Word. Shelter me from attempts by Satan to disarm my shield of strength that protects me from all adversities. Without you as my strength and refuge, I cannot call upon the power of the Holy Spirit to regenerate others into the faith. Yet, because of your steadfast love for me and my confidence in my Redeemer, Jesus Christ, I can do all things you set before my path. Praise to you, my God. Amen.

REFLECTIONS

What does it mean to regenerate others into a living faith in Christ?

Please use the space below to write down any thoughts or comments you may have.

"May God Bless You,
As you live your Life for Christ,
Empowered by The Holy Spirit."

May 12

2 Peter 1:5-7 NIV.

[5] For this very reason, make every effort to add to your faith goodness; and to goodness, knowledge; [6] and to knowledge, self-control; and to self-control, perseverance; and to perseverance, godliness; [7] and to godliness, mutual affection; and to mutual affection, love.

Light of the world, my Holy Messiah, hear the songs of praise upon my heart. The tenderness of your love has provided me with the assurance of faith that I am your child. The warmth of your embrace has given me the security to know that I can do all things through you. Instill in me all the qualities of a faithful servant; goodness, knowledge, self-control, perseverance, godliness, mutual affection, and the most significant attribute of all, the love of Christ.

Father, remove from me any thorns in my side that may impede the ministry of your Word. Remove from me the selfish nature that focuses on myself and not the needs of my fellow man. Remove from me the sin of pride that tears down the message of your love and postures me higher than a lowly servant. For I am your servant, to do your will, show your grace, share your compassion, and embrace your love with all your children. Here is my song to you, O Christ, to live for you, willingly die for my faith, and proclaim the message of your Gospel to the world. Praise to you, my Lord. Amen.

REFLECTIONS

What would be a Christian hymn or praise song that would be your song of praise to God.

Please use the space below to write down any thoughts or comments you may have.

*"May God Bless You,
As you live your Life for Christ,
Empowered by The Holy Spirit."*

May 13

1 Peter 5:10 NIV.

[10] And the God of all grace, who called you to his eternal glory in Christ, after you have suffered a little while, will himself restore you and make you strong, firm, and steadfast.

O Christ, my wonderful counselor, lend your ear upon me as I share the words upon my heart. My heart is weary from the stresses of the past. Forgiveness has escaped my lips, and I wallow in a sea of confusion and pain. Bless me with the spirit of wisdom and revelation coupled with the courage to risk forgiving those that have caused uncertainty in my life.

Restore my soul and lift me to the pinnacle of forgiveness so I may faithfully and without hesitation forgive those that have grieved my heart. Cleanse me from all unrighteousness in my thoughts and behavior so that I may be a faithful servant and follower of my Lord, Jesus Christ. Help me realize that an unforgiving heart is a burden upon my soul and that I cannot faithfully serve you when I have this transgression against those who have caused me pain. I rejoice in you, O Lord, for you are the Way, the Truth, and the Life, and in you do I place my faith. Amen.

REFLECTIONS

How do you feel when you have an unforgiving heart?

Please use the space below to write down any thoughts or comments you may have.

"May God Bless You,
As you live your Life for Christ,
Empowered by The Holy Spirit."

May 14

John 8:31-32 NIV.

[31] To the Jews who had believed him, Jesus said, "If you hold to my teaching you are really my disciples. [32] Then you will know the truth, and the truth will set you free."

O Great Redeemer, Lord of my life, I come before you on humble knees asking for your divine presence as I seek to be a faithful disciple of your Word. Allow the Truths of your scriptures' to be embedded in my heart. Cleanse my heart and soul from all impurities so I may not tarnish the words you lay upon my heart. Grant me the spirit of wisdom and revelation so I can enlighten others to live their lives as faithful disciples of Jesus Christ.

You are the Almighty God. The one true God. The God of Abraham and the Father of my Lord and Savior, Jesus Christ. Let me wear the truth of your Word as a shield to protect me from the ploys of Satan. And if I should succumb to his evil ways, rescue me through the power of the Holy Spirit so I may once again be free to live my life for you. Grant these things, I pray. Amen.

REFLECTIONS

What does it mean to be a Disciple of Christ?

Please use the space below to write down any thoughts or comments you may have.

"May God Bless You,
As you live your Life for Christ,
Empowered by The Holy Spirit."

May 15

Psalm 9:9 NIV.

[9] The Lord is a refuge for the oppressed, a stronghold in times of trouble.

Blessed Lion of Judah, I worship you, and I magnify you. From your Word, I gain the strength and encouragement to live my life for you. From your Word, I boldly find the power and wisdom to proclaim the Truth of your Holy Scriptures. I am but a servant among my Christian brothers and sisters in Christ, a servant that loves you and seeks to glorify you in all I say and do.

When oppressed, I lean on your Word to gain the strength needed to sustain my faith. When I am overwhelmed with joy, I proudly acknowledge you have been the source of my happiness. Glory to you, O Christ. Your love is ceaseless and knows no boundaries for those that remain in Christ. Let me be an instrument of faith-building to the unchurched so they too may know the same joy I have in my heart for you. I ask these things in the name of the Father, Son, and Holy Spirit. Amen.

REFLECTIONS

Read Revelation 5:5. Describe what it means to be the Lion of Judah.

Please use the space below to write down any thoughts or comments you may have.

"May God Bless You,
As you live your Life for Christ,
Empowered by The Holy Spirit."

May 16

Philippians 4:6 NIV.

[6] Do not be anxious about anything, but in every situation, by prayer and petition, with thanksgiving, present your requests to God.

O God, how grateful my heart is. This world has known so much turmoil and uncertainty. Yet by faith, I have the assurance that all things will work together for those who love the Lord. Among the nations of this world, there is war, conflict, terrorism, and persecution of your people. In the name of Jesus Christ and the Holy Spirit, extend your hand of reconciliation to calm the seas of anger and instill peace and righteousness to the lands of this earth.

Restore your people's devotion to the truth of your Word. Set them free from all persecution to the spreading of your Gospel. Lift those that do not know you and grant them a revelation that you are the true God so they may claim your Son as their eternal Savior. Grant these petitions in the spirit of hope and faith that your will shall come to pass. In Christ's name, I pray. Amen.

REFLECTIONS

Share what you would do if you were persecuted for your beliefs?

Please use the space below to write down any thoughts or comments you may have.

May 17

James 1:22 NIV.

[22] Do not merely listen to the word, and so deceive yourselves. Do what it says.

Precious Christ, Redeemer of my soul, as you walked this earth, you set the example for your children to live in the Truth of your love and Word. You always extend your grace to me even though I am unworthy.

Let me be a beacon of light and hope not only by listening to your Word but by my actions toward others. Restore me on the path of righteousness when I falter and do not comprehend the gravity of my sins. Awaken me so I may have the crystal clarity and knowledge I need to know when I am off the path of righteousness.

When I am consumed with doubt and depression, restore my mind and soul so I may once again rejoice in the love of my Lord and Savior, Jesus Christ. You are the Great Physician, the trustworthy source of healing power not only for my physical and mental illness but also for my soul's spiritual regeneration. Praise to you, O Lord. My heart is full of love for you. Amen.

REFLECTIONS

Do you understand the gravity of your sins and how they displease God?

Please use the space below to write down any thoughts or comments you may have.

"May God Bless You,
As you live your Life for Christ,
Empowered by The Holy Spirit."

May 18

Psalm 126:3 NIV.

[3] The Lord has done great things for us, and we are filled with joy.

Father, there is joy in my heart because of all the great things you have done for me. You have always been there to love and care for me despite my sinful nature. When I have been at my lowest point, consumed with anger and depression, you saw me through my self-absorption and self-destructive behavior. You then saw fit to rescue me through your tender mercies.

Praise to you, O Christ. Where would I be today if not for your enduring love? My gratitude and love for you are pale compared to the magnificence of your love and grace. You have given me a foothold into your kingdom. I shall prepare myself by humbly submitting myself to your pruning.

I will always love you and, with your help, forsake the temptations of this world. Extend your grace, I pray, so I may continue to be worthy of the bloodshed by your Son on the Cross of Calvary. Praise to you, O Christ. Amen.

REFLECTIONS

Describe the joy in your heart that you have for all God has done for you.

Please use the space below to write down any thoughts or comments you may have.

May 19

Romans 8:5-6 NIV.

[5] Those who live according to the flesh have their minds set on what the flesh desires; but those who live in accordance with the spirit have their minds set on what the spirit desires. [6] The mind governed by the flesh is death, but the mind governed by the spirit is life and peace.

O Most Gracious God, thank you for the gift of Salvation. Thank you for the power of the Holy Spirit, which guides me along the path of righteousness. Father, your Word serves as food for my soul and quells my hunger for the temptations placed in my way by Satan. Lord, when I keep my mind on the things of your kingdom, my heart is content. When my mind is consumed with lustful desires of the flesh, I am incomplete and lack fulfillment.

Grant me, O Christ, an earnest desire to always walk alongside you, to forever cherish your Word, and to always safeguard my heart with the joy of living for Christ. Praise to you, O Lord. For it is through the gifts of the Holy Spirit that I can rise above my sinful state and squash the power of Satan over me. In Jesus' name, I pray. Amen.

REFLECTIONS

How can things of the flesh keep you from being faithful to Christ?

Please use the space below to write down any thoughts or comments you may have.

"May God Bless You,
As you live your Life for Christ,
Empowered by The Holy Spirit."

May 20

Luke 10:20 NIV.

[20] However, do not rejoice that the spirits submit to you, but rejoice that your names are written in heaven.

Abide in me, O Christ, my Lord, and my Savior. Praise to your most high name. Thank you for writing my name down on the door of your kingdom. Thank you for giving me a rock to cling to in times of duress and fatigue. Thank you for loving me when I act like a spoiled child with concern only for myself. Thank you for walking beside me when I am consumed with depression and see no hope.

You are always with me, my Lord, even when I think I am alone. When the glory of your kingdom seems far away, I am reminded of the sacrifice your Son paid on the Cross of Calvary. Christ is my Redeemer and my Sanctuary. I am forever grateful for your love. Praise to you, O Christ.! Let me be a faithful child of yours even when I am in the throes of despair. In Christ's name, I pray. Amen.

REFLECTIONS

When the kingdom of God seems far away, how can you draw closer to His kingdom?

Please use the space below to write down any thoughts or comments you may have.

May 21

Romans 2:7 NIV.

[7] To those who by persistence in doing good seek glory, honor, and immortality, he will give eternal life.

Merciful Father, your Word promises eternal life in Heaven for those that love you and believe in your Son, Jesus Christ. I do not know when Jesus will come again, but I do know by faith, I will one day be surrounded by your angels in Heaven singing songs of praise and glory to your Holy Name. Prepare my heart and soul for that day, Lord, by shaping my virtues and character into a faithful reflection of your Son's glorious life.

Let me be full of love, compassion, and grace for my fellow man even when my patience is put to the test, and I am weary from the ploys of Satan. Lead me down the path of righteousness emboldened with the shield of the Holy Spirit as my protection so I may fend off all adversity that crosses my path. In all my ways, may I be persistent so I may prevail and claim victory through Jesus Christ, my Lord? Amen.

REFLECTIONS

What does eternal life mean to you? Have you accepted Jesus Christ as your Savior?

Please use the space below to write down any thoughts or comments you may have.

"May God Bless You,
As you live your Life for Christ,
Empowered by The Holy Spirit."

May 22

Galatians 5:5 NIV.

[5] For through the spirit we eagerly await by faith the righteousness for which we hope.

My Loving Faithful Lord Jesus, as this day begins, let me wait upon your voice to lead me by righteousness through the valleys of darkness. Let me hear your voice, O Lord, so I will be comforted and assured that I can overcome any obstacle in my path that threatens to cause me to stumble off my walk with you. Grant me the spirit of wisdom and revelation to know the truth of your Word as I struggle with the sinful nature that beckons me with sins of the flesh. Grant me the moral fortitude to squash the enemy and prevail over Satan as I soar like an eagle to victory through Christ.

Praise to you, my Lord, for you are faithful to me even when I have stumbled off the path of righteousness. And when I have regained my footing, you delight in my victory and send your angels to sing songs of joy and praise. All glory to you, O Lord. All praise to you. Amen.

REFLECTIONS

When you are consumed with your sinful nature, what do you need to do to please God?

Please use the space below to write down any thoughts or comments you may have.

May 23

Psalm 92:1-2 NIV.

[1] It is good to praise the Lord and make music to your name, O Most High, [2] proclaiming your love in the morning and your faithfulness at night.

Hallelujah, O Christ my King! I come before you this morning rejoicing in the love you bestow so graciously upon me. Because of your enduring love, I can rest assured that nothing is impossible if I cling to you. You are my Savior, my Redeemer, and the Truth by which I live. Fill me now with the power of the Holy Spirit as I proclaim your love, grace, and endless mercies.

O Father, your voice is sweet music to my ears. I listen for your whisper and hear the calling of your gentle voice. I come before you in fear because I am in awe of your love, grace, and forgiveness. Praise to you, O Lord. May I always be fruitful in my calling to serve you. May I permanently forsake the sins of this world and cling to your promises of eternal happiness in Heaven. And may I always have a repentant heart that turns from the evil one, so I may claim victory in Christ, my Lord. Hallelujah, O Christ my King! Hallelujah. Amen.

REFLECTIONS

- *Is your heart and mind open to hearing God's sweet music? If so, describe the music.*

Please use the space below to write down any thoughts or comments you may have.

"May God Bless You,
As you live your Life for Christ,
Empowered by The Holy Spirit."

May 24

Colossians 3:16-17 NIV.

[16] Let the message of Christ dwell among you richly as you teach and admonish one another with all wisdom through psalms, hymns, and songs from the spirit, singing to God with gratitude in your hearts. [17] And whatever you do, whether in word or deed, do it all in the name of the Lord Jesus, giving thanks to God the Father through him.

Glorious Prince of Peace, my risen Lord Jesus, my heart is filled with gratitude and love for the countless blessings you have showered upon me. So many benefits, my Lord, that I am awestruck by the outpouring of your love and grace.

Heavenly Father, I am a faithful servant of yours, who is willing to spread the message of your Gospel and ready to submit myself to your Lordship. My withered branches are dead and serve no purpose in glorifying you.

Continue to shape me into the child of God you intended me to be so I may teach and share with others the joy of knowing Christ. Whatever I do, O Christ, let me always sing praises to your Holy Name. You are the Alpha and the Omega, the beginning and the end, and in your name does my hope rest. Amen.

REFLECTIONS

What withered branches are keeping you from a closer relationship with Christ?

Please use the space below to write down any thoughts or comments you may have.

"May God Bless You,
As you live your Life for Christ,
Empowered by The Holy Spirit."

May 25

Psalm 86:11 NIV.

[11] Teach me your way, Lord, that I may rely on your faithfulness; give me an undivided heart, that I may fear your name.

Blessed Jesus, my Lord, and Redeemer, I give thanks for the seasons of life. These seasons give me the opportunity for personal growth and test my faith and love for you. Lord, without these seasons, my faith could become stagnant and unfruitful. I am your child, willing to be pruned of withered branches no matter what the season.

I rejoice in knowing there is a blessing for those who surrender their lives to you. I am a wretched sinner redeemed by the blood of your Son, Jesus Christ, who died so I may have eternal life with you in Heaven. How gracious and merciful is your love. I rejoice in knowing you and the joy of being able to praise you. Let me always be fruitful as I devote my life to service in your name. In the name of the Father, Son, and Holy Spirit. Amen.

REFLECTIONS

What areas of service or fruits of the Holy Spirit is Christ calling you to use?

Please use the space below to write down any thoughts or comments you may have.

"May God Bless You,
As you live your Life for Christ,
Empowered by The Holy Spirit."

May 26

Ephesians 3:20 NIV.

[20] Now to him who is able to do immeasurably more than all we ask or imagine, according to his power that is at work within us.

My Blessed Lord Jesus, I praise you for the sacrifice you paid on the Cross of Calvary for my sins. I commend you for the beautiful lessons of love and grace you have taught me. I praise you for being there along my path in life when I need to cry out for comfort and guidance. There is none like you, my God, no none like you. You are the Great Comforter. When I am caught up in the ways of this world, you speak to my heart and gently guide me back into your fold.

What more could I ask for, O Christ? You are the source of my strength, the foundation of my hope, and the beginning of eternal peace. Praise to you, my Lord. May the power of the Holy Spirit always guide and comfort me as I put on the coat of armor to shield me from the ploys of Satan. In your name, I pray. Amen.

REFLECTIONS

Are you feeling spiritually weak today? If so, how can God help you?

Please use the space below to write down any thoughts or comments you may have.

"May God Bless You,
As you live your Life for Christ,
Empowered by The Holy Spirit."

May 27

Matthew 7:7-8 NIV.

[7] "Ask and it will be given to you; seek and you will find; knock and the door will be opened to you. [8] For everyone who asks receives; the one who seeks finds; and to the one who knocks, the door will be opened.

Most Merciful God, through your Son, Jesus Christ, I am a redeemed sinner who loves you and prays for your constant strength to live out my faith untarnished. Lord Jesus, you said, "Ask and it will be given to you, seek and you will find…" Father, I ask that you open the gates of Heaven and let your Holy Spirit descend upon me. Help me to be loyal in my walk with you and be able to hear your admonishment when I falter. Let me not be caught up in the lusts of the world, be it sexual lusts or the lust for money.

I am your child, lost without you, but fulfilled when I keep my eyes and heart on you. Grant me the spirit of wisdom and revelation so I may discern the truth of your Word. And give me the courage to live my life in an honorable and faithful manner to your Word. In the name of your Son, Jesus Christ, grant now my petition. Amen.

REFLECTIONS

"Ask, and it will be given to you…" Does that mean anything you ask for God will give you?

Please use the space below to write down any thoughts or comments you may have.

"May God Bless You,
As you live your Life for Christ,
Empowered by The Holy Spirit."

May 28

Matthew 5:6 NIV.

[6] Blessed are those who hunger and thirst for righteousness, for they will be filled.

Wonder, Faithful and Blessed Lord Jesus, I come before you today with a hunger and thirst for righteousness. Grant me, I pray, the moral fortitude to be faithful to your Word and live out my Christian life in an honorable and holy manner. Lord, you know the grasp Satan has on my life. He is always seeking to tear me down and to break me away from my walk with Christ. The closer I get to you; it seems he tempts me more and more and intrudes upon my life by placing more temptations before me.

Thank you, Lord, for the strength of your Word that I can use to rebuke him and stay on the path of righteousness. Always stay with me, O Christ, so I may have the shield of your strength to fight off Satan's attacks. And when I falter in my walk, send your Holy Spirit's whisper to guide me back to you and your loving embrace. Amen.

REFLECTIONS

When Satan has a strangle-hold on you, is it possible to break free of him?

Please use the space below to write down any thoughts or comments you may have.

"May God Bless You,
As you live your Life for Christ,
Empowered by The Holy Spirit."

May 29

Isaiah 41:13 NIV.

[13] For I am the Lord your God who takes hold of your right hand and says to you, do not fear; I will help you.

O Faithful and Just God, you are the light that shines in the darkness. When I am consumed with fear, you are always there to calm my soul and uplift me with your tender Words of love. You are my refuge and the one whom I go to when confronted with thoughts that tear down my will to live for you. I will not allow Satan to be the breeder of dark news in my life. I will not allow Satan to hold me captive to the temptations of worldly sins. I will persevere and conquer his evil ways by clinging to the truth of your Word and by calling on the power of the Holy Spirit to deliver me from his clutches.

You are the Almighty God. You are the one I serve. You are the one I love. Empower me now, through the Holy Spirit, with a moral compass and the personal integrity to always be faithful in my walk with you. Amen.

REFLECTIONS

- *Is it difficult to see God's light when you are consumed with the darkness of the world?*

Please use the space below to write down any thoughts or comments you may have.

"May God Bless You,
As you live your Life for Christ,
Empowered by The Holy Spirit."

May 30

Proverbs 12:8 NIV.

[8] A person is praised according to their prudence, and one with a warped mind is despised.

My loving Christ, my precious Redeemer, grant unto me this day the spirit of wisdom and revelation so, I may be wise and prudent in all the choices I make. Lord, the evil one is a constant threat to my happiness. Despite how much I love you and worship you, the forces of Satan wear me down. This world is corrupt and vile because it has turned away from you.

O Lord, let me take on your armor to be successful against any attacks by Satan on my character. Turn me towards my faithful brothers and sisters in Christ when I need admonishment and correction in my behavior. Lead me through my dark days, so I may see the glorious light of your kingdom waiting for me at the end of the day. Let me always praise you for your love, forgiveness, and eternal grace. In the name of the One who gave his life for me, Jesus Christ. Amen.

REFLECTIONS

- *How important to you is protecting your character from attacks by Satan? Why?*

Please use the space below to write down any thoughts or comments you may have.

"May God Bless You,
As you live your Life for Christ,
Empowered by The Holy Spirit."

May 31

Romans 13:1 NIV.

[1] Let everyone be subject to the governing authorities, for there is no authority except that which God has established. The authorities that exist have been established by God.

Blessed Lord Jesus, by your hand, you grant authority to those whom I live under. Grant me now the spiritual wisdom to discern man's righteousness versus the righteousness of the Almighty God. Your Holy Word has been defiled by mankind. It bleeds a culture that bends its morals and values to suit their own desires rather than living by the truth of your Word. Forgive me when I succumb to these senseless rationalizations that try to usurp your Word.

Grant me the spirit of wisdom and revelation to faithfully discern righteousness and to submit to your authority in all matters of faith. Build me up in character and faithfulness so I may always be steadfast in my devotion to you. And if I should stumble, lovingly admonish me, and restore me on the path of righteousness. In the name of the Father, Son, and Holy Spirit. Amen.

REFLECTIONS

Have you witnessed recent attempts by man to usurp God's Word? If so, how?

Please use the space below to write down any thoughts or comments you may have.

"May God Bless You,
As you live your Life for Christ,
Empowered by The Holy Spirit."

June 1

Romans 3:25 NIV.

[25] God presented Christ as a sacrifice of atonement, through the shedding of his blood, to be received by faith. He did this to demonstrate his righteousness, because in his forbearance he had left the sins committed beforehand unpunished.

Precious Christ, by your cross and resurrection, you have set me free from the torment of sin. By the shedding of your blood, you are the atonement, by faith, of a living sacrifice given by the grace of God. When caught up in the sins of the world, I look to you as my refuge and source of righteousness. What joy there is in my heart, knowing that I find Salvation in you and through you. What peace is in my heart knowing you are the Son of the Living God, the source of all Truth and the absolute authority of all that is good and righteous.

Praise to you, O Lord. For you are my King, my hope and strength when I falter and lay prostrate on the ground crying out for your mercies. How can I be worthy of your love, my God? It is only through your Son, Jesus Christ, and your endless love, grace, and forgiveness. Bless me now, this day. In Christ's name, I pray. Amen.

REFLECTIONS

What does it mean to you to know that Christ was a living sacrifice for you?

Please use the space below to write down any thoughts or comments you may have.

"May God Bless You,
As you live your Life for Christ,
Empowered by The Holy Spirit."

June 2

James 2:13 NIV.

[13] because judgment without mercy will be shown to anyone who has not been merciful. Mercy triumphs over judgment.

Holy Lord, gracious and most merciful, by the Holy Spirit, you have implanted in my heart undying hope to love, serve, and obey your Word. Father, there are days when I am overcome with frustration and want to react inappropriately to situations that cross my path. Where I should extend mercy and grace, I look inwardly and think only of myself. When people act in ways that cause anxiety and leave me in a state of uncertainty, I want to run and seek solace from worldly ways.

Forgive me, Lord Jesus, for my weak spirit. Forgive me for being selfish and insensitive to the plight of others. Bless me with your forgiveness and mercy. Restore me on the path of understanding, so I may be a faithful servant of yours no matter what adversity I may face. For the truth of your Word is the longing and fulfillment of my heart's desire. Renew me and through your saving grace, look upon me once again with favor. Amen.

REFLECTIONS

Have you ever acted in ways that caused anxiety in others? How did that make you feel?

Please use the space below to write down any thoughts or comments you may have.

"May God Bless You,
As you live your Life for Christ,
Empowered by The Holy Spirit."

June 3

2 Corinthians 7:10 NIV.

[10] Godly sorrow brings repentance that leads to Salvation and leaves no regret, but worldly sorrow brings death.

Heavenly Father, at the beginning of another day, I come before you with a heart full of remorse and sadness, sadness from my inability to lead an utterly faithful life devoted to living out the truth of your Word. I have succumbed to sins of lust and frustration, sins that grieve my heart and yours. Forgive me of these transgressions and restore me on the path of righteousness so I may bear the fruits of the Holy Spirit.

Let me be sincerely repentant this day as I venture forth confident that I can accomplish all things through your Son, Jesus Christ. It is only through your Son that I will be able to be faithful in my walk. Praise to you, O Lord, for your admonishment and correction as I submit to your will for my life. In the name of the One who delivers me, Jesus Christ. Amen.

REFLECTIONS

What does it mean to be delivered by Christ?

Please use the space below to write down any thoughts or comments you may have.

"May God Bless You,
As you live your Life for Christ,
Empowered by The Holy Spirit."

June 4

John 14:26 NIV.

[26] But the Advocate, the Holy Spirit, whom the Father will send in my name, will teach you all things and will remind you of everything I have said to you.

Gracious God, Father of my Lord Jesus Christ, through your advocate the Holy Spirit, you enable me to live a fruitful life of obedience to your Word. Through the Holy Spirit, I hear your whisper when Satan breaches the door of my conscience. And through your love and endless mercies, you give me the power to resist Satan in all his forms so I may be safe from the perils of an ungodly life. Praise to you, O Lord, for without you, I am lost and tossed about in a sea of rebellion.

Thank you for the gift of redemption that comes from a life in Christ. Thank you for your precious grace that is bestowed upon me even though I do not deserve it. And thank you, dear Lord, for the ability to live a life of righteousness on this earth so I can attempt to model my life after yours. Let me be fruitful in my desire to faithfully live as you did, full of hope, faith, and love for all your people on this earth. Amen.

REFLECTIONS

Describe the life of one that is in faithful obedience to Christ.

Please use the space below to write down any thoughts or comments you may have.

"May God Bless You,
As you live your Life for Christ,
Empowered by The Holy Spirit."

June 5

Psalm 119:9 NIV.

[9] How can a young person stay on the path of purity? By living according to your word.

My Lord God, the Creator of the Universe, send now your Holy Spirit to revive my soul so I may bear the fruits in my life that can serve your people. Help me to stay pure and live according to your Word, so I may be a faithful disciple of your Son, Jesus Christ. Create in me an earnest desire to reach out to the lost and to touch their lives with the grace and love you so generously shower upon me. Lead me down the path of righteousness so I may be a faithful example of one whose walk is in Christ. Grant these petitions in the name of the one who gave his life for me, my Lord and Savior, Jesus Christ. Amen.

REFLECTIONS

Have you ever felt the need for God to revive your soul? If so, what did you do?

Please use the space below to write down any thoughts or comments you may have.

"May God Bless You,
As you live your Life for Christ,
Empowered by The Holy Spirit."

June 6

Hebrews 4:15-16 NIV.

[15] For we do not have a high priest who is unable to empathize with our weaknesses, but we have one who has been tempted in every way, just as we are---yet he did not sin. [16] Let us then approach God's throne of grace with confidence, so that we may receive mercy and find grace to help us in our time of need.

Heavenly Father, in my weakness, I come to you asking for your help. I know without the armor of the Lord, I am utterly useless in fighting the temptations of the evil one. I know if I am healthy, Lord Jesus, I can do all things through the power of the Holy Spirit. I would be doomed to a life of misery, loneliness, and failure in my ability to serve you without the saving grace of my Lord and Savior, Jesus Christ.

Help me, Father, by giving me the strength and courage to get through the trials I face. Lift me up, gracious Lord, so I may be a shining example of one who loves you and is prepared to give his own life to defend my faith. Praise to you, O Christ. Let me go forth this day triumphant in my victory over sin and in serving you as the Lord and Master of my life. Amen.

REFLECTIONS

Share with God some weaknesses in your life you need His help with

Please use the space below to write down any thoughts or comments you may have.

"May God Bless You,
As you live your Life for Christ,
Empowered by The Holy Spirit."

June 7

Deuteronomy 20:4 NIV.

[4] For the Lord your God is the one who goes with you to fight for you against your enemies to give you victory.

Holy Father, through my Savior, Jesus Christ, I give you thanks with a grateful heart for your steadfast love. I give you thanks for your Word that promises me that I can overcome any temptation if I call upon your name. How strong am I, O Lord? Through your Son, Jesus Christ, I am strong enough to defeat the enemy that causes my weakness. Through you, I can overcome any temptation by remembering to always be mindful that I am a child of God. You are there to defend me with the truth of your Word.

What a glorious feeling to know I am free from the dominion of Satan, who wants nothing more than to destroy your kingdom on earth. Raise up the Sword of Truth and slay the evil one so he may never again cause me to falter in my walk with Christ. Praise to you, my Lord, as I go about this day confident in my victory through your Son, Jesus Christ. Amen.

REFLECTIONS

Do you feel confident through hrist that you can have victory over Satan?

Please use the space below to write down any thoughts or comments you may have.

"May God Bless You,
As you live your Life for Christ,
Empowered by The Holy Spirit."

June 8

Romans 9:1 NIV.

[1] I speak the truth in Christ---I am not lying, my conscience confirms it through the holy spirit. [2] I have great sorrow and unceasing anguish in my heart.

Precious Lord Jesus, Son of Righteousness, shines into my heart and life today. Lord, I am weary and feel much sorrow in my heart because I think I am unworthy of your love. Father, Jesus, I am a sinner caught up in the sins of this world. Your love is so great, so faithful, that no matter what my sinful state may be, you are right and devoted to your Word to welcome me into your presence.

Lord, you have chosen me to be worthy of your love and sacrifice on the Cross of Calvary. You have taken me from the clutches of Satan and, through baptism into the Holy Spirit, brought me into the kingdom of God. Father, I praise you for the gift of Salvation, the power of your redeeming blood, and the joy of being in your presence through the offering of grace and faith. Forgive me of all my transgressions as I enter another day in service to your Holy Name. Amen.

REFLECTIONS

What does the baptism of the Holy Spirit mean to you?

Please use the space below to write down any thoughts or comments you may have.

"May God Bless You,
As you live your Life for Christ,
Empowered by The Holy Spirit."

June 9

Psalm 105:3 NIV.

[3] Glory in his Holy Name; let the hearts of those who seek the Lord rejoice.

Glory to you, O Lord, my King, and my Savior! Praise to your Holy Name. I come before you are today confident my sins are forgiven and optimistic that I can be a faithful crusader for Christ. You have saved me from the perils of corruption. You have given me a taste of your Holy kingdom. You have made me alive through your Son, Jesus Christ, so I can be bold in my witness before my family, friends, and neighbors.

Who am I to question your will for my life? Who am I to doubt the wonders of your creation? I rest on the Truth of your Holy Word and place my faith in your Son, Jesus Christ, to be my Rock of faith. What more could I ask, my God? I love you. I praise you. And I will glorify your name before all men until my judgment day comes and I arrive in your kingdom. Thank you, my God. All praise and glory to your name. Amen.

REFLECTIONS

Sometimes, family or friends may question your faith. Is it hard to be bold before them?

Please use the space below to write down any thoughts or comments you may have.

"May God Bless You,
As you live your Life for Christ,
Empowered by The Holy Spirit."

June 10

Proverbs 13:6 NIV.

[6] Righteousness guards the person of integrity, but wickedness overthrows the sinner.

Holy God, my loving Father, keep me; I pray from temptation today. I do not know what tricks Satan may use to deceive me, but I ask you to protect me with a Shield of Armor so strong that any sin that does come may bounce off my chest and leave me free from its grasp. I am weak, O Lord, but you are powerful. I am lost, but through your Son, I have a place in your kingdom on earth and eternal peace in Heaven. I am your child whom you love. And with all my heart, O Christ, I give my love to you. No matter what temptations may cross my path, I am capable of repentance and spoiling the attempts of Satan to defile me. Yes, Lord, I am your child, a child of the Almighty God, and a child who knows his Father in Heaven. Praise be to your name. Amen.

REFLECTIONS

- *How can you build up your shield of armor to protect you from demonic attacks?*

Please use the space below to write down any thoughts or comments you may have.

"May God Bless You,
As you live your Life for Christ,
Empowered by The Holy Spirit."

June 11

Acts 13:52 NIV.

[52] And the disciples were filled with joy and with the holy spirit.

Holy and Faithful Father, thank you for the gifts of love and friendship. Thank you for Christian brothers and sisters in Christ who are faithful to your Word. Thank you for your affection, grace, and forgiveness that restores me spiritually and keeps me in your loving embrace. You are the Almighty God whom I love to glorify and sing praises to.

Praise to you, O Christ, for the angels of Heaven proclaim you are coming again on the appointed day. I wait with anticipation for that day and know in my heart that not by my good works, but by faith and grace, I shall one day be among your angels basking in the warmth of your love with eternal peace. Glory to you, O Lord. Amen.

REFLECTIONS

Can you feel God's love for you when you are consumed with sin?

Please use the space below to write down any thoughts or comments you may have.

"May God Bless You,
As you live your Life for Christ,
Empowered by The Holy Spirit."

June 12

Colossians 3:1-4 NIV.

[1] Since, then you have been raised with Christ, set your hearts on things above, where Christ is, seated at the right hand of God. [2] Set your minds on things above, not on earthly things. [3] For you died, and your life is now hidden with Christ in God. [4] When Christ, who is your life, appears, then you also will appear with him in glory.

Glorious Christ, my faithful Redeemer, I exalt you and praise you for your steadfast love and unending grace. I stand before you firm in my passion and conviction for the truth of your Word. I stand before you boldly proclaiming you are the Son of the Living God, the Alpha and Omega, and the Living Water that nourishes my soul. I will not abandon my faith nor falter in my strength as I stand up for what I believe. My heart is set on things of your kingdom, and with your help, I will remain loyal and faithful to your Word. Give me the strength to rise above pettiness that does little to further your kingdom on earth. I shall always love you and stand up for my faith when the enemy of your Word seeks to destroy me. Praise to you, O God. Amen.

REFLECTIONS

With all the satanic influences in the world, how can you remain firm in your faith?

Please use the space below to write down any thoughts or comments you may have.

"May God Bless You,
As you live your Life for Christ,
Empowered by The Holy Spirit."

June 13

Colossians 3:5-8 NIV.

[5] Put to death, therefore, whatever belongs to your earthly nature: sexual immorality, impurity, lust, evil desires, and greed, which is idolatry. [6] Because of these, the wrath of God is coming. [7] You used to walk in these ways, in the life you once lived. [8] But now you must also rid yourselves of all such things as these: anger, rage, malice, slander, and filthy language from your lips.

O Lord, my most awesome God, the Great Comforter, I come before you overcome with the grievous nature of my sins. I come before you laden with heartache and remorse because I have not been as faithful in my walk with Christ as I long to be. I come before you begging to forgive my sins of the flesh, sins of anger and discord, and sins of malice toward others. How grievous my sins must be upon your heart, O Christ? I am saddened by the words that come from my lips and the behaviors I have exhibited.

Grant me absolution, I pray, so I may once again be looked upon with favor in your eyes. Restore my heart and my soul to the place that honors and loves you by actively pursuing Holy motives that bring honor and glory to your name. I pray these things earnestly, O God, in the name of the Father, Son, and Holy Spirit. Amen.

REFLECTIONS

What divine motive could you pursue today that would please Christ?

Please use the space below to write down any thoughts or comments you may have.

*"May God Bless You,
As you live your Life for Christ,
Empowered by The Holy Spirit."*

June 14

2 Corinthians 13:11 NIV.

[11] Finally, brothers and sisters, rejoice! Strive for full restoration, encourage one another, be of one mind, live in peace. And the God of love and peace will be with you.

Loving and Merciful Lord Jesus, your love transcends any love I have ever known. Your soft voice embraces me with peace and contentment that nourishes my soul. You are my Lord. I love you and praise you for all you have done for me. Please hear my prayer this day. I need peace in my heart and soul. I need you to watch over my household and extend all the tender mercies I need. I need to be restored so I may be a faithful witness of your love. Help me, O God, to navigate the uncharted waters of this day with courage, patience, and hope so I may succeed in my honoring of your Word. Praise to you, O Christ, my Lord, and my Redeemer, for all your blessings. Amen.

REFLECTIONS

What would give you peace and contentment today?

Please use the space below to write down any thoughts or comments you may have.

"May God Bless You,
As you live your Life for Christ,
Empowered by The Holy Spirit."

June 15

Psalm 30:4 NIV.

[4] Sing the praises of the Lord his faithful people; praise his Holy Name.

Precious Lord Jesus, the Christ, Author, and Finisher of my faith, be with me today as I demonstrate my love and trust in your Word. I thank you for being my Deliverer and the Rock upon which I stand. You are my Lord! I love you. I Praise you. I give thanks to your Holy Name for all the blessings you generously shower upon me. Apart from you, I am a worthless sinner, but in you and through you, I am a child of God worthy of your love and grace. Why you love me as you do is a mystery to me. Still, I am eternally grateful for your presence in my life and the enduring love and mercies you continuously bless me with.

As this day begins, fortify me with the Shield of the Almighty God so I may be able to fend off the evil one and his desperate ploys to separate me from your love. Praise to your Name, O Christ, for you are the eternal God. Amen.

REFLECTIONS

Why do you love God? Is He worthy of your love? Are you worthy of His love?

Please use the space below to write down any thoughts or comments you may have.

June 16

1 Samuel 12:23 NIV.

[23] As for me, far be it from me that I should sin against the Lord by failing to pray for you. And I will teach you the way that is good and right.

Blessed Lord and Savior, Jesus Christ, teach me the ways of grace so I may extend to others the same blessings you have extended to me. Teach me how to love unconditionally, so my love is pure and fruitful as I witness to others. Show me the path of righteousness so I may point others to the same way. Allow me, my Lord, the spirit of wisdom and revelation that I need to explain to others how they too can have a loving relationship with you. Allow me to grow in faith, love, and charity so I may always be a real victor in my battle against Satan. And may I always enjoy your blessings as I faithfully bring others to Christ. Point me now to the next person whose life you want me to touch. In the name of the Father, Son, and Holy Spirit. Amen.

REFLECTIONS

Is there someone you know whose life can be touched with the Good News of Jesus Christ?

Please use the space below to write down any thoughts or comments you may have.

"May God Bless You,
As you live your Life for Christ,
Empowered by The Holy Spirit."

June 17

1 John 2:16 NIV.

[16] For everything in the world---the lust of the flesh, the lust of the eyes, and the pride of life---comes not from the Father but from the world.

O Holy Spirit and my faithful Lord and Savior, Jesus Christ, you beckon me to live a life of righteousness and purity. You beckon me to forsake the sins of the flesh, lust in my heart, and worldly pride that can cause me to falter in my walk with you. You beckon me to love you above all earthly goods and to glorify your name in all I do. I come before you, my Lord, a sinner by nature but redeemed in your sight through the blood of Christ.

Lead me forward this day, confident in my ability to fend off the evil one and in my ability to have victory over my sins. Protect me from myself and my self-indulgent pride that fails to honor your Word. You are the Almighty God, maker of Heaven and earth, and it is into your hands that I place all my faults so you can wipe them clean. Praise to you, O Christ. Let me be a blessing to others this day as I live my life for you? Amen.

REFLECTIONS

Has pride interfered with your walk with Christ?

Please use the space below to write down any thoughts or comments you may have.

"May God Bless You,
As you live your Life for Christ,
Empowered by The Holy Spirit."

June 18

Psalm 51:11 NIV.

[11] Do not cast me from your presence or take your holy spirit from me.

My Lord God, my Father in Christ Jesus, I do not know what today has in store for me, but I am not afraid because I have you. In your Word, you have promised me your continued presence through all trials and tribulations I may face. The evil one continually seeks to destroy me, but I can claim victory through Jesus Christ because of my faith in you. In you, I can do all things. And because of you, I can claim victory in life situations that cause me to stumble in my Christian walk.

Lead me always, my Lord, down the path of righteousness so I may not only conquer my fears and failings but so I can be mindful of your continued presence in my life. Father, I delight in the fruits of the Holy Spirit. I pray that your blessings will always keep the Holy Spirit upon me so I may be a faithful witness of one who is in Christ Jesus. Amen.

REFLECTIONS

- *You never know when a challenging situation in life will come up. What can you do when it does?*

Please use the space below to write down any thoughts or comments you may have.

"May God Bless You,
As you live your Life for Christ,
Empowered by The Holy Spirit."

June 19

Exodus 19:4 NIV.

[4] 'You yourselves have seen what I did to Egypt, and how I carried you on eagles' wings and brought you to myself.

O Christ, my Lord, and my Redeemer, hear the pleas of my heart. I am lost without your constant watch over me. Without you, I wander from your Word and get caught up in the cesspool of life that tears down the moral fiber of my character. I do not want to be lost and enslaved to the ways of this world. Free me, my Lord, from myself and the evil intentions of Satan. Build me up strong in character and with the strength of one who is victorious over sin.

I am your child and belong not to the ways of the flesh but as one who wants to live to glorify your name. Enable me, my God, with the power of the Holy Spirit, so I may always be mindful of my walk. And when I fall off the path of righteousness, let me rise like an eagle and soar to new heights in my faith and love for your Son, Jesus Christ. I ask these things in the name of the One who paid the ultimate price for my fallen nature, Jesus Christ. Praise to you, O Lord. Amen.

REFLECTIONS

What can you do to build up your Christian character?

Please use the space below to write down any thoughts or comments you may have.

June 20

Nehemiah 2:2 NIV.

[2] so the king asked me, "Why does your face look so sad when you are not ill? This can be nothing but sadness of heart." I was very much afraid, ...

Glorious Father, my heart awakens today with the pain of loneliness. I look to fill my life with sins of the flesh but find no fulfillment. I am empty, and I am wallowing in a sea of despair. Where am I without you, O Lord? Is there a place in your kingdom for a sinner as wretched as I am? I try to overcome my sinful nature to find contentment and joy in living my life for you, but the clouds of depression come over me. Lift this cloud of darkness from my eyes, O Lord, so I may receive your eternal love and forgiveness through your Son, Jesus Christ.

Let me not succumb to sins of the flesh. Fill me instead with the power of the Holy Spirit so no matter how depressed I may be, I can still see the light of your Truth through my darkness. Rescue me, O God, and take this burden of depression from my heart so I may indeed find comfort, love, and security in the arms of my Lord. Restore my relationship with Jesus Christ. As a child of God, I walk down the righteous path singing songs of praise and speaking words of adoration. Love me, my Lord, when I find it difficult to love myself. In the name of the Father, Son, and Holy Spirit. Amen.

REFLECTIONS

Describe the clouds of darkness that may be keeping you from God's eternal love.

Please use the space below to write down any thoughts or comments you may have.

"May God Bless You,
As you live your Life for Christ,
Empowered by The Holy Spirit."

June 21

Luke 9:26 NIV.

[26] Whoever is ashamed of me and my words, the Son of Man will be ashamed of them when he comes in his glory and in the glory of the Father and of the holy angels.

Great Father in Heaven, I give thanks for your Holy Word and my Savior, Jesus Christ. I stand before you unabashedly devoted in my love and my willingness to lay down my life for you. You are my God, the one whom I turn to when confronted with the frustrations of this world. So many people, my Lord, turn from you and your loving grace. Many people want nothing more than to pursue this world's interests at the expense of eternal life with you.

I will not be ashamed of loving you, my God. I will not turn from your loving grace and live a sinful life. While I am weak, with my faith in you, I can do all things. I can rise above my sinful nature and see the promise of redemption by living my life for you. I am your child. Shape me, Lord Jesus, into a faithful disciple of your Word. Shape me into one who is obedient to your Word even at the expense of earthly pleasures. Comfort me when I am weak and in despair and lead me always to victory through Christ Jesus. Amen.

REFLECTIONS

In what ways does God need to shape you? Will you let Him?

Please use the space below to write down any thoughts or comments you may have.

"May God Bless You,
As you live your Life for Christ,
Empowered by The Holy Spirit."

June 22

Psalm 54:2 NIV.

[2] Hear my prayer, O God; listen to the words of my mouth.

O Precious Lord Jesus, hear the cries of my heart. I come before you through prayer, asking for your Divine Intervention. Lord, you know my heart. You know my needs. Lord, I often have difficulties sharing my thoughts with you because of the sin in my life. Because I am often led astray by the ways of this world, I have allowed a wedge to come between me and your presence. I do not want to be like this, my Lord. I want to be able to whisper to you my deepest thoughts and fears and to be able to hear your sweet whisper of love and assurance that you will always love me.

Forgive me, Lord, when I have been led astray and when I fail to come before you in faithful prayer. Give me the assurance that you will hear me and answer my prayers in your way and timing. I love you, O Christ, and ask that you fortify my character against the evil in this world. Let me not be consumed by fears and doubts when I struggle in my prayer life. Give me the faith and hope that I may come to have a closer relationship with you through prayer. Restore my heart through the power of the Holy Spirit, so I may know with confidence that you are my God in whom I place my trust. Amen.

REFLECTIONS

How important is your prayer life for you to have a personal relationship with Christ?

Please use the space below to write down any thoughts or comments you may have.

"May God Bless You,
As you live your Life for Christ,
Empowered by The Holy Spirit."

June 23

Proverbs 20:7 NIV.

[7] The righteous lead blameless lives; blessed are their children after them.

Heavenly Father, hear the prayers of my heart. I want nothing more than to serve you in reverence and awe and to be a faithful witness of your Holy Word. Lord, I want to live a blameless life and to be an authentic example of one in Christ so I can lead others to Jesus. I wish I did not fail so often, my Lord, because I know it grieves your heart. I wish I could be more like Jesus and turn the other cheek when confronted with adversity. I wish I were more faithful in proclaiming the message of your Gospel to strangers I come upon. But I am weak, and although I fail you so often, please forgive me for my transgressions and lift me up in your grace so I may be a better person.

I love you, my God. And although I struggle with personal failings, know I am and always will be your servant, devoted to you and to the service of others through Christ Jesus. My heart is yours, and although it sometimes is held captive by sin, I will continue to fight to break free of the shackles that bind me to the ways of this world. Bless me, Father, as I live my life for you, through Christ Jesus. Amen.

REFLECTIONS

- *Why is it difficult to turn the other cheek when confronted by someone who hurts you?*

Please use the space below to write down any thoughts or comments you may have.

"May God Bless You,
As you live your Life for Christ,
Empowered by The Holy Spirit."

June 24

Psalm 91:2 NIV.

[2] I will say of the Lord, "He is my refuge and my fortress, my God, in whom I trust."

O Great Jehovah, in whom I trust, you are my refuge and my fortress from which I gather my strength to fend off the enemy. With you as my Advocate, I can do all things. With you as my Rock, I remain grounded in the truth of your Word. With your Son, Jesus Christ, as my Savior, I am free from the burdens of my sins and can look forward to the day I spend eternal life with you.

Praise to you, O Lord, for your faithfulness and unending grace. Thank you for being the foundation of my trust. Thank you for giving me the confidence to faithfully live my life as I place all my trust in your Holy Word. Thank you for the redemption I find through the body and blood of my Lord and Savior, Jesus Christ. Let me go forth this day, knowing with certainty that you are the God above all creation. Let me forever be blessed for my faithfulness to your Word. Praise to you, O Christ. Glory to you, my Lord. Amen.

REFLECTIONS

What does it mean to have God as your advocate?

Please use the space below to write down any thoughts or comments you may have.

June 25

James 4:4 NIV.

[4] You adulterous people, don't you know that friendship with the world means enmity against God? Therefore, anyone who chooses to be a friend of the world becomes an enemy of God.

My Lord, my God, in whom I seek solace and peace. I come to you seeking a ray of hope among those lost and who do not know you as their personal Savior. Please help me because keeping company with those who do not know you can be dangerous to my relationship with you. Because I can be susceptible to influences that tear me away from my oneness in Christ, I need your divine presence. Lord, I seek your Divine Intervention and pray your Holy Spirit will be upon me as I witness to those who do not know you.

Present me with precious opportunities to see them in a spirit of love and humility. Bring me the words to share so their hearts may be touched by the power of the Holy Spirit. Grant me a hedge of protection from the evil one, so I may be on guard against those influences that detract from my witness. Let your love, grace, and forgiveness be extended to all those I meet so they, too, may know the joy of living their lives for Christ. Amen.

REFLECTIONS

Have you ever been afraid to witness a non-believer? If so, why?

Please use the space below to write down any thoughts or comments you may have.

"May God Bless You,
As you live your Life for Christ,
Empowered by The Holy Spirit."

June 26

1 Peter 2:25 NIV.

[25] For "you were like sheep going astray," but now you have returned to the Shepherd and Overseer of your souls.

O Christ, my Redeemer, take my hand this day and lead me forward, knowing that I can be confident in my victory over Satan if I follow your walk. Lead me with a firm hand so I may not wander from the path of righteousness as a lamb may from its shepherd. Guide me over gravelly soil and rocks so I may not stumble in my walk with you. Fill me with the power of the Holy Spirit so I may see with clarity the truth of your Word.

Grant me the spirit of wisdom and revelation as I seek to learn and obey the validity of your written Word. Be my faithful companion as I reach out to hold your hand when an obstacle crosses my path. I am your child, my God. I will always love you and glorify your Holy Name. Praise to you, O Lord. Glory to you, my Living Shepherd. Amen.

REFLECTIONS

What does it mean to be a lamb led by the Good Shepherd?

Please use the space below to write down any thoughts or comments you may have.

"May God Bless You,
As you live your Life for Christ,
Empowered by The Holy Spirit."

June 27

2 John 1:6 NIV.

[6] And this is love: that we walk in obedience to his commands. As you have heard from the beginning, his command is that you walk in love.

Most merciful God, I rejoice at the sound of your trumpet calling me to follow you through the dark valleys of confusion. I rejoice that through your Son, Jesus Christ, I am made alive through the blood spilled on the Cross of Calvary. I rejoice that Jesus paid it all, and because of His sacrifice, my sins are forgiven. I am so unworthy of this great love, my Lord, and the promise of eternal life with you in Heaven. I praise you for these gifts and dedicate my life, my heart, and my good works to the glory of your kingdom.

Why do you love me so, my God? Why do you look beyond my sins and see the creation you made? Why am I so important to you, O Christ? I see the angels of the Lord proclaiming your great love for me. Let me walk in the knowledge that your grace is sufficient for the cleansing of all my sins. Because of your fondness for me, I see the wonders of your creation and know I am your child — a child of the Almighty God. Amen.

REFLECTIONS

What more can you give to honor and glorify God? What have you given so far?

Please use the space below to write down any thoughts or comments you may have.

"May God Bless You,
As you live your Life for Christ,
Empowered by The Holy Spirit."

June 28

Isaiah 45:24 NIV.

[24] They will say of me, 'In the Lord alone are deliverance and strength. All who have raged against him will come to him and be put to shame.

O Gracious Lord Jesus, with one voice, I cry out to you for the forgiveness of my sins. I ask for your strength to guide and deliver me from perils I may face today. Father, you know all too often the path I walk and the dangers I encounter. Free me, my Savior, from my troublesome self and my notion that I can solve my own problems. I cannot accomplish anything without the Holy Spirit guiding and directing my walk.

Instill in me the presence of the Holy Spirit, so I may glorify you by the fruits I bear. Lift me up when I am downtrodden and find myself unable to withstand the forces of the evil one. Let me rejoice when I am victorious and have beaten back the ravages of sin. Always, my God, let me remain humble in spirit, so my pride does not taint the glory I give to you. Hallelujah, O Christ! Let me always be mindful that you are my Creator and that my strength comes from living a life in Christ. Amen.

REFLECTIONS

- *As you face perils today, remind yourself that you are a child of the Almighty God.*

Please use the space below to write down any thoughts or comments you may have.

"May God Bless You,
As you live your Life for Christ,
Empowered by The Holy Spirit."

June 29

Job 1:8 NIV.

[8] Then the Lord said to Satan, "Have you considered my servant Job? There is no one on earth like him; he is blameless and upright, a man who fears God and shuns evil."

O Lord God, my Father in Christ Jesus, I do not know what today has in store for me. I am not afraid, though, because of my faith and trust in your Holy Word. While the world is spiraling out of control: wars, famines, terrorism, hatred, and an unending compulsion to turn from the truth of your Word, I am alive and hopeful because you are my Almighty God. You are the source of all righteousness and the source of my Salvation. Praise to your Holy Name! Let me always be comforted during trying times by your steadfast love and unending grace. Let me remember that no one comes before you except through your Son, Jesus Christ. Let me be a true reflection of your character as I live my life daily for you.

Give me the strength and encouragement to weather any storms that may cross my path so I will still be standing upright, having conquered my fears and doubts after they pass. Through Christ Jesus, I can do all things, and because of my love for you, I will stand my ground and lay down my life for you if I am called. Praise to you, O Christ. Amen.

REFLECTIONS

What does it mean to you to stand your ground when your faith is challenged?

Please use the space below to write down any thoughts or comments you may have.

"May God Bless You,
As you live your Life for Christ,
Empowered by The Holy Spirit."

June 30

Psalm 104:1 NIV.

[1] Praise the Lord, my soul. Lord my God you are very great; You are clothed with splendor and majesty.

Heavenly Father, Lord of all Creation, I thank you for the privilege of being able to come to you in prayer. I thank you for being willing to always listen to the needs of my heart. I know I can be difficult, Lord Jesus, because I am a work in progress. I stumble often, and I forget to always reflect the life of Christ to others in this world. How you can love a sinner like me so dearly that you would send your Son, Jesus Christ, to die on the Cross of Calvary is beyond human comprehension. But that is what you did. You sacrificed your Son so I may be saved and forever seen pure in your sight.

Let me always be honorable to your Word and steadfast in my love so I may continue to be worthy of the grace you so freely give. Praise to you, O Lord! I give all glory to your Holy Name. Bless me now, as I go forth this day in service to you. Amen.

REFLECTIONS

As you start your day, ask God how you can be of service to Him.

Please use the space below to write down any thoughts or comments you may have.

July 1

Hebrews 6:1 NIV.

[1] Therefore let us move beyond the elementary teachings about Christ and be taken forward to maturity, not laying again the foundation of repentance from acts that lead to death, and of faith in God,

Eternal Lord, the Father of all Creation, grant now the prayers of my heart. Lord, I often do not look at the big picture. I often look at things from a worldview perspective and not from a heavenly perspective. I want so much to grow in spiritual maturity and to have a countenance that is upright, patient, and Godly.

Forgive me for falling short of reaching the desires of my heart. Forgive me for falling short of reaching the desires of my Almighty God. Instill in me the spirit of wisdom and revelation so I may be the child of God you intended me to be. Guide me by the Holy Spirit in all my ways and in all the opportunities I can to express my love and faith in your Son, Jesus Christ.

Open the eyes, ears, and hearts of those I witness to so they may also grow and have a loving relationship with you. Let me not falter in my walk, so I do not shame myself in the presence of my Lord. Fill me now with a love and passion for serving you and glorifying your name as I am called to do in your Holy Word. Amen.

REFLECTIONS

What do you believe God has called you to do with your life? Will you do it?

Please use the space below to write down any thoughts or comments you may have.

"May God Bless You,
As you live your Life for Christ,
Empowered by The Holy Spirit."

July 2

Romans 1:16-17 NIV.

[16] For I am not ashamed of the gospel, because it is the power of God that brings Salvation to everyone who believes: first to the Jew, then to the Gentile. [17] For in the gospel the righteousness of God is revealed—a righteousness that is by faith from first to last, just as it is written: "The righteous will live by faith."

My Precious Lord, gracious and most merciful God, you have implanted in my heart undying faith in your Son, Jesus Christ, by your Holy Spirit. Lord, so many of your children, reject the Gospel of Jesus Christ and fail to understand the ramifications for their eternal life. Help me be a faithful disciple of your Holy Word, so I may bring others into fellowship with you. I am not ashamed, my Lord, of the profound impact my relationship with you, has meant to me. I am your child, a child of the Living God, and the one whom I will always follow.

Lord, guide my footsteps as I walk into the abyss of unbelievers. Father, please help me call upon the Holy Spirit to renew my strength, and faith, as I witness to those who are lost. Open their hearts so the Word of God through my lips may touch the core of their souls. I rejoice in the opportunity to share my faith and my hope in the Gospel of Jesus Christ. Bless me now as I look for Divine Opportunities. Amen.

REFLECTIONS

If you witness to someone and they refuse to accept Christ, have you failed in your witness?

Please use the space below to write down any thoughts or comments you may have.

"May God Bless You,
As you live your Life for Christ,
Empowered by The Holy Spirit."

July 3

2 Corinthians 3:17 NIV.

[17] Now the Lord is the spirit, and where the spirit of the Lord is, there is freedom.

My Holy God, Father of my Lord and Savior, Jesus Christ, I pray you will hear my heartfelt prayer. On this, the day before the anniversary of our nation's birth, I bring before you the turmoil our country finds itself embroiled in. Lord, our men, and women are fighting daily to preserve the freedoms others have paid for with their lives. For over two centuries, our country has seen war abroad and division at home. I ask for your Divine Intervention to protect all our military men and women as they serve our country and safeguard our freedoms.

I ask for your healing power to be present among all the injured who suffer from war's psychological traumas. Bless them, Lord Jesus, with the anointing of the Holy Spirit as they recover from the wounds of battle. Help them to fight to have their lives physically and emotionally restored. Bless also, the families of the wounded. Give them the peace and assurance that they and their loved ones will persevere through the grace of God.

Father, Son, and Holy Spirit restore our country to the faithful roots upon which our nation was founded. Grant our leaders the spirit of wisdom and revelation as they work toward the ending of all hostilities. Bless now all the people of our nation. Give them peace and harmony so that we can join in unity to preserve the values we hold dear to our hearts. Amen.

REFLECTIONS

Ask God to heal the hearts and minds of all those who have sacrificed for our country.

Please use the space below to write down any thoughts or comments you may have.

"May God Bless You,
As you live your Life for Christ,
Empowered by The Holy Spirit."

July 4

1 Peter 2:16 NIV.

[16] Live as free people, but do not use your freedom as a cover-up for evil; live as God's slaves.

Blessed Father, today, America celebrates its freedom. Let us be mindful of the cost of freedom since our nation was founded. For over two centuries, America has been a nation that has embraced freedom for all its people. Unfortunately, there have been periods where we as a nation have failed to see that the arms of liberty welcomed everyone. Lord, as we pause to remember and celebrate our freedom, let us give thanks for all the blessings you have bestowed on us.

O Christ, our nation would have been doomed to fall years ago had it not been founded on Christian beliefs. It has succeeded because it has become a beacon of hope for all other countries around the world. Let us not forget, as we are now caught up in a state of uncertainty, with values that seem to be diminishing, that we are one nation under God. Let us remember that the real test of any nation's greatness is its willingness and strength to preserve the values upon which it was founded. Lord, we are a nation that has failed to always follow the truth of your Word.

We need your help as we go forth this day, renewed in a spirit of greatness and with a heart that will encourage our children to fight for our nation's moral and spiritual growth. Empower our leaders with the spirit of wisdom and revelation to faithfully lead America through tumultuous times. Forgive our country and its people for straying from the truth of your Word. Keep our nation safe from domestic and foreign dangers and protect our troops from all threats until, at long last, peace is restored. Bless America, Heavenly Father, and continue to lead and guide her as she navigates the rough waters ahead. Let us as a nation always rejoice that God has indeed blessed America. Amen.

"May God Bless You,
As you live your Life for Christ,
Empowered by The Holy Spirit."

REFLECTIONS

Do you believe America is still one nation under God? If not, why?

Please use the space below to write down any thoughts or comments you may have.

*"May God Bless You,
As you live your Life for Christ,
Empowered by The Holy Spirit."*

July 5

Romans 12:12-13 NIV.

[12] Be joyful in hope, patient in affliction, faithful in prayer. [13] Share with the Lord's people who are in need. Practice hospitality. ...

Heavenly Father, the Caretaker of my soul, I come before you today giving thanks and praise for all the blessings you have bestowed upon me. You are my God, the strength and pillar of my faith through your Son, Jesus Christ. Praise to you, O Lord. Your blessings never cease. You are there for me to turn to when I feel alone and caught up in a cycle of depression. You are there when I am joyful and reflect upon all your love and grace. You are always there, my Lord, and I humbly thank you for your continued presence in my life.

I am thankful for my family and for all my brothers and sisters in Christ who bless me with acts of love and kindness. I am grateful for the strangers I come upon who unknowingly bless me with their presence and ability to show love and grace to those they do not know personally. I am thankful, most of all, for my Salvation and for the promise of eternal life through your Son, Jesus Christ. Please forgive me when there are days when I forget your blessings and do not share them with others. Love me, forever, my God, and instill in me a heartfelt desire to love and serve you always. Through Christ's name, I pray. Amen.

REFLECTIONS

- *When depression strikes, how can your personal relationship with Christ help you?*

Please use the space below to write down any thoughts or comments you may have.

*"May God Bless You,
As you live your Life for Christ,
Empowered by The Holy Spirit."*

July 6

Romans 6:17 NIV.

[17] But thanks be to God that, though you used to be slaves to sin you have come to obey from your heart the pattern of teaching that has now claimed your allegiance.

O Great Jehovah, accept my thanks for your steadfast love during times that are both turbulent and peaceful. Accept my gratitude for your Gospel's message and the teachings of my Lord and Savior, Jesus Christ. Where would I turn to if you were not there for me? Where would I turn if my path were rocky and unstable? Where would I turn if Satan put his daggers in me? Lord, you are my refuge, my source of strength, my source of comfort, and my source of redemption through your Son, Jesus Christ. You are the only one I can turn to that will love me and care for me in times of frustration and confusion.

You are the Great Comforter! You alone — not family, not friends, nor anything of this world can bring me the happiness and security of the steadfast love, forgiveness, and mercy you provide. Praise to you, O Lord, for always being there for me. Thank you for all the gifts of the Holy Spirit and the blessings of love you shower upon me. I humbly submit my stubborn will for a daily crucifixion and pray your grace will continue to sustain me when I am weak and discouraged. Praise to you, O Christ, for you are the way, the Truth, and the life. Amen.

REFLECTIONS

Where would you be right now if you did not have a personal relationship with your Lord, Jesus Christ?

Please use the space below to write down any thoughts or comments you may have.

*"May God Bless You,
As you live your Life for Christ,
Empowered by The Holy Spirit."*

July 7

James 1:19-20 NIV.

[19] My dear brothers and sisters, take note of this: Everyone should be quick to listen, slow to speak and slow to become angry, [20] because human anger does not produce the righteousness that God desires.

Most merciful Heavenly Father, send your Holy Spirit upon me as I begin a new day in service to you. Lord, while this day is full of uncertainty, the one constant I can count on is the love, grace, and forgiveness of my Lord and Savior, Jesus Christ. When fear consumes me, you are my calming hand. When doubt takes hold of me, you rescue me from my anxiety. When anger takes hold of my breath, you quell my unrest with your intense whisper. You are my Almighty God. My refuge to whom I must turn to if I am to reflect the life of Christ.

Praise to you, O God, for being the rock upon which I stand. Glory to you, O Lord, for being able to sing praises to your Holy Name. Praise to you, my Father in Heaven, for the righteousness of your hand when I am disobedient to your Word. Guide me now as I go forth this day, secure in my faith and secure that you are a righteous and loving God who will love and protect me from myself. Thank you, O Christ. I give all of myself to your glory. In Christ's name, I pray. Amen.

REFLECTIONS

When anger takes hold of you, what might you say to God? Will you let Him help you?

Please use the space below to write down any thoughts or comments you may have.

"May God Bless You,
As you live your Life for Christ,
Empowered by The Holy Spirit."

July 8

John 13:34-35 NIV.

[34] "A new command I give you: Love one another. As I have loved you, so you must love one another. [35] By this everyone will know that you are my disciples if you love one another."

Blessed Father, your Word says I should love one another as you have loved me. Forgive me, Lord, for not always being faithful to this command. I am your disciple who has committed himself to service in your name. I understand the power of love because of the love you so generously bestow on me. Yet, in my human frailty, I get caught up in anger that hinders my ability to express love.

Cleanse me, O Lord, of this spirit of anger so I may faithfully fulfill your teachings. Wrap your arms around me as I go forth this day, confident of your love for me so I can fully express love, mercy, and kindness to my fellow man. Grant me the spirit of humanity where I can understand the difficulties your children go through. When I fail to express my love, correct me so I may once again be your faithful disciple. I ask these things in the name of the One who laid down his life for me, Jesus Christ. Amen.

REFLECTIONS

Is it difficult for you to understand the difficulties others go through? If yes, why?

Please use the space below to write down any thoughts or comments you may have.

"May God Bless You,
As you live your Life for Christ,
Empowered by The Holy Spirit."

July 9

Philippians 2:3-4 NIV.

[3] Do nothing out of selfish ambition or vain conceit. Rather, in humility value others above yourselves, [4] not looking to your own interests but each of you to the interests of the others.

O Christ, the Shepherd of my heart, lead me forth this day full of compassion and love for my fellow man. Let me not be filled with vanity or conceit or selfishness that would undermine my witness to others. Instead, let me go forth in humility and with grace and place others' needs before my own. Grant me the spiritual countenance that will be a Godly display of righteousness before others. Lead me through any obstacles that may deter me from walking in your light. Guide me with the power of the Holy Spirit through any attempt by Satan to tarnish my witness before others.

I know, my Lord, that I can accomplish your will for my life by being faithful to your Word and by calling on the armor of the Lord to be my shield of strength. Grant me the peace and assurance that through a life full of devotion to your Son, Jesus Christ, that I will prevail in all my efforts to live a Godly life. In the name of the One who gave his life for me. Amen.

REFLECTIONS

As you go about your day, how can you place the needs of others before your own?

Please use the space below to write down any thoughts or comments you may have.

"May God Bless You,
As you live your Life for Christ,
Empowered by The Holy Spirit."

July 10

Psalm 119:114 NIV.

[114] You are my refuge and my shield; I have put my hope in your word.

My Lord God, I come before you as a sinner knowing I can never be one with you until I repent of my sins. I come before you with the hope that by claiming the truth of your Word, I can overcome my sinful nature. Help me, through the Holy Spirit, to prune myself of the withering branches in my life. I come before you with a repentant heart knowing that I claim you as my Savior because you first claimed me.

You are my Redeemer, and nothing I can do of myself can pay the penalty for my sins. You are my refuge and my shield against all attempts by Satan to destroy the faith and trust I have in you. Praise to you, O God, for my heart is in the palm of your hand to shape into the likeness of your Son, Jesus Christ. Grant me the desire to be developed into the kind of servant that will use my gifts to share with my fellow man. Grant me the spirit of truth that will forever lend my voice to your angels by proclaiming you are the Son of the Living God, and in you do I place my trust. Amen.

REFLECTIONS

How willing are you to be shaped by God into the likeness of Christ?

Please use the space below to write down any thoughts or comments you may have.

"May God Bless You,
As you live your Life for Christ,
Empowered by The Holy Spirit."

July 11

Job 3:26 NIV.

[26] I have no peace, no quietness; I have no rest, but only turmoil.

Precious Jesus, I need you every hour. I call out your name, and you are there beside me. Your presence is always felt by my side. When I find myself struggling with temptations, you are the rock I turn to. When I am depressed and can see no other way out of my despair, you are the Great Counselor. In you, I can find complete solace and peace in my life. Your Word is like a life raft tossed out into the turbulent sea waiting for me to grab hold of and once again be safe and secure.

I praise you, O Christ, for I would be lost and prey for Satan without you. But with you, I can rebuke him and cast him from my life. You are the Almighty God, and through Christ, I can do all things. No matter the difficulty, the situation, or the hopelessness I may feel, you are the one I will turn to because my strength is through Jesus Christ. Praise to you, O Lord. Yes, Praise to you! Amen.

REFLECTIONS

If you were afloat in a life raft, tossing about at sea, what book would you want to read?

Please use the space below to write down any thoughts or comments you may have.

"May God Bless You,
As you live your Life for Christ,
Empowered by The Holy Spirit."

July 12

1 Corinthians 15:57 NIV.

[57] But thanks be to God! He gives us the victory through our Lord Jesus Christ.

Dear Savior, Lord of my life, I am troubled by my sinful state. I am troubled by the sins I commit and the sins of omission I neglect to confess. Help me, Lord, to be aware of all the evils in my life so I may confess them and be purified by the blood of my Savior, Jesus Christ. Grant me the courage to rise above my sins and to conquer the evil one who tries continuously to entrap me with his devious ploys. I do not want to sin. I do not want to humiliate myself. I do not want to shame myself. I do not want to be a blight upon my Christian witness. Help me when I cry out for your guidance.

Comfort me, Lord, when I cry out for your compassion. Calm me when I cry out for your mercy and forgiveness. And walk with me as I try to become a more faithful and obedient Christian. Give me the courage, O Christ, to demonstrate my love and faithfulness to you by prostrating myself daily before your cross. Let me know true humility and steadfast devotion to your Holy Word. Grant me the spirit of wisdom and revelation as I go forth this day proclaiming you are the Son of the Living God, and in you will I place my trust. Amen.

REFLECTIONS

When caught up in a sinful state, what concerns you the most?

Please use the space below to write down any thoughts or comments you may have.

*"May God Bless You,
As you live your Life for Christ,
Empowered by The Holy Spirit."*

July 13

Acts 26:17-18 NIV.

[17] I will rescue you from your own people and from the Gentiles. I am sending you to them [18] to open their eyes and turn them from darkness to light, and from the power of Satan to God, so that they may receive forgiveness of sins and a place among those who are sanctified by faith in me.

My Faithful Christ, my Lord, and Redeemer, I am troubled by my sins of the past. I am troubled by my flagrant sins and in my sins of omission. Lord, you know the path life has taken me. You know the temptations the evil one has placed in my path. You see the difficulty I have had in forsaking the sins of this world. Forgive me, Lord. Forgive me for not having a deeper relationship with you. I wish I could be more assertive in my ability to fight off Satan's attacks. I am lost without you and need you to convict my heart of these sins and seek your forgiveness when I commit them.

I also need you to forgive me for those sins that I did not recognize at that time. Enlighten me, O Lord, so I may see them with crystal clarity and be willing to lay them before you and seek your forgiveness. You have sent your Son, Jesus Christ, to die on the Cross of Calvary for my sins. Let me rejoice in this extraordinary gift and confess with my heart all my sins so I may be seen pure in your eyes. Thank you, Lord, for your grace and unending love for me. I lift your name and sing hallelujah! Praise be to God. Amen.

REFLECTIONS

Is it possible for you to not see some of the sins you have committed? If so, why?

Please use the space below to write down any thoughts or comments you may have.

"May God Bless You,
As you live your Life for Christ,
Empowered by The Holy Spirit."

July 14

Isaiah 54:10 NIV.

[10] Though the mountains be shaken, and the hills be removed, yet my unfailing love for you will not be shaken nor my covenant of peace be removed," says the Lord, who has compassion on you.

Lord Jesus, I am troubled by many things, and sometimes I fear for my faith. In my human understanding, when I see the devastation caused by floods, tornados, and other extreme weather, I often wonder where your hand is amid tragedy. I wonder how you can allow the suffering of your children, especially those that have been faithful to your Word. Where are you, O Lord, when families are torn apart by tornados? Where are you, O Lord, when the lives of your children are entirely uprooted and are now homeless and without shelter? Where are you, O Lord, when your people cry out to you for mercy?

And then I remember you are always there restoring their lives through the acts of kindness by their fellow man. You are still there, comforting them during their times of sorrow. You are always there, walking side-by-side with each of your children as they rebuild their lives. And then, my faith is renewed because you are a Great God. A God of love, mercy, and grace. You are the Master of the Universe. There is nothing you cannot restore because you created everything in the beginning. You are a loving God, and through my Savior, Jesus Christ, I will build up a stronghold of faith to weather all the storms in my life. Amen.

REFLECTIONS

Describe some storms in your life and how God helped you through their turmoil.

Please use the space below to write down any thoughts or comments you may have.

"May God Bless You,
As you live your Life for Christ,
Empowered by The Holy Spirit."

July 15

Matthew 6:24 NIV.

[24] "No one can serve two masters. Either you will hate the one and love the other, or you will be devoted to the one and despise the other. You cannot serve both God and money.

Precious Lord, you are the Almighty God. I humbly submit myself to your authority. I call upon you and claim you as the Lord and Master of my Heart. Unfortunately, I often fail to exhibit the Christian characteristics that reflect one in complete submission to your will. Father, I get caught up in so many ways of the world. I often find myself allowing my desire for money to overrule areas that should be utterly devoted to you. I often fail to contribute the resources needed by your kingdom on earth to sustain themselves. I allow myself to let my lust for money control my desires and my heart's wants. And I neglect to use my resources to further your work among your people.

Forgive me, my Lord. I know I cannot serve two masters. Either I will give myself entirely to you, or I will bring dishonor on myself. Forgive me, O Lord, as I wrestle with the sins associated with money and the temptations it leads me to. Cleanse my spirit, O Christ, and renew me through the Holy Spirit. Renew me in ways that will purge me from this desire to forsake your kingdom by using money as a substitute for your glory. I cannot overcome this weakness on my own and plead for your strong hand in controlling my impulses. I claim victory in this sin in the name of the Father, Son, and Holy Spirit. Amen.

REFLECTIONS

How has the desire for money kept you from experiencing all God wants for you?

Please use the space below to write down any thoughts or comments you may have.

"May God Bless You,
As you live your Life for Christ,
Empowered by The Holy Spirit."

July 16

Psalm 91:4 NIV.

[4] He will cover you with his feathers, and under his wings you will find refuge; his faithfulness will be your shield and rampart.

Faithful Lord Jesus, it is so comforting that you are with me no matter what adversity I may be facing. As I walk through life, you, in your infinite kindness, are always there walking beside me. Praise to you, my Lord, for your steadfast love, grace, and forgiveness. I call upon you now to restore my heart and soul and to give me the same compassion for showing love, grace, and forgiveness that you extend. Let me be a true reflection of your life so I may be a faithful witness of your enduring love.

While I know I will falter in my walk from time to time, forgive me when I do, and correct my path so I may be a faithful disciple of yours. Let me be a true warrior for Christ, ready to stand up for my convictions. Prepared to witness to others. And prepared to lay down my life, if need be, to demonstrate that my belief in you, the Living God, is not for the weak of heart. Let me go forth this day, confident in my victory through Christ that no matter what challenges I face, I will prevail in my witness through your Son, my Lord, Jesus Christ. Amen.

REFLECTIONS

During your walk with Christ today, in what area are you most likely to stumble?

Please use the space below to write down any thoughts or comments you may have.

"May God Bless You,
As you live your Life for Christ,
Empowered by The Holy Spirit."

July 17

Psalm 13:6 NIV.

[6] I will sing the Lord's praise, for he has been good to me.

O Christ, my Beautiful Savior, how I adore you. From the days of my youth, until now you have been steadfast in your love for me. When troubles crossed my path, you were there beside me. When anger filled my heart, you quelled its fury. When loneliness gripped my soul, you fulfilled my need for love.

O Lord, what a faithful God you are — so kind, so loving, so patient, and so precious. When I felt I had no haven during times of rebellion, you were with me. Why you have so much love for me is beyond my comprehension? Yet, you are a God of infinite love and mercy. I adore you. I love you. And I will always praise you for the gift of Salvation you graciously bestowed on me. Praise to you, O Christ! Praise to you, my Lord! Amen.

REFLECTIONS

In your youth, did you live your life for Christ? If yes, who or what influenced you?

Please use the space below to write down any thoughts or comments you may have.

July 18

Psalm 73:26 NIV.

[26] My flesh and my heart may fail, but God is the strength of my heart and my portion forever.

Lord God, Heavenly Father, whom do I have on this earth that is more loving than you? Whom do I have that will walk with me through the valleys of my darkness, other than you? And whom, O Lord, will suffer my transgressions for the sins of my unrighteousness? Oh yes, Lord, you are the Great One! You are the only one who will love me unconditionally despite any faults I may have. Praise to you, O Christ! Glory to you, my Redeemer, and the Rock upon which I rely upon.

This day, I call upon you to lift me out of any demise I may come upon so I will not succumb to the ploys of the evil one who wants nothing more than to destroy my faith in you. Rescue me, Lord, before I need rescuing. Let me wear the armor of God so I can fend off any attacks by Satan. Father, it is the evil ones of this world who want nothing more than to see my faith crumble. Send your Holy Spirit and guardian angels to form a protective shield of love and strength around me. No matter what adversity I encounter today, let me prevail through your Son, Jesus Christ. Amen.

REFLECTIONS

Why does God love you? Do you deserve His love? If so, why? If not, why?

Please use the space below to write down any thoughts or comments you may have.

"May God Bless You,
As you live your Life for Christ,
Empowered by The Holy Spirit."

July 19

Psalm 9:1 NIV.

[1] I will give thanks to you, Lord, with all my heart; I will tell of all your wonderful deeds

My most merciful Lord Jesus, accept my thanks, O God, for the joy of your Gospel Message. Allow me, this day, to spread the message of God's love for all humanity. Let me do this by the attitude of my heart and conviction for the truth of your Word. Let my voice be an instrument that sings your praises and shares your love and grace to others by the example of your life on earth.

Instill in me the power of the Holy Spirit, so I may discern the Truth and the Divine Opportunities you lay before me. Grant me a heart of love and forgiveness, especially to those I hold a hardness of the heart toward and whom I have not yet extended forgiveness to. Bless me as I, in turn, bless those whose lives are turned toward the evil one and who need the peace and love offered by my Lord and Savior, Jesus Christ. My heart sings songs of praise to your Holy Name, and I pray now that every syllable I utter may bring honor and glory to your precious name. Amen.

REFLECTIONS

If you meet someone today who is sorely tempted by Satan, should you turn and run?

Please use the space below to write down any thoughts or comments you may have.

"May God Bless You,
As you live your Life for Christ,
Empowered by The Holy Spirit."

July 20

I Peter 2:24 NIV.

[24] He self-bore our sins" in his body on the cross, so that we might die to sins and live for righteousness: "by his wounds you have been healed.".

Gracious Father in Heaven, hear my songs of praise to you. You are the Almighty God, the Father of my Lord and Savior, Jesus Christ. Thank you for loving me so much that you sent Jesus to die on the Cross of Calvary for my sins. Thank you for being my friend, my confidant, the one I can turn to in times of distress. Nowhere in my earthly life is someone I can trust like you, not family, not friends, not even brothers and sisters in Christ. As much love as I receive from them, it pales in comparison to your great love.

I give you thanks and praise, O Lord, for your steadfast love, grace, and endless mercies. Be with me now, O Christ, as I go about my day, confident that I can do all things through you. Be with me as I battle the temptations Satan places before me so I can rise victorious, like an eagle, over my sins. Bless me now, in the name of the Father, Son, and Holy Spirit, as I shout out to the world, "My God is a Great God, a Great God indeed." Amen.

REFLECTIONS

Why is it that you cannot trust people of this world like you can with God?

Please use the space below to write down any thoughts or comments you may have.

"May God Bless You,
As you live your Life for Christ,
Empowered by The Holy Spirit."

July 21

1 Thessalonians 1:4-5 NIV.

[4] For we know, brothers and sisters loved by God, that he has chosen you, [5] because our gospel came to you not simply with words but also with power, with the holy spirit and deep conviction. You know how we lived among you for your sake.

O Lord, my faithful Redeemer, I pray for you to enter my heart daily. Let me, through the meditation of your Word and my wholehearted devotion to living my life as an obedient and loving Christian, be faithful to you. I pray you will instill in me the spirit of wisdom and revelation so I may know your will for my life. Grant me the patience to respond to others in a spirit of love so I may be the kind of Christian witness I should be. Grant me the courage and moral fortitude to persevere in times of calamity, so I do not forget the love and grace you freely give in challenging times.

Protect me from the ploys and devious tactics of Satan when he tries his best to undermine your Belt of Truth and Strength. Lift me up in my times of weakness and restore me on the path of righteousness so I may once again be strong in your Word. And after I have regained my strength in the Lord, let me rejoice with thanksgiving for all your blessings and countless mercies. I ask these things in the name of the One who gave his life for me, Jesus Christ. Amen.

REFLECTIONS

What is the best way to be a Christian witness of God's love?

Please use the space below to write down any thoughts or comments you may have.

July 22

2 Timothy 2:22 NIV.

[22] Flee the evil desires of youth and pursue righteousness, faith, love, and peace, along with those who call on the Lord out of a pure heart.

Faithful Redeemer, send now your Holy Spirit upon me as I lift my concerns of the world to you. Father, our young people are faced with challenges and choices far different from those I had in my youth. They live in a world of technology that is stripping them of their moral compass. They have fallen victim to a new social norm that allows many traditional values to be compromised in the name of tolerance. I fear for them, my God, that they will lose sight of the need to know their Savior, Jesus Christ, and have the one genuine relationship in life that is most important.

Lord, I pray you will deliver them from the clutches of Satan and that you will enlighten our youth to the Truth of your Holy Word. Bless them and set them on the path of righteousness that will free them from all impediments to living a Godly life. Give them the courage to forsake peer pressure that undermines a Godly character and that turns them away from you. Bless them, Lord, and give them the knowledge they need to successfully live in a world that is shifting from God. In the name of the One who gave his life for us all, Jesus Christ. Amen.

REFLECTIONS

What are some of the traditional values from your youth that are no longer true for you?

Please use the space below to write down any thoughts or comments you may have.

"May God Bless You,
As you live your Life for Christ,
Empowered by The Holy Spirit."

July 23

2 Corinthians 11:3 NIV.

[3] But I am afraid that just as Eve was deceived by the serpent's cunning, your minds may somehow be led astray from your sincere and pure devotion to Christ.

Faithful Father, strengthen my desire to love and serve you with a steadfast devotion to your Word. Remove from me any thorns or thistles that may impede my Christian walk. Help me to look inward to see the sweet love of my Lord and Savior, Jesus Christ. Stir my heart into action when it has been dormant in reaching out with love and compassion to my fellow man. Help me remember that your children are crying out for someone to touch their lives and bring them into the assurance of faith in Christ Jesus. Help me to remember the pain and suffering of your people across this land and our world.

Move me to pray for them and for the conditions that are afflicting their lives. Let me rejoice in the fact that you are the Almighty God, and you can restore the lives of all your children into perfect harmony with your will. Let me not take for granted the truth of your Word. Please do not let me succumb to complacency and drift into the trappings of the evil one. I am yours, O Faithful God. I rejoice in your Word. I praise you for your love, and I surrender my stubborn will to be shaped into the embodiment of one who personifies a person who walks in the light of Christ. Amen.

REFLECTIONS

Have you noticed the pain and suffering in the world? If yes, in what ways can you help?

Please use the space below to write down any thoughts or comments you may have.

"May God Bless You,
As you live your Life for Christ,
Empowered by The Holy Spirit."

July 24

Galatians 6:7-8 NIV.

[7] Do not be deceived: God cannot be mocked. A man reaps what he sows [8] Whoever sows to please their flesh, from the flesh will reap destruction; whoever sows to please the spirit, from the spirit will reap eternal life.

Dear Father in Heaven, I thank you for all the blessings of body, mind, and spirit you have showered upon me. Help me remember to keep my sight on being true to myself as a disciple of Christ, not as one of this world. Help me to understand myself, know my failings, and have the courage to pick myself up and correct my thoughts and behavior when they lead me astray. Teach me to recognize that my failure to make the most of myself is often due to jealousy and comparing myself to others. Let me not be consumed with the need to seek approval from this world but to have the assurance by faith that I am genuinely worthy in Christ.

In all my doings, let me always remember to rejoice in my daily communion with you by lifting you up in praise and adoration. Let the world know I love you and am prepared to lay down my life for my Christian values and beliefs. Let me not be ashamed to publicly profess that you are the Almighty God and that I am alive through the blood of your Son, Jesus Christ. Amen.

REFLECTIONS

- *Being prepared to lay down your life for Christ is serious. Why would you do that?*

Please use the space below to write down any thoughts or comments you may have.

"May God Bless You,
As you live your Life for Christ,
Empowered by The Holy Spirit."

July 25

Isaiah 25:9 NIV.

[9] In that day they will say, "Surely this is our God; we trusted in him, and he saved us. This is the Lord, we trusted in him; let us rejoice and be glad in his Salvation."

Gracious Lord, I thank you for the gift of Salvation through the light of the world, Jesus Christ. Thank you for your endless love, grace, and forgiveness that is more precious to me than I ever thought possible. No longer am I consumed with material goods to find joy and happiness in my life. No longer will I be sad over things I cannot control. No longer do I need to face the uncertainties of life without the assurance you are walking beside me. You are my faithful God! You are the Rock upon which I stand. My love for you will never dwindle, for there is no other love like yours. No matter how dark it may seem, even in my darkest hour, I can see the light of hope reaching out to me. I rejoice, for no longer will I allow the dark one to rob me of the comfort and knowledge of my Lord and Savior, Jesus Christ. Praise to you, O Christ! Glory to your Holy Name. Amen.

REFLECTIONS

What material goods have kept you from finding joy in Christ?

Please use the space below to write down any thoughts or comments you may have.

"May God Bless You,
As you live your Life for Christ,
Empowered by The Holy Spirit."

July 26

Psalm 119:28 NIV.

My soul is weary with sorrow; strengthen me according to your word.

Most merciful, Lord Jesus, I come before you weary and confused. With so much in my life to rejoice about, I have become a slave to my worries. I long for days where I can be free of those burdens and completely relax in the comfort and love of your bosom. I long for days where I am no longer held hostage to this world because of my refusal to completely surrender my will to you. Free me, O Lord, from this human condition I feel compelled to live in. I should know better, O Christ, because of the great sacrifice and eternal promises you made to me.

Lift me up out of this darkness and restore the light unto my path so I may see with clarity the brightness of your kingdom. Ban the forces of Satan from my life, so I have no excuse to doubt or fear your Word. Allow me to live in your will and to have complete assurance of your promises.

I cannot do this on my own, my God. I need your help. I need your patience with me. I need your strength and encouragement to weather the darkest storms in my life. Forgive me of my transgressions and lead me now and forever in the Truth and Light of your Word. Bless me in the name of the One who died on the Cross of Calvary, Jesus Christ, my Lord. Amen.

REFLECTIONS

What are some of the fears that are keeping you from having a fruitful relationship with Christ?

Please use the space below to write down any thoughts or comments you may have.

"May God Bless You,
As you live your Life for Christ,
Empowered by The Holy Spirit."

July 27

1 John 3:10 NIV.

This is how we know who the children of God are and who the children of the devil are: Anyone who does not do what is right is not God's child, nor is anyone who does not love their brother and sister.

O Lord, my precious God, I arise today full of hope and anticipation. I am ready to start my day with you by my side. I will not allow myself to use the evil one to perpetrate sins that dishonor my God. I will not forsake loving others as you first loved me. I will not wander from the path of righteousness because I know I can do all things through your Son, Jesus Christ. I am your child, O God, to shape into the kind of person you intended me to be. I live expectantly knowing while I am a sinner, I am forgiven by the grace of my loving God.

Send now your Holy Spirit as I go forth this day to serve you humbly and with the reverence deserving of a powerful God. Bless me now, through the power of the Holy Spirit. Let me go forth with my burdens free of fear so I may glorify your Holy Name. I ask these things through the One who is the light of the world, Jesus Christ. Amen.

REFLECTIONS

Have you been living expectantly for Christ? If so, how has this blessed you?

Please use the space below to write down any thoughts or comments you may have.

"May God Bless You,
As you live your Life for Christ,
Empowered by The Holy Spirit."

July 28

Revelation 12:8 NIV.

[8] But he was not strong enough, and they lost their place in heaven.

Great God, Lord of my life. I come before you today with sadness in my heart. Sorrow for those that do not know you or refuse to believe you are the one true God, creator of the Heavens and the earth. I come before you, crying out for their lost souls and for their refusal to accept the Truth of your Gospel Message. Lord, you know the hearts of the lost. You know how hardened they are. You know if there is a crack in their soul waiting to be split open so your message can finally touch their lives. Lead me to their hardened hearts so I may be a vehicle of your Truth for their lives. Provide me a divine opportunity to connect the life of at least one lost soul today to Jesus Christ. Find me a lost soul who is weary and who can be blessed by the comfort and love that can only come from a personal relationship with your Son.

Let me be mindful and observant of those who cross my path, whose faces may carry the burdens of hardship and pain only you can heal. Let me have a heart full of compassion and love that is ready to say to this lost soul, "God loves you, and so do I." When I come across this soul if there is any sin in my life that can taint my witness, purge it immediately from my life. Send your Holy Spirit to remind me I can only serve one Master, and that is you. Let me go forth hopeful and expectant that I would have touched the life of one of your children by the close of this day. In Jesus's name, I pray. Amen.

REFLECTIONS

Are you prepared to lead a lost soul to Christ? Can the Holy Spirit help you? If so, how?

Please use the space below to write down any thoughts or comments you may have.

"May God Bless You,
As you live your Life for Christ,
Empowered by The Holy Spirit."

July 29

Matthew 26:28 NIV. [28]

This is my blood of the covenant, which is poured out for many for the forgiveness of sins.

O Gracious Lord, I thank you for all the blessings you have brought into my life. I especially give thanks to family, friends, and my brothers and sisters in Christ. Lord, you know the trials and conflicts that can occur with those you love. You know that disagreements arise over petty issues that only undermine the love and unity within a family. Show those who are wallowing in pain and anger the joy of forgiveness. Send your Holy Spirit upon them so their relationships with each other can be restored. Spread the gift of love and forgiveness into their hearts so they may live in harmony and peace.

Help me to understand the power of love and the price of forgiveness paid for by my Lord and Savior, Jesus Christ. Do not let me take for granted the precious gift of grace you so freely extend to your children. Restore my heart and soul with a spiritual renewal that can survive the most difficult seasons of conflict. I pray, my Lord, that your grace will spill over on me and that I may touch the lives of your children through my devotion to your Word and the message of your Gospel. In the name of the Father, Son, and Holy Spirit. Amen.

REFLECTIONS

Is grace from God something you have taken for granted?

Please use the space below to write down any thoughts or comments you may have.

*"May God Bless You,
As you live your Life for Christ,
Empowered by The Holy Spirit."*

July 30

Proverbs 3:3 NIV.

[3] Let love and faithfulness never leave you; bind them around your neck, write them on the tablet of your heart.

O Great Emmanuel, the light of the world, be with me today as I go forth in service to you. Be with me as I open the door of my heart to hear the message of your Gospel. Be with me as I lift my voice to sing praises to your Holy Name. O Christ, I love you so dearly. My whole life would be empty and void of joy if not for your constant presence. I am so grateful for your love and the forgiveness you continuously extend to cover my sins. Where would I be, my Lord, if not for your faithfulness? Where would I go when I am consumed with doubt and fear if not into your loving arms?

No matter how grievous my sins are, you are faithful to your Word that you will cover my sins with the belt of forgiveness and restore my heart and soul so they will be pleasing to your precious name. Can I ask for anything more from my Savior? Can I be more grateful for your love? Can I be more secure in the assurance of my faith through the One sent to die on the Cross of Calvary? O Christ, the truth of your Word covers all my questions of faith. You are the Almighty God in whom I will forever place my trust. Bless me now as I go forth this day confident in my relationship with you and my heartfelt desire to love and serve you. Amen.

REFLECTIONS

Is there something more you need from God that you have not asked for? If so, what is it?

Please use the space below to write down any thoughts or comments you may have.

"May God Bless You,
As you live your Life for Christ,
Empowered by The Holy Spirit."

July 31

1 Thessalonians 2:11-12 NIV.

[11] For you know that we dealt with each of you as a father deals with his own children, [12] encouraging, comforting, and urging you to live lives worthy of God, who calls you into his kingdom and glory.

My Lord, my God, hear the heartfelt pleas of my heart as I go about this day serving and loving you. Many perplexing thoughts run through my mind that disturbs and irritate me. When I go about my day, some people show a lack of courtesy when I am driving. These are people who seem to care about nothing but themselves. There are those that, by their words and actions, cause my heart to race with anxiety. These people are your children too, O Lord, but they seem to have wandered far off the path of righteousness. In my human condition, I want to react in ways not appropriate for a Christian. What am I to do, O Christ? Your Word cautions me to respond in ways that are loving and bear the fruits of the Holy Spirit. Your Word says I am to show grace toward those I am at odds with.

Take hold of me, dear Lord, and create in me a desire and the strength to respond in love and kindness toward those that offend me. Renew my spiritual countenance so I am genuinely reflective of one whose life is in Christ. Help me to extend grace to those in need just as you continuously extend it toward me. Remind me, O Lord, that I am a sinner, desperately in need of your forgiveness and grace. Do not let me fall into a trap where I judge others but instead leave their judging to you. I need your help. I need your wisdom. I need your patience. Prepare my heart today, so I have the courage and civility to live by the example of your Son, Jesus Christ. In his name, I pray. Amen.

REFLECTIONS

Find one person you know and extend grace to him that you would not normally do.

Please use the space below to write down any thoughts or comments you may have.

"May God Bless You,
As you live your Life for Christ,
Empowered by The Holy Spirit."

August 1

1 Samuel 8:12 NIV.

[12] Some he will assign to be commanders of thousands and commanders of fifties, and others to plow his ground and reap his harvest, and still others to make weapons of war and equipment for his chariots.

Most merciful Lord Jesus, my heart is heavy because of concern for my country and its military. Tensions among nations have been building, and severe conflict is looming. Lord, I know that sometimes war is inevitable and that it can be a means of establishing your order on earth. I pray, Lord, that your hand is always present in whatever situation occurs and that a peaceful and sustained resolution can be found among all involved. I also pray for the military and political leaders within our nation. I pray they will be given the wisdom, courage, and power to discern when to use and not use their enormous arsenal of weapons to accomplish your will. I pray they will use restraint when necessary but be bold in dire need to protect our homeland.

The cost of war is tremendous, O Lord, not only in monetary cost but more importantly in the price of human lives that can be taken needlessly. Protect them, my God, and keep them from imminent danger. Give them the courage to faithfully serve our country and bear the cost of hardship with as little physical and emotional turmoil as possible. Protect the people of our land as the real threat and reality of war can be brought to our homeland. Give me the peace and assurance that you are always in control and that your will can be accomplished no matter what happens. Bless the United States of America as it struggles to live according to your plan. Forgive its transgressions, so it may be spiritually awakened. Let America once return to the values it once held dear to its heart. Be with me now as I ask that the pain of uncertainty be lifted from me. Give me the peace and assurance that your love will sustain me no matter the outcome of this or any conflict. I ask these things in the name of the genuine Peace Maker, my Lord, Jesus Christ. Amen.

"May God Bless You,
As you live your Life for Christ,
Empowered by The Holy Spirit."

REFLECTIONS

The power of prayer in times of war is mighty powerful. Is this a time to pray?

Please use the space below to write down any thoughts or comments you may have.

"May God Bless You,
As you live your Life for Christ,
Empowered by The Holy Spirit."

August 2

Psalm 25:8 NIV.

[8] Good and upright is the Lord; therefore, He instructs sinners in his ways.

O God, who delights in a clean heart, be with me today as I do my best to walk down the path of righteousness. Be with me as I search my heart for obstacles that may hinder my walk with you. Lead me through every trial I face with the assurance of God's promises that He is always with me no matter what my sinful state may be. Infuse me with the power of the Holy Spirit, so I may be constantly aware of your presence, and so I can overcome and wipe out the sin that binds me to the world. Release me from the straps of Satan that hold me hostage to faulty thinking and behavior that dishonors your name.

Father, help me to rejoice in your Holy Word. As I go about this day, confident in my relationship with Jesus Christ, let me be optimistic that I can do all things through him. You are my Almighty God! You alone soothe my heart and soul with a love that transcends any human intervention that attempts to ease the burdens of my heart. How I love you, my God! I praise you. I adore you. I lift my hands in joyful jubilation so the world may know I am your child, a child of the Almighty God. Amen.

REFLECTIONS

- *If you come upon a difficult conflict or trial today, what is the best way to cope with that adversity?*

Please use the space below to write down any thoughts or comments you may have.

*"May God Bless You,
As you live your Life for Christ,
Empowered by The Holy Spirit."*

August 3

Mark 6:34 NIV.

[34] When Jesus landed and saw a large crowd, he had compassion on them, because they were like sheep without a shepherd. So, he began teaching them many things.

Eternal Lord, Master of the Universe, I come before you recognizing there is so much more, I need to know about your Word. The scriptures teach so much, but my comprehension of your Word is sometimes challenging to grasp. I ask that you reveal to me the Truths of your Word that you want me to understand so I may be better equipped to defend your Word against those that seek to tear it down. Send your Holy Spirit upon me as I study your Word.

Let my spirit be enlightened and edified so I may be able to acknowledge your Gospel's message and Truths. Grant me the spirit of wisdom and revelation. When I speak your Word, let others recognize through me that you are the Living God, Master of the Universe, and Lord of all creation. My heart sings praise to your name and rejoices when it hears your spoken message and can apply the Truths of your Word to my life. Praise to you, O Christ! All Glory to you! Amen.

REFLECTIONS

How do you know if the truth of God's Word is valid today? How would you defend it?

Please use the space below to write down any thoughts or comments you may have.

"May God Bless You,
As you live your Life for Christ,
Empowered by The Holy Spirit."

August 4

Isaiah 55:8-9 NIV.

[8] "For my thoughts are not your thoughts, neither are your ways my ways," declares the Lord. [9] "As the heavens are higher than the earth, so are my ways higher than your ways and my thoughts than your thoughts. ...

My Lord, my God, I come before you, seeking peace in my heart. I need your guidance and steady hand as I face the trials of the unknown in the days to come. Lead me, Father, as I seek to fulfill my duties as a Christian so all may know I am a child of God. Cast me not away when I falter in my walk but pick me up and steady my steps so I may stay on the path of righteousness and be able to claim victory through Christ my King. Lord, your love is so powerful and faithful that I rejoice in my faith and desire to live my life honorably. I am so weak in some areas of my life, but I know that I can conquer any doubts or fears I may face through your grace and forgiveness.

You are my Almighty God! I love you and praise your Holy Name. Send now your Holy Spirit so with the armor of the Lord I may be decisive in my faith, strong in my witness, and firm in my desire to serve you. As I come upon any trials, let me face them with the confidence of a convicted Christian who is willing to lay down his life for you. Let the righteousness of your Word be upheld. Instill in me the spirit of one whose faith has been tested and yet survived the temptations of the evil one. Bless me now as I start my day full of anticipation so I can face the unknown without fear or trepidation. I ask these things in the name of the one who sacrificed his life on the Cross of Calvary, Jesus Christ, my Lord, and my Savior. Amen.

REFLECTIONS

How can you gain confidence that you have the faith to conquer any fears or doubts?

Please use the space below to write down any thoughts or comments you may have.

"May God Bless You,
As you live your Life for Christ,
Empowered by The Holy Spirit."

August 5

Romans 15:29 NIV.

[29] I know that when I come to you, I will come in the full measure of the blessing of Christ.

Dear Lord, my heart is full of gratitude and joy for the blessings you have bestowed upon me. I have often taken for granted the gifts and blessings you have showered upon me. Your Word says all things work together for those that place their trust in you. As I go about this new day, let me be a vehicle of your love to others that need blessings. Let me seek out Divine Opportunities to touch their lives by sharing the Gospel message of your Son, Jesus Christ.

Through the power of the indwelling Holy Spirit, let me be a force of righteousness so I can bring others to know and accept the gift of Salvation. You are my Almighty God. I seek you every moment of the day and rejoice that you are with me even when I am led astray by the temptations of this world. My heart is ever grateful for your steadfast love and your continuing grace. Bless me now as I awaken with a newfound joy that you are the Son of the Living God I love and adore. Amen.

REFLECTIONS

When you witness toward others, what would you do if they walk off and show no interest?

Please use the space below to write down any thoughts or comments you may have.

"May God Bless You,
As you live your Life for Christ,
Empowered by The Holy Spirit."

August 6

1 Corinthians 2:14 NIV.

[14] The person without the spirit does not accept the things that come from the spirit of God but considers them foolishness and cannot understand them because they are discerned only through the spirit.

Heavenly Father, I praise you for your Holy Word — the Word of God that sustains me and that lifts me up in songs of adoration to your Holy Name. What a joy it is to have a personal relationship with you. You are my Father in Heaven. You are my friend. You are the One I can turn to when I am sad or need the comfort of your arms. Praise to you, O Christ. For without your saving grace, I would be lost forever. When I am confronted with seasons of doubt, you remain faithful to me. When I am riddled with humanity's sins, you look beyond my sins and see the redeeming blood of your Son, Jesus Christ. How can I not be grateful for your enduring love? It is a love so sweet, so fragrant, so beautiful that your angels proclaim your glory to all your creation. Yes, my God, Praise to your Holy Name!

May I always be faithful in honoring your Word, and may I still remember the peace and joy that comes from serving you. Today, as I start a new day, may I reflect on the life of Christ in all I say and do. May I filter my words and my thoughts, so only the message of your love and the gift of Salvation comes from my lips. Let me be filled with the power of the Holy Spirit so no matter what adversities I face, I will respond to others in a spirit of true love. Thank you, Lord, for your enduring love, grace, and forgiveness. Amen.

REFLECTIONS

How can you bring honor to God today? Are you willing to humble yourself if necessary?

Please use the space below to write down any thoughts or comments you may have.

"May God Bless You,
As you live your Life for Christ,
Empowered by The Holy Spirit."

August 7

Galatians 6:10 NIV.

[10] Therefore, as we have opportunity, let us do good to all people, especially to those who belong to the family of believers.

O Majestic God, Lord of all creation, send now your Holy Spirit upon me so I may face this new day with renewed faith, hope, and joy. Open my eyes to the beauty of your creation. May I see the face of Christ in all those I encounter, and may I look for Divine Opportunities to share God's soft whisper so they may come to know you as I do. Awaken in me, my sleeping soul, so I may recognize the beauty within all your children, regardless of their human condition.

Let me be a force of good where I can influence those that are depressed, weary, or caught up in the sins of this world with the truth of your Word. Let me help guide them to the comfort of your loving arms, where they can feel the warmth and compassion you have for them. Help them to realize that you are their Heavenly Father who loves them and wants them to rejoice in their newfound relationship with you.

Grant them the spirit of wisdom and revelation, so when I am no longer with them, they may seek the truth of your Word through your Holy Scriptures. Encourage them to seek out their brothers and sisters in Christ who can help them grow closer to you. And may I keep them in my prayers and thoughts as they discover for themselves the wonders of your love. In Christ's name, I pray. Amen.

REFLECTIONS

When you look at God's creation, what do you marvel at?

Please use the space below to write down any thoughts or comments you may have.

"May God Bless You,
As you live your Life for Christ,
Empowered by The Holy Spirit."

August 8

James 5:7 NIV.

[7] Be patient, then, brothers and sisters, until the Lord's coming. See how the farmer waits for the land to yield its valuable crop, patiently waiting for the autumn and spring rains.

My God, Lord of all, I come before you with anticipation of the day Jesus Christ returns. I wait anxiously because the world is caught up in more sin than ever before. Children of yours are turning to soothe themselves with things of this world rather than the Word of God. As for myself, I, too, get caught up in sins that dishonor your name. I fail you often. I make choices that are not in keeping with those who are followers of Christ. While I long to lead a sinless life, I know I am doomed to fail. It is only because of your love and unending grace that I am found acceptable in your eyes.

Help me, my Lord, to surrender my stubborn will and to live a righteous life. Give me the patience not only for others but also for myself to live a life complete with the Holy Spirit's gifts. Allow me to have my branches pruned when there are thorns that hinder my Christian walk. Push evil and unclean thoughts from my mind so I may have the countenance of a Godly child — one who loves you, adores you, and serves you with reverence and honor. Bless me, O Faithful God, so I may be an instrument of yours to further the kingdom of Christ. Amen.

REFLECTIONS

How has your stubborn will kept you from being faithful to Christ?

Please use the space below to write down any thoughts or comments you may have.

"May God Bless You,
As you live your Life for Christ,
Empowered by The Holy Spirit."

August 9

Psalm 25:7 NIV.

[7] Do not remember the sins of my youth and my rebellious ways; according to your love remember me, for you, Lord, are good.

Precious Lord Jesus, you have brought joy and happiness into my heart. You have given me countless blessings I feel I do not deserve. The beauty of your love is sweet, fragrant, and so enduring that I am truly humbled by the wonder of your love. Thank you, dear Lord, for, without you, my life would be full of sadness and remorse. But with you, I have the promise of eternal life and a multitude of angels to surround me with your righteousness.

O Lord, how grateful I am for your Holy Spirit. How grateful I am for the gifts you have blessed me with, especially the gifts of love and compassion. For without these gifts, my heart would be hardened and not able to touch the lives of your children with the love they desperately need. I thank you for the outpouring of love that I can share with my family, friends, and even the strangers among me through you. You are the Almighty God, the one whose love I cherish and adore. Thank you, Lord Jesus, for being my personal Savior and guiding me through all the trials in life I encounter. In Jesus's name, I pray. Amen.

REFLECTIONS

Can you imagine living your life without God as your refuge and source of comfort?

Please use the space below to write down any thoughts or comments you may have.

"May God Bless You,
As you live your Life for Christ,
Empowered by The Holy Spirit."

August 10

Ephesians 1:7 NIV.

[7] In him we have redemption through his blood, the forgiveness of sins, in accordance with the riches of God's grace.

My God, my God, my love for you is so great. You have blessed me beyond measure. You have instilled in me the Truth of your Holy Word so that I can use your scriptures as a shield against the forces of Satan. You have surrounded me with a hedge of guardian angels to protect me from all adversities that can detract me from my service to you. And when I have led been astray, you gently call me back into your fold so I may receive the redemption of your blood and the forgiveness of my sins.

You are indeed a God full of grace and wonder. How can I imagine a life without you? How could I navigate the turbulent waters of this world without your firm hand to calm the seas? You are majestic in every sense of the word. You give me hope when others may see complete darkness. You have blessed me with faith when I could have been caught up in the doubts promulgated by mankind. With a grateful heart, I seek the power of your Holy Spirit, so I may continue to live my life in reverent and submissive service to you. Glory to you, O Lord. Praise to your Holy Name. Amen.

REFLECTIONS

When surrounded by turbulent waters, can the storms of your heart be calmed? If so, how?

Please use the space below to write down any thoughts or comments you may have.

"May God Bless You,
As you live your Life for Christ,
Empowered by The Holy Spirit."

August 11

Proverbs 25:20 NIV.

[20] Like one who takes away a garment on a cold day, or like vinegar poured on a wound, is one who sings songs to a heavy heart.

Father in Heaven, I come before you today with a heavy heart. A sadness has crept into my soul. A frustration with situations that leave me in a quandary. Where am I to turn, O Lord, but to you to find solace for my aching heart? I long for the peace that will ease this burden. I long for your direction to overcome my uncertainty and to quell any discontent. I need you, O Lord. Come into my heart and take my burdens upon you so I can find peace in my soul. Lead me from this period of darkness so once again I can see the light and hope found in my Lord and Savior, Jesus Christ.

I praise you, Father, for your steadfast faithfulness to me. I rejoice in you for your enduring love. I praise you that no matter what fears I may have or questions of life, that you will send your Holy Spirit to uplift me and to guide me through these troubling waters. Praise to you, O Lord! For without you in my heart, I would be lost and a slave to my fears. Thank you for your precious gifts of love, grace, and forgiveness. In Jesus' name, I pray. Amen.

REFLECTIONS

- *Living with an aching heart is difficult. How can you ease the burden that may be consuming you?*

Please use the space below to write down any thoughts or comments you may have.

"May God Bless You,
As you live your Life for Christ,
Empowered by The Holy Spirit."

August 12

Psalm 35:27 NIV. [27]

May those who delight in my vindication shout for joy and gladness; may they always say, "The Lord be exalted, who delights in the well-being of his servant."

My God, how great Thou Art. In your capacity for love and forgiveness, you continue to shower your mercies upon me. Because I am a wretched sinner, I am not worthy of your love and compassion. Yet through the crucifixion of your Son, Jesus Christ, on the Cross of Calvary, I become blameless and pure in your sight. What greater joy is there than to know your Son and to have a personal relationship with Him. When I am feeling lonely, He is there. When I am frustrated, you send Your Holy Spirit to calm my soul. When I am caught up in the ways of the world, you remind me, I can only serve one Master.

What an honor it is to do your will, my God! Let me always be mindful that you are the Living God, the Father of my Redeemer, and the Great Comforter. I seek you before anything else and pray I may be vital in my faith as I take on the shield of your righteousness to protect me from the ploys of the evil one. Bless me now, my Lord, as I go about this day, vigilant in my quest to avoid the pitfalls of humanity so I can continue to love, honor, and serve you. In the name of the Father, Son, and Holy Spirit. Amen.

REFLECTIONS

What does it mean to be vigilant in your quest to avoid the pitfalls of humanity?

Please use the space below to write down any thoughts or comments you may have.

"May God Bless You,
As you live your Life for Christ,
Empowered by The Holy Spirit."

August 13

Ezekiel 11:19 NIV.

[19] I will give them an undivided heart and put a new spirit in them; I will remove from them their heart of stone and give them a heart of flesh.

Father in Heaven, send now your Holy Spirit upon me. Speak to me in your soft whisper so I may receive comfort from your voice. Lord, my heart is consumed with disappointment and resentment because I fail to reflect the same grace to others you have given to me. Lord, this is wrong behavior, and I beg your forgiveness. You sent your Son, Jesus Christ, to die for my sins even though I am totally undeserving of this gift of grace. Yet, in my human condition, I struggle with this weight upon me.

Lift this burden from me, O Christ, so I will find peace and comfort through the One who is the Great Comforter. Help me realize I cannot control the actions of others so they will appease my longings. Help me understand that people will always fail me and face their frustrations and difficulties relating to others. Help me rejoice now in a spirit of thanksgiving for all your blessings that have touched my life. Let me not focus on the negative but look at each situation's positive side so I may respond with grace to others. As I go about this new day, may I be filled with a spirit of grace and forgiveness as I look to you for eternal joy? In Jesus' precious name, I pray. Amen.

REFLECTIONS

Extending grace to someone can be a challenge. Why does God want us to extend grace?

Please use the space below to write down any thoughts or comments you may have.

"May God Bless You,
As you live your Life for Christ,
Empowered by The Holy Spirit."

August 14

Psalm 5:11 NIV.

[11] But let all who take refuge in you be glad; let them ever sing for joy. Spread your protection over them, that those who love your name may rejoice in you.

Lord Jesus, my Almighty God, through the power of the Holy Spirit, I seek your blessing as I go about another day in service to you. Your love is always there to sustain me and to lift me up when forces of the evil one drag me down in despair. I praise you that nothing is impossible, no matter the distressing situation in my life. Father, hear my prayer for the lives of all emergency care workers in our country. Protect our police, firemen, EMS workers, and all those that put their lives in danger so your people can be protected. I pray for a hedge of protection to be placed around them and that they may come to know you as their personal Savior.

Protect them, O Lord, from all dangers they encounter. And if they find themselves in a situation where their lives are in peril, send your guardian angels upon them so they may know your divine healing and protection. Help them to always do your will and to preserve the righteousness that is entrusted to them. I ask these things in the name of the Great One, the Great Comforter, and the Great Physician. In the precious name of Jesus, I pray. Amen.

REFLECTIONS

Not knowing Jesus can be more dangerous than facing imminent danger in this world. Why?

Please use the space below to write down any thoughts or comments you may have.

"May God Bless You,
As you live your Life for Christ,
Empowered by The Holy Spirit."

August 15

Matthew 6:33-34 NIV.

[33] But seek first his kingdom and his righteousness, and all these things will be given to you as well. [34] Therefore do not worry about tomorrow, for tomorrow will worry about itself. Each day has enough trouble of its own. ...

Faithful Father, Lord of all creation, I come before you today with a heart filled with gratitude. When there is despair in my life, you lift me out of the darkness and into the light. When I struggle against the forces of evil, it is you that gives me the courage to break free of the shackles Satan binds me with. When I search for answers to life's questions, it is you who provides the solutions through your soft whisper and the Words of your Holy Scriptures. What a glorious and faithful God you are! How could I not be grateful for all the mercies and grace you extend to me?

I ask you now, my God, to continue to be my faithful companion and to bless me this day with the power of the Holy Spirit. Let me be an instrument of yours as I minister to those that do not know your Son, Jesus Christ, as their personal Savior. Let me sing with a joyful heart the glory of your kingdom and the riches of Heaven promised in your Word. For you, my God, are the way, the Truth, and the life for all your children to follow. Bless me now, my great King, as I joyfully submit to your will for my life. Bless me now, my God, as I stand firm in my faith and say to the world, "I am a child of God, and in Him will my heart's desires remain." Amen.

REFLECTIONS

What answers to life's questions has God revealed to you?

Please use the space below to write down any thoughts or comments you may have.

"May God Bless You,
As you live your Life for Christ,
Empowered by The Holy Spirit."

August 16

2 Corinthians 13:5-6 NIV.

[5] Examine yourselves to see whether you are in the faith; test yourselves. Do you not realize that Christ Jesus is in you -- unless, of course, you fail the test? [6] And I trust that you will discover that we have not failed the test. ...

O Great God, Father of my Lord and Savior, Jesus Christ, awaken my spirit lying dormant and in need of renewal. Consider my heart and soul and see where I have been failing to love and serve you as a faithful witness of Jesus Christ. Take me, O Christ, and shake me loose from all cobwebs that have entrapped me and are keeping me entangled in the web of lies and deceit of Satan. Renew my heart with a passion for loving and serving you and walking down the path of righteousness where no evil can befall me if I remain in Christ.

You are my Almighty God! I love you, and I dedicate my life to service in your name. Bless me now this day as I seek to bless others through prayer and Divine Opportunities. Show me where I can touch the lives of those in need of your love and grace. Forgive me when I fail to live out your call to love others as you first loved me. And when the darkness of Satan threatens to undermine my calling from Christ, cast him into a fiery pit where he can no longer have dominion over me. Grant these things in the name of the One who gave His life for all, Jesus Christ. Amen.

REFLECTIONS

Describe the cobwebs that keep you entangled in the lies and deceit of Satan.

Please use the space below to write down any thoughts or comments you may have.

"May God Bless You,
As you live your Life for Christ,
Empowered by The Holy Spirit."

August 17

I Philippians 2:5-8 NIV.

[5] In your relationships with one another, have the same mindset as Christ Jesus: [6] Who, being in very nature God, did not consider equality with God something to be used to his own advantage; [7] rather, he made himself nothing by taking the very nature of a servant, being made in human likeness.

My Faithful Father, I rejoice in being a servant of my Almighty God. I delight in the Truth of your Word that emanates from your Holy Bible. I rejoice in my ability to grow closer to Christ, so I can strive to have the same mindset as Him. Father, I am but a sheep being led by the Great Shepherd. Let me always search my heart and soul for my real motive in being of service to you. It is not out of complete fear but joy in knowing you are the Son of the Living God. Let me always be mindful of the mind of Christ, to love and serve those that do not have a personal relationship with you.

Father, I ask that you fill me with the power of the Holy Spirit. And, when I encounter the forces of the evil one, may I break his hold on me with a cry of freedom that is, like a trumpet, heard all among your creation. Bless me, Father, as you lead me down the path of righteousness so I may faithfully reflect the love and mind of Christ. Help me to greet others as I attempt to lead them to Christ with a spirit of humility, love, and understanding. Keep me from turning them away from the message of your Gospel. And when my day is done, help me to find peace knowing I served you well. In Christ's name, I pray. Amen.

REFLECTIONS

- *What is your real motive for serving Christ? Has your reason brought Glory to God?*

Please use the space below to write down any thoughts or comments you may have.

"May God Bless You,
As you live your Life for Christ,
Empowered by The Holy Spirit."

August 18

Deuteronomy 28:20 NIV.

[20] The Lord will send on you curses, confusion and rebuke in everything you put your hand to, until you are destroyed and come to sudden ruin because of the evil you have done in forsaking him.

O Lord, my Father in Heaven, I come before you today with a weary body and mind consumed with confusion. I live in a world full of hate, violence, and a lack of compassion and understanding for my fellow man. This was not part of your plan. O God, you meant for your creation to live in harmony with each other from the beginning. But because of Adam and Eve, your children must bear the cost of their disobedience. All over the world, discord and war are tearing apart the fabric of righteousness intended to heal and restore your order among your creation. People turn from your Word's Truth and look to false Gods to justify their hate and violence.

When will this end, O Christ? When will you come again to restore peace and harmony? When will the word of Truth replace the action of violence? Father, I pray you send your Holy Spirit upon the people of all nations to quell the spirit of unrest and to instill in them a heartfelt desire to love and serve you. Grant them the strength needed to forsake their rebellion and seek the Truth found in your Holy Word. Be with me now as I go about this day to find the peace and comfort needed to soothe my weary body and confused mind. I ask these things in the name of the Great Peacemaker, Jesus Christ. Amen.

REFLECTIONS

Why is it so difficult for God's children to live in harmony?

Please use the space below to write down any thoughts or comments you may have.

"May God Bless You,
As you live your Life for Christ,
Empowered by The Holy Spirit."

August 19

1 Corinthians 9:23 NIV.

[23] I do all this for the sake of the, that I may share in its blessings.

Gracious God revives my heart this day and awakens it from its slumber. This is a day you have made, and I rejoice in it. There is so much gratitude in my heart for all the blessings you have given to me. Benefits of health, strength, finance, love, perseverance, and so much more. How can I not bow down before you, my Almighty God? Send now your Holy Spirit upon me so I may be an instrument of your blessings to others in need. Shower me with your grace until it spills over unto all those searching and in need of your divine grace.

Let me be faithful in my desire and sincere devotion to love and serve my fellow man. Give me the passion of heart to love others as you first loved me. As I walk beside you, show me the miracles of your love in humanity and your creation. Let me not get jaded in my walk with you so that I fail to recognize the magnificence of all your wonders you have created. Let me have a joyful heart where I cry out to the world, "You are the Almighty God, Creator of Heaven and Earth." And when this day has passed, let me reawaken to the beauty of your love and faithfulness. Amen.

REFLECTIONS

How would one get jaded in their walk with Christ? Have you fallen into this trap?

Please use the space below to write down any thoughts or comments you may have.

"May God Bless You,
As you live your Life for Christ,
Empowered by The Holy Spirit."

August 20

Joshua 1:7 NIV.

[7] "Be strong and very courageous. Be careful to obey all the law my servant Moses gave you; do not turn from it to the right or to the left, that you may be successful wherever you go.

Gracious Jesus, thank you for being my Savior. Thank you for being the one true friend I can turn to in times of confusion and uncertainty. I praise you daily for your love, grace, and forgiveness. Where would I turn to when I am filled with despair if not to you? On this day, Lord Jesus, my heart cries out for those in need of your grace. Lord, you know who they are. You know the trials they are presently enduring and the pain that is in their hearts. I pray for your Holy Spirit to come upon them and to revive their hearts, their souls, and their joy in living.

Bless them with hearts of happiness so they may go about their daily tasks confident you are walking beside them and will not forsake them. Grant them peace and serenity so their confusion does not lead them astray and into the claws of Satan. I pray they will come to have a personal relationship with you. I pray they will always be filled with the strength and courage needed to weather any storms they may encounter in life. Praise to you, O God, for being the Great Provider and for always being there in times of need. May I be fruitful in my walk with you today, so I may influence others to claim the promises and Truth of your Holy Word by my example. In Jesus's name, I pray. Amen.

REFLECTIONS

What trials are you presently going through that you need God's help with?

Please use the space below to write down any thoughts or comments you may have.

"May God Bless You,
As you live your Life for Christ,
Empowered by The Holy Spirit."

August 21

Psalm 23:4 NIV.

[4] Even though I walk through the darkest valley, I will fear no evil, for you are with me; your rod and your staff, they comfort me.

Precious Jesus, my loving Redeemer, your Word says you will be with me even when I am walking through the darkness that consumes my heart and soul. How grateful I am for your presence in my life and the blessings you continuously bestow on me. I ask for your strength and courage to accompany me today as I venture forth in service to you. Let me be a powerful vehicle so no matter what obstacles cross my path, I can persevere and conquer my fears. I long to be a faithful servant, quick to love others, and quick to serve them with a spirit of humility.

Nothing in my earthly life is as essential as helping my fellow man as you instructed me in your Holy Word. Give me Divine Opportunities and the spirit of wisdom and revelation so I may know where there is a lost soul in need of your love. Grant me the patience of heart to listen to your children's pleadings so I may effectively witness to them. And when this day has passed, allow me to rest in the security and comfort of your love with the assurance I have served you well. In Christ's name, I pray. Amen.

REFLECTIONS

Can you think of a few Divine Opportunities you might have missed recently?

Please use the space below to write down any thoughts or comments you may have.

"May God Bless You,
As you live your Life for Christ,
Empowered by The Holy Spirit."

August 22

Colossians 3:12-14 NIV.

[12] Therefore, as God's chosen people, holy and dearly loved, clothe yourselves with compassion, kindness, humility, gentleness, and patience. [13] Bear with each other and forgive one another if any of you has a grievance against someone. Forgive as the Lord forgave you. [14] And over all these virtues put on love, which binds them all together in perfect unity. ...

Precious God, Father of my Lord and Savior, Jesus Christ, reveal to me, your obedient child, the spirit of wisdom and revelation. Let me go forth this day filled with love for my fellow man expressed through the virtues of compassion, kindness, humility, gentleness, and patience. Lord, you know those my heart bears grudges against. Forgive me for not extending the same love and grace to them you have blessed me with.

Console my heart as it struggles to find within it the compassion and humbleness that will allow me to touch their lives in a spirit of Godly love. Speak to their hearts so they will receive the blessing of forgiveness I extend to them. But more importantly, my Lord, break down the shackles of imprisonment to this world that binds me and others captive to the snares of Satan. Ban Satan from my life and cause him to flee when he hears me cry out for your Divine Intervention. Bless me with your enduring love and presence, so I can confidently face my enemies with a shield of love and patience. I ask these things in the name of the Great Peacemaker, Jesus Christ. Amen.

REFLECTIONS

What is something, becoming of a Christian, you can scream out when Satan tempts you?

Please use the space below to write down any thoughts or comments you may have.

"May God Bless You,
As you live your Life for Christ,
Empowered by The Holy Spirit."

August 23

Psalm 143:10 NIV.

[10] Teach me to do your will, for you are my God; may your good spirit lead me on level ground.

O Christ, send now your Holy Spirit upon me. Fill me with the spirit of love, patience, and mercy for my fellow man. Lord, there is so much sadness in this world. Some of your children do not have their basic needs met to feed their families, clothe themselves, or have access to medical care to preserve their health. Some of them have minimal financial resources to pay for these basic needs and often must rely on government assistance to make ends meet.

I pray, Lord, that as the Great Provider, you will ease their burdens and provide them with the resources to properly care for themselves and their loved ones. Teach me, Lord, to have a heart of love and mercy so if presented with an opportunity to personally ease their burdens, your will may be done. You are not only my God, but you are the God of all creation. Keep me steadfast in your command to love others as you first loved me. May I be strong in my faith and devotion to service in your name, and may I always reflect the face of Christ as I look for Divine Opportunities to show your love. In Christ's name, I pray. Amen.

REFLECTIONS

If God is the Great Provider, do you have anything to worry about?

Please use the space below to write down any thoughts or comments you may have.

"May God Bless You,
As you live your Life for Christ,
Empowered by The Holy Spirit."

August 24

Acts 17:26-27 NIV.

[26] From one man he made all the nations, that they should inhabit the whole earth; and he marked out their appointed times in history and the boundaries of their lands. [27] God did this so that they would seek him and perhaps reach out for him and find him, though he is not far from any one of us. ...

Great God, your Holy Scriptures are the blueprint for living my life. Your Word gives me the instructions to guide my footsteps along the path of Christ. Your Word is the food that feeds my soul. How great Thou art! Come now and provide America with the nourishment it needs to grow, prosper, and achieve peace among the world's nations. Let America be responsive to the plight of other countries whose people suffer from malnutrition and poverty. For among the world's nations, there is so much division. There is so much turmoil and conflict, yet you are in control.

I profess I do not understand why things in America are unfolding as they are. Still, I have faith your hand will ultimately reign supreme and restore order to this chaos. I pray, Father, that you will always keep America close to your heart. Prune America and its leaders of any thorns that impede its ability to be a great nation and a guiding light to the world. Help the leaders of America restore the Christian roots that made our country great and help us remember we cannot be great if we turn from God's Word. Renew America's greatness so no matter what adversity it faces, it will remain faithful to the guiding principles that made it great. In Christ's precious name, I pray. Amen.

REFLECTIONS

Have you helped those that are suffering from poverty and malnutrition? What did you do?

Please use the space below to write down any thoughts or comments you may have.

"May God Bless You,
As you live your Life for Christ,
Empowered by The Holy Spirit."

August 25

Psalm 139:23-24 NIV.

[23] Search me, God, and know my heart; test me and know my anxious thoughts. [24] See if there is any offensive way in me and lead me in the way everlasting. ...

O Gracious God, consider my heart and see the love and joy I have in serving you. You are my Creator, my Comforter, my King, and my Lord. I willingly place my life in your hands for the pruning it needs to be strong in my faith and firm in my resolve to always honor you. You know my heart, Lord Jesus, and you know how it sometimes trembles with anxiety. If there is anything in my life causing me to have anxious thoughts, I pray you will lift this burden from me and root it out from my heart and mind.

I pray for your constant direction in my life. Help me have clarity in my life and listen to your soft whisper so I may have no doubt where my heart's desire lies. I pray for spiritual wisdom so I may have a complete understanding of your will for my life. If there is anything offensive within me, strike it down and cause me to bow down, seeking your forgiveness and grace. I love you, my God, and praise your name for all the blessings you have bestowed upon me. In Christ's name, I pray. Amen.

REFLECTIONS

- *Are you willing to let God prune you of the branches that need pruning? If so, why?*

Please use the space below to write down any thoughts or comments you may have.

"May God Bless You,
As you live your Life for Christ,
Empowered by The Holy Spirit."

August 26

Leviticus 19:18 NIV.

[18] "Do not seek revenge or bear a grudge against anyone among your people but love your neighbor as yourself. I am the Lord.

Most merciful Lord Jesus, it is so easy to get caught up in anger and retribution when I find myself being offended. It is so easy to respond in cruel and destructive ways. And it is so easy to cast blame on others rather than holding myself responsible. Lord, you are the Great Mediator! You alone can soothe wounded spirits and teach me to respond to others' offenses in a spirit of true love and mercy. I pray you will take my heart and wring from it the soreness of anger that floods from my heart. Cause my heart and soul to respond in love and gratitude to your command to love others as you first loved me. Wipe from my mouth any foul or hurtful language that dishonors your name.

I implore you to fill me with your continuing presence, so I will hear your soft whisper reminding me I am a child of God. I am called to love and serve others with compassion, humility, mercy, and kindness. May I go forth this day, strong in my faith and firm in my resolve to faithfully reflect the life of Christ. Amen.

REFLECTIONS

How should you respond to others when they have offended you?

Please use the space below to write down any thoughts or comments you may have.

"May God Bless You,
As you live your Life for Christ,
Empowered by The Holy Spirit."

August 27

Psalm 86:15 NIV.

[15] But you, Lord, are a compassionate and gracious God, slow to anger, abounding in love and faithfulness.

Most Merciful God, Lord of all creation, and Lord of my heart thank you for your faithfulness to me and your endless grace. I know I am undeserving of your love and grace save for the blood of Christ. Yet, in your infinite mercy, you are slow to anger when I sin against you. Amazingly you still love me despite my failings. What a glorious God and Savior you are! Let me go about this day exhibiting a measure of the same love and faithfulness to my fellow man.

When I am confronted by those who do not know you and who try to pull me into the snares of Satan, may I be strong in my faith and strong in my courage to forsake temptations that dishonor you? May I be filled with the power of the Holy Spirit so I may discern your Truth and have a revelation of what is pure and righteous in your name.

Grant me a heart full of love and obedience to you, so I may dwell in your eternal home in Heaven when my time on earth passes. And if I should falter in my walk with Christ, awaken and correct me. Guide my behavior, so it is brought into alignment with your will for my life. I ask these things in the name of the One who gives my life purpose, my Lord and Savior, Jesus Christ. Amen.

REFLECTIONS

- *What is it that gives you purpose in life? Is it something of the world or God's kingdom?*

Please use the space below to write down any thoughts or comments you may have.

"May God Bless You,
As you live your Life for Christ,
Empowered by The Holy Spirit."

August 28

1 Peter 2:19 NIV.

[19] For it is commendable if someone bears up under the pain of unjust suffering because they are conscious of God.

My God, my precious Lord, my heart is heavy with the burden of sorrow for my fellow man. So many of them are experiencing anguish and discontent because of circumstances beyond their control. Their lives are caught up in confusion and pain they long to be free of. Help them, O Mighty God, to see that you are always there to comfort and love them through their trials no matter how bad things are. Wipe from their eyes the tears flowing and restore their hearts so they may be assured they are not alone in their grief.

Grant them the clarity of vision so they may see the light of hope and the prospect of a new tomorrow free of anguish and hopelessness. Provide them with the hope of your Word so they can rejoice in knowing all things work together for those that love the Lord. And by the power of the Holy Spirit, raise up the armor of the Lord, and let peace transcend all earthy confusion. And with voices lifted high, sing, "Alleluia, all glory to my God and King." Amen.

REFLECTIONS

- *When tears flow from your eyes, do you feel God there to comfort you? Will you let Him?*

Please use the space below to write down any thoughts or comments you may have.

August 29

Galatians 5:22-23 NIV.

[22] But the fruit of the spirit is love, joy, peace, forbearance, kindness, goodness, faithfulness, [23] gentleness and self- control. Against such things there is no law.

Gracious Savior, I praise you for the gifts of the Holy Spirit. I thank you for the opportunity to use my talents to touch the lives of your children. Let me greet them in the name of the One who created all things. Father, so many of your children, need your love. They need to feel the assurance that you are there in the direst of circumstances. Across our nation, tragedy has befallen so many. People's lives are being uprooted. What was once a semblance of peace and harmony has now placed their lives in peril. Father, you alone can provide for those in need. Use your people, O Christ, to minister to those without shelter or food. Use your people to bring medical care to those who are suffering. Use your people to ease the emotional turmoil they may be going through. And, Father, use your people to pray diligently for all those dealing with afflictions, whatever the cause might be.

And throughout these trials, help us all to remember that with you, all things are possible. Help us to remember the power of prayer, the one way to share with you all our concerns and fears. But let us not forget to praise you for all your blessings, so we do not take for granted the beautiful mercies and love you shower upon us. Thank you, dear Lord. Thank you for your gifts of grace. In Christ's name, I pray. Amen.

REFLECTIONS

What ways can God use you to minister to those who are in need?

Please use the space below to write down any thoughts or comments you may have.

"May God Bless You,
As you live your Life for Christ,
Empowered by The Holy Spirit."

August 30

Mark 11:23-24 NIV.

[23] "Truly I tell You, if anyone says to this mountain, 'Go, throw yourself into the sea,' and does not doubt in their heart but believes that what they say will happen, it will be done for them. [24] Therefore I tell you, whatever you ask for in prayer, believe that you have received it, and it will be yours.

Gracious Lord, your Word says if I believe something will happen in my heart, that it will be so. Father, I pray for deliverance from the influences of Satan, his cunning ways, insidious onslaught, and from his constant attack on my character. Lord, I am weak and need your strength. I am lost without your constant presence. And I am shamed by the intrusive thoughts that fill my head and are dishonoring to your name.

Cleanse my heart and soul and purge from them all thoughts and behaviors that fail to reflect the character of one who loves your Son, Jesus Christ. Fill me with the presence and power of the Holy Spirit so I may quash Satan in his tracks and ban him from my life. Through the Holy Spirit and through your grace, I believe in my heart you will rescue me from Satan's devious ploys. Hear my plea, my Father in Heaven, so I may find peace and rest as I trust in the One who gave his life for me, my Lord and Savior, Jesus Christ. Amen.

REFLECTIONS

What sin or shame has been challenging for you to hand over to God?

Please use the space below to write down any thoughts or comments you may have.

"May God Bless You,
As you live your Life for Christ,
Empowered by The Holy Spirit."

August 31

Psalm 145:8 NIV.

[8] The Lord is gracious and compassionate, slow to anger and rich in love.

My Lord, my God, I come before you as a sinner and a child of yours that is not slow to anger. Father, this sin grieves me, and it is dishonoring to your Holy Name. Forgive me, O Lord, for I seek a heart like yours, slow to anger and rich in love. Show me how to be gracious and compassionate to others so I may exemplify my life as a faithful Christian. Bring me to my knees and let me feel your gentle prod that stimulates patience and forbearance within me.

Arouse within me the love of Christ and His great compassion. And may I touch the lives of others with the integrity of a Christian who is strong in his faith. I humbly submit my stubborn will before your Cross so it may be crucified and buried once and for all. Let me be a beacon of light to others who have similar trials in their lives. And through the grace of my Lord, Jesus Christ, may I be empowered with the Holy Spirit to accomplish your will. Amen.

REFLECTIONS

How can a Christian influence those that do not believe in God? What would you do or say?

Please use the space below to write down any thoughts or comments you may have.

"May God Bless You,
As you live your Life for Christ,
Empowered by The Holy Spirit."

September 1

Psalm 145:1 NIV.

[1] I will exalt you, my God the King; I will praise your name for ever and ever.

Gracious God, I bow before you in humble repentance of my sins. I seek to be free of all things that hinder the flow of my gifts from the Holy Spirit. Empower me through the same spirit to break the shackles of Satan and to ban him from all things in my path. Lead me, O Lord, on the path of righteousness so I may delight in your will. Let me always exalt your name and sing praises that will let people know I am a child of the Living God. A God, who through His gift of grace, sent His only begotten Son, Jesus Christ, to pay the penalty for my sins.

As I go about this new day, O Christ, let me take on the shield of righteousness so I may be faithful and true in my witness to the world. Instill in me a heartfelt desire to show love and compassion, especially to those whose lives are tormented by forces beyond their control. Awaken my eyes and heart to see their needs and to have the courage to touch their lives with a true spirit of love, compassion, and grace. In your name, I pray. Amen.

REFLECTIONS

- *Why is the shield of righteousness necessary to be an effective witness of Christ?*

Please use the space below to write down any thoughts or comments you may have.

"May God Bless You,
As you live your Life for Christ,
Empowered by The Holy Spirit."

September 2

John 15:2 NIV.

[2] He cuts off every branch in me that bears no fruit, while every branch that does bear fruit, he prunes so that it will be even more fruitful.

Lord God, what a joy and privilege it is to love and serve you. You are my Master, the one whom I bow down before to seek forgiveness and to humble myself, so I may be pleasing in your sight. Father, I know you have blessed me with the fruits of the Holy Spirit. Sometimes, my Lord, I find myself caught up in day-to-day life issues that hinder my fruit from being nurtured.

Please prune my branches of worthless twigs that do nothing to develop my spiritual growth. Replace them, O Mighty God, with roots that nourish my limbs with the fruits of the Holy Spirit. Cultivate within me the strength and moral fortitude I need to develop strong branches. If a part of me should fall by the ploys of Satan, let a new one grow in its place more robust and more fruitful than the one that failed.

Help me to always remember that the fruits of the Holy Spirit are a gift from you to share with all your children so they too may enjoy the fruits they yearn for. Bless me now, this day, as I go forth seeking your face. Present me with Divine Opportunities to share your Gospel's message and the love of my Savior, Jesus Christ. Amen.

REFLECTIONS

Describe a worthless branch in your life that needs pruning by the Holy Spirit.

Please use the space below to write down any thoughts or comments you may have.

"May God Bless You,
As you live your Life for Christ,
Empowered by The Holy Spirit."

September 3

Psalm 18:32-34 NIV.

[32] It is God who arms me with strength and keeps my way secure. [33] He makes my feet like the feet of a deer; he causes me to stand on the heights. [34] He trains my hands for battle; my arms can bend a bow of bronze. ...

Blessed Father, because of your great love for me and through your grace and the power of the Holy Spirit, I can do all things. You give me the strength of a lion to fight off attacks by Satan. And you give me the capability of an eagle to soar high above the problems of this world. If I remain in my Lord and Savior, Jesus Christ, nothing can keep me bound to the ways of the world. You have given me the strength to break free of Satan's hold on my tongue, my behavior, and anything else that would compromise my love for you and the truth of your Word.

Through your grace, I can survive any conflict, any adversity, and any attempt by Satan to tear me from the warm embrace of your love. How can I not praise your Holy Name? Because of your great love for me, I can stand on the highest mountain top and proclaim, "My God, my God. How great Thou art." What a privilege and honor it is to be your faithful and obedient servant. May I always be loyal and devoted to your Holy Word and be led by the Holy Spirit. In Christ's name, I pray. Amen.

REFLECTIONS

When your tongue is loose, and you say things you shouldn't, how can God help you?

Please use the space below to write down any thoughts or comments you may have.

"May God Bless You,
As you live your Life for Christ,
Empowered by The Holy Spirit."

September 4

Matthew 16:24 NIV.

[24] Then Jesus said to his disciples, "Whoever wants to be my disciple must deny themselves and take up their cross and follow me.

Most Merciful God, your Word says if I am to be your disciple, I must deny myself and take up your cross and follow you. Father, I pray for your constant strength. Let me be a faithful disciple capable of denying myself and willing to bear your cross, no matter what the cost, so I may faithfully follow you. You know my sinful life and all the things of this world that have corrupted me and led me astray. You know the things I have found earthly pleasure in that are abhorrent to you and offensive to my Christian walk. Purge from my wayward life all those things that undermine my character and my personal profession that you are the Lord of my life.

Instill in me the truth of your Word, so I may be a living witness of your love, grace, and eternal forgiveness. Let the world see through my life the joy of one who loves the Lord and who gladly bears the weight and burdens of one in Christ. Forgive me, my Lord, of all my transgressions and my inability to remain strong in times of trial. This day blesses me with the fruits of the Holy Spirit, so I may find victory through the Cross of my Savior, Jesus Christ. Amen.

REFLECTIONS

Are there things in your life that are so offensive to God that you cry out in shame to Him, or do you run?

Please use the space below to write down any thoughts or comments you may have.

"May God Bless You,
As you live your Life for Christ,
Empowered by The Holy Spirit."

September 5

Job 31:33 NIV.

[33] if I have concealed my sin as people do, by hiding my guilt in my heart...

O Lord, my precious Savior, hear the concerns of my heart. Father, in your Word, you say the wages of sin are death. You also say when I confess my sins and repent, you are faithful to your Word to forgive them. My life has been riddled with corruption, my Lord. But despite countless requests that you excuse me of my sins, I still sin. How can you love me when each day I sin again and again and grieve your heart? How do I get over the guilt of my sins and rest with the assurance that you will be faithful to your Word and wipe my slate clean as snow?

Father, because of your great love for me and because of your endless grace and mercy, I can claim your promises and know in my heart, you are faithful and true to your Word. There is no other hope for me than to rely on the promises of your Word. I can do nothing by myself. I am totally incompetent in my efforts to free myself of those sins. Thank you for sending your Son, Jesus Christ, as my personal Savior and the perfect atonement for my sins. Let me always glorify your name as I strive to live my life in perfect harmony with your Word and with the freedom that comes from one who is in Christ. Amen.

REFLECTIONS

Why do you think God loves you so much despite your constant tendency to sin?

Please use the space below to write down any thoughts or comments you may have.

"May God Bless You,
As you live your Life for Christ,
Empowered by The Holy Spirit."

September 6

Psalm 128:2 NIV.

[2] You will eat the fruit of your labor; blessings and prosperity will be yours.

O Merciful Lord Jesus, your grace is utterly extraordinary. All over your creation, evidence of your love and grace is a constant reminder that you are my Almighty God. In all my walks, I see the truth of your Word. I see the beauty of living a life in Christ. Thank you for being my God. Thank you for being my strength. Thank you for being my comforter. And thank you, Lord, for loving me despite my sinful nature and the sins I commit. You are unique, and I vow to always love you and always try to live my life in faithful obedience to your Word.

As I go about this day, plant your seed of love within my heart. Plant the power of your grace in those dealing with crisis after crisis. Be with them as they seek comfort from the emotional and financial toll on their lives. Bless me with the gift of compassion as I seek opportunities to speak the soft whisper of your voice to those in need. Let me be a true ambassador of your Word as I seek out Divine Opportunities to touch the lives of others. Bless me, Lord, as I seek to do your will. Amen.

REFLECTIONS

If you were to name the seeds of love you need, what would be some of their names?

Please use the space below to write down any thoughts or comments you may have.

*"May God Bless You,
As you live your Life for Christ,
Empowered by The Holy Spirit."*

September 7

Psalm 118:5-8 NIV.

[5] When hard pressed, I cried to the Lord; he brought me into a spacious place. [6] The Lord is with me; I will not be afraid. What can mere mortals do to me? [7] The Lord is with me; he is my helper. I look in triumph on my enemies. [8] It is better to take refuge in the Lord than to trust in humans. ...

Hallelujah, O Christ, my King! I rejoice in the undeniable truth of your Word. I rejoice knowing that because of my Savior, Jesus Christ if I remain in him, I will spend eternity in paradise with you. You alone are my sovereign King. I bow down before you with great humility. Lord, you are my helper in times of need, and you look over me with a watchful eye as I traverse the many roads along life's way.

Praise to you, O Christ! It is in you that I take refuge and know that, unlike humans, I can always rely on your love and guiding presence. Where would I be, my Lord, without you? Where would I turn to in moments of despair? Where would I go when no one would offer me the love and compassion I need? Only to you, O faithful Christ. Only to you.

Bless me now with the anointing of the Holy Spirit. Bless me so I may carry with me the power of the Holy Spirit to ward off all attempts by Satan to lead me away from your Word. Let me not fall victim to the influences of the evil one that waits in hiding to corrupt my heart and soul. Praise to you, O Christ! Hallelujah to your Holy Name. Amen.

REFLECTIONS

What does God's guiding presence mean to you? Are you willing to be guided by Him?

Please use the space below to write down any thoughts or comments you may have.

*"May God Bless You,
As you live your Life for Christ,
Empowered by The Holy Spirit."*

September 8

Job 16:20 NIV.

[20] My intercessor is my friend as my eyes pour out tears to God...

O Christ, my King, I confess with a heavy heart that I often fail to put you first as I go about my day. I admit I am a fallen sinner with the frailty of one who has a broken spirit that needs your abiding grace. I confess I am lost without your enduring love and mercy. As a fallen child of yours, I petition you to continue to love me despite my many faults. I implore you to shower me with your grace so I may bear the fruits of the Holy Spirit. And I petition you to let me be a faithful follower of Christ, resolute in my conviction and love for your precious Son.

Lord, as much as I need your personal mediation, I ask that you bless those who are less fortunate and whose needs are far greater than mine. You know the ones whose lives I encounter on my daily walks. Send now your Holy Spirit upon them to awaken them to newness in life that can only come from having a personal relationship with Jesus Christ. I thank you, my God, for always being there to comfort me, to love me, and to guide my footsteps in good times as well as bad. I thank you for being my God, whom I can always trust with my heart.

I thank you for my Salvation and the price your Son paid on the Cross of Calvary. How can I not praise you for your precious love? How can I not praise you for your endless mercy and gifts of the Holy Spirit? And how can I not praise you for your steadfast faithfulness to always be by my side and to love me despite my failings? Praise to your name, O Christ! Let me be strong in my faith as I go about this day, loving you and praising your Holy Name. Amen.

REFLECTIONS

If you have a broken spirit, how can it be healed? Do you have faith God can heal you?

Please use the space below to write down any thoughts or comments you may have.

"May God Bless You,
As you live your Life for Christ,
Empowered by The Holy Spirit."

September 9

Psalm 31:5 NIV.

[5] Into your hands I commit my spirit; deliver me, Lord, my faithful God.

Glory to you, O Christ! Praise to your Holy Name. What a joy it is to be your servant and to know you personally as my Savior. Without you, I would be lost among the wolves of humanity. Without you, I would not have the assurance of faith that all things work together for those that trust in your promises. Although my faith is strong, my Lord, I still have fears and doubts that cloud my thinking and cause me to fall off the path of righteousness. When I succumb to these fears, awaken within me the truth of your Word, so I may again know you will not fail me.

Give me the courage to love you and be strong in my faith no matter what obstacles may be in my path. Give me the strength to weather any storms that threaten my relationship with you and undermine my character. And when these storms have passed, let me rejoice with jubilation that you are my Almighty God, my Savior, and my King. Through the power of the Holy Spirit, I can say it is well with my soul. Yes, Lord, it is well with my soul. Amen.

REFLECTIONS

When your thinking is cloudy, how can you lift the clouds so you can think clearly?

Please use the space below to write down any thoughts or comments you may have.

September 10

2 Peter 2:19 NIV.

[19] They promise them freedom, while they themselves are slaves of depravity---for "people are slaves to whatever has mastered them."

Blessed Lord Jesus, I long to faithfully love you with a devotion becoming of one in Christ. It is my heart's desire to be a faithful servant of your Word. Lord, through the death of your Son, Jesus Christ on the Cross of Calvary, you have given me newness in life. You have promised that whoever believes in Jesus Christ and repents from their sins will have their sins forgiven. Father, I praise you for this gift of forgiveness. I know, though, that I remain unworthy of your forgiveness because of my constant failure to faithfully turn from my sins.

Forgive me, O Lord, for my weakness to completely forsake my sins. In my heart, I wish I could completely turn from my sins and live a sinless life. But I know your Son, Jesus Christ, was the only one capable of living an innocent life. Without Christ in my life, I would be forever lost to Satan's influences and subject to his demonic hold on my life. Please do not give up on me, my God, for I will continue to strengthen my resolve to forsake all my sins and to do my best to turn from them so I will be pleasing in your sight.

Light my path to freedom from Satan's influences and keep me firm in my faithfulness to your Word. Take from my life any evil that has the propensity to cause me to falter in my walk with Christ. And when I find myself succumbing to sin, I claim the blood of Christ as my substitute and the only right path to your heavenly kingdom. Amen.

REFLECTIONS

Do you think because of your sinful nature, God would ever give up on you? If not, why?

Please use the space below to write down any thoughts or comments you may have.

"May God Bless You,
As you live your Life for Christ,
Empowered by The Holy Spirit."

September 11

Jeremiah 8:18 NIV.

[18] You who are my comforter in sorrow, my heart is faint within me.

Most gracious and loving God, I pray for the souls of all those lost in the terrorist attacks on September 11, 2001. I pray for the families and loved ones of those who lost their earthly lives on that fateful day. I pray you will soothe and comfort their emotions as they remember with fondness and sorrow the memories they shared. I rejoice in the firefighters' courage. My heart goes out to the EMS workers, the police, and all the other emergency responders, especially those who lost their lives responding to this tragedy. I praise you for their incredible bravery. May we never forget their sacrifice and the families and loved ones they left behind.

Lord, why this tragedy had to happen is beyond human comprehension. But I do believe that amid this horrifying day, the hand of your grace was upon them. You are a God of love! Through your hands, you deliver your children from the fires of Satan and the perpetrators of the evil one. For those that have accepted you as Lord of their lives, fire and brimstone cannot keep them from eternal life with you. For those that did not know you, I pray an intercessory prayer that you welcomed them into your kingdom. You are a God of grace, forgiveness, and great mercy. Thank you, Lord, for this day of remembrance. Thank you for your enduring love and comforting words. As America pauses to celebrate the lives of all those lost on this day of sadness, I thank you for the hedge of protection you continue to provide. Let your love and grace continue to soothe the hearts of those who lost loved ones on this day. In Christ's name, I pray. Amen.

REFLECTIONS

If you lost a loved one on 9/11, have you been calling on God to soothe your pain?

Please use the space below to write down any thoughts or comments you may have.

"May God Bless You,
As you live your Life for Christ,
Empowered by The Holy Spirit."

September 12

Psalm 111:10 NIV.

[10] The fear of the Lord is the beginning of wisdom; all who follow his precepts have good understanding. To him belongs eternal praise.

Blessed Father, send now your Holy Spirit upon me. Place the words on my lips that I should whisper to those that do not know your Son, Jesus Christ, as their personal Savior. Let me be a vehicle of your Truth, firm in my beliefs that you are the Almighty God, creator of all that is good and righteous in this world. Within my soul, stir the cup of wisdom and love that can be used to steer the misguided and lost. Bless me as I open my ears to hear others' plight and let them not fall deaf to their pleadings.

There is a great love for your children within my heart and a sincere desire to love them as you first loved me. Grant me the patience to hear their forlorn words so I do not dismiss them and lead them down the path of Satan's ploys. You are the Almighty God in whom I place my trust and faith. Preserve me in the Truth that whoever believes in your Son, Jesus Christ, will find eternal life in your heavenly kingdom. And let me not waver in my devotion to your Word as I go about this day. Let me be confident that through your Son, Jesus Christ, I can accomplish all things. In His name, I pray. Amen.

REFLECTIONS

When you hear of others' plight, what spiritual gifts can you use to ease their pain?

Please use the space below to write down any thoughts or comments you may have.

"May God Bless You,
As you live your Life for Christ,
Empowered by The Holy Spirit."

September 13

1 John 3:16 NIV.

[16] This is how we know what love is: Jesus Christ laid down his life for us. And we ought to lay down our lives for our brothers and sisters.

As I go about this new day, Blessed Lord Jesus, fill me with the spirit of wisdom and revelation. Let me be keenly aware of the great love you have for me as I try to share that same love with my family, friends, and strangers. Let me remember you paid the supreme sacrifice for my sins by laying down your life on the Cross of Calvary.

Lord, there is so much stress, conflict, and hatred among your children. In your precious mercy, purge from my life anything that goes contrary to your will. Purge from my life any doubt I may have that you can restore my heart and mind. Let me be free of anything that deters me from being a loving and faithful child of yours. Instill in me a stronghold of faith and obedience so no matter what adversities I may face, I will be prepared to lay down my life for your glory.

O Christ, when my time on this earth is done, and the angels of Heaven part the gates to your kingdom, receive me as a faithful and obedient child that loves you and sings praises to your Holy Name. Amen.

REFLECTIONS

- *How can you build up a stronghold of faith and obedience? Could the Holy Spirit help you? If so, how?*

Please use the space below to write down any thoughts or comments you may have.

"May God Bless You,
As you live your Life for Christ,
Empowered by The Holy Spirit."

September 14

Galatians 6:9 NIV.

[9] Let us not become weary in doing good, for at the proper time we will reap a harvest if we do not give up.

O Holy Father, let me not get weary or discouraged in my service to your name. The glory of your kingdom is a treasure I want to tell others about so they too may share in the gift of Salvation. Through your Son, Jesus Christ, I have been redeemed and have found forgiveness of my sins. Through your Son, I can see the strength and hope that no matter how many obstacles I encounter as I try to share your Gospel Message, you will open the hearts of those I try to touch. Through the power of the Holy Spirit, let them receive the good news of your Gospel with joy and jubilation.

Let me be faithful, O Lord, in planting the seeds of faith so when your Word has time to grow within the hearts of those whom I touch, your name will be glorified. Let me hear the soft voice of my Lord, Jesus Christ, so as I lift your Holy Word, the ears upon which they fall may know you are the Almighty God, and through your Son, all things are possible. In the name of the Father, the Son, and the Holy Spirit. Amen.

REFLECTIONS

How will you know if the seeds of faith you helped plant in someone blessed God and them?

Please use the space below to write down any thoughts or comments you may have.

"May God Bless You,
As you live your Life for Christ,
Empowered by The Holy Spirit."

September 15

Luke 22:44 NIV.

[44] And being in anguish, he prayed more earnestly, and his sweat was like drops of blood falling to the ground.

Merciful Lord Jesus, I come before you on bent knees and with a humble heart. I come before you with a heart full of intercessory prayer for those whose bodies are consumed with injury, illness, and disease. Lord, your healing hand is needed upon all those struggling with health issues, both physical and emotional. Through the power of the Holy Spirit, send now your guardian angels and, through Divine Intervention, heal those in need so their health may be fully restored.

Lord, you are the Great Physician. My trust is in you that through a heart full of love for your Son, Jesus Christ, you may hear my petitions and grant the healing upon the bodies that are afflicted. May I be a faithful instrument of your love, so through my words of consolation and prayer, I may be a source of comfort and strength to all those in need. And when my tears of compassion have subsided, let me look upon your gracious miracles and rejoice that you are the Almighty God, and in your arms, do I rest. Amen.

REFLECTIONS

If your heart is weary, can you still be a source of comfort and strength to those in need?

Please use the space below to write down any thoughts or comments you may have.

"May God Bless You,
As you live your Life for Christ,
Empowered by The Holy Spirit."

September 16

Psalm 119:125 NIV.

[125] I am your servant; give me discernment that I may understand your statutes

Father God, in your mercy, you see beyond my human faults to the blood of your Son, Jesus Christ. When I am engaged in sinful thoughts and deeds, you cover them with the blood of Christ and look upon me with a heart full of compassion and love. I deserve no forgiveness, but despite my sinful condition, when I confess my sins, you are quick to forgive them. As you wrap your arms around me, draw me close to the bosom of your chest. O Lord, your mercy is so great! Praise to you, O Christ, for setting me free of my transgressions and leading me back to the path of righteousness.

I rejoice in your precious name and offer myself as a devoted servant with a heart bent toward service in your name. Grant me another day in faithful service and love to my fellow man so I may exemplify the character of one who is in Christ. And if I should falter, as I will, may I be awakened and gently corrected. Let me recognize my sin and turn with a repentant heart back on the path of righteousness. In Christ's name, I pray. Amen.

REFLECTIONS

- *If your sins are covered by the blood of Christ, does that give you permission to sin?*

Please use the space below to write down any thoughts or comments you may have.

"May God Bless You,
As you live your Life for Christ,
Empowered by The Holy Spirit."

September 17

Hebrews 10:4 NIV.

[4] It is impossible for the blood of bulls and goats to take away sins.

Most Merciful Lord Jesus, you have chosen me to be worthy of your love and sacrifice on the Cross of Calvary. You have taken me from the clutches of Satan and, through baptism into the Holy Spirit, brought me into the kingdom of God. I praise you, Father, for the gift of Salvation, the power of your redeeming blood, and the joy of being in your presence through the precious gifts of grace and faith.

Lord, I am a sinner caught up in the sins of this world. Because your love is so great and so faithful, no matter what my sinful state is, you are loyal and devoted to your Word to welcome me into your presence. Praise to your name, Lord Jesus! Let me always be grateful for the love and grace you continuously bestow upon me. Grant me the peace, assurance, and security in your Word when my actions may cause me to doubt the gift of Salvation. In Christ's name, I pray. Amen.

REFLECTIONS

- *What are some circumstances in your life where you have doubted the gift of Salvation?*

Please use the space below to write down any thoughts or comments you may have.

"May God Bless You,
As you live your Life for Christ,
Empowered by The Holy Spirit."

September 18

John 14:6 NIV.

[6] Jesus answered, "I am the way and the truth and the life. No one comes to the Father except through me.

Gracious God, the truth of your Word is evident in my heart. You are my Lord, my Savior, and my hope for complete restoration of my body, mind, and spirit. You alone are the source of righteousness in this world full of deceit, wickedness, and all sources of evil. You stand alone as the one to turn to for guidance when I am lost in the mayhem caused by mankind.

Lord Jesus, I give you thanks, that I can always turn to you when I am lost and bewildered by situations in life of my doing and those beyond my control. Let me be a vessel of hope and righteousness as I serve as an ambassador of your Truth to those that may not know you. Father, cleanse from my heart and soul all impurities that may impede my ability to touch your children's lives. Bless the lives of those in need of your love and grace. And, in your Name, let me be a blessing to all those that hear my words, see my actions, and whose lives I interact with as I seek out Divine Opportunities to share my faith. In Christ's name, I pray. Amen.

REFLECTIONS

How do you know you can be an actual vessel of hope and righteousness to those who are lost?

Please use the space below to write down any thoughts or comments you may have.

"May God Bless You,
As you live your Life for Christ,
Empowered by The Holy Spirit."

September 19

Romans 5:21 NIV.

[21] so that, just as sin reigned in death, so also grace might reign through righteousness to bring eternal life through Jesus Christ our Lord.

O Holy Father, I praise you for your endless grace and my undeserved mercy. I confess it is not always easy to follow your example by extending the same understanding to those in need. I wrestle with my emotions, fears of the unknown, and my sense of loss with the erosion of societal values I held dear to my heart. I grapple with changing lifestyles that undermine the sanctity of your Word. And I wonder where will it all end? The struggle within my heart is very genuine. There seems to be no hope for those caught up in sinful lifestyles that shred and compromise your Word. But then I remember your grace, and your gift of Salvation is for everyone. Even those who are lost and confused. Who am I when I repeatedly sin only to claim your forgiveness and mercy to restore myself with you?

Help me remember, my Lord, that those who are caught up in sins of the flesh, those that are caught up in lifestyles that offend you, and those who are non-repentant are still in need of your grace. Let me be an instrument of your love. When I encounter those caught up in the ways of the world and who are being manipulated by Satan, let me wear the hat of mercy, not judgment. The shield of righteousness, not permissiveness. The face of love, not hate, And may I always remember you are still a merciful God — full of love, grace, and forgiveness. No matter what sins my brothers and sisters are engaged in, let your Truth resound within their hearts. May they someday recognize the path to your heavenly kingdom is paved by obedience to your Holy Word. Give them souls that are cracked, not harden, or sealed, so the truth of your Word can find its way into their hearts and lead them toward eternal peace and life with you. In Christ's name, I pray. Amen.

"May God Bless You,
As you live your Life for Christ,
Empowered by The Holy Spirit."

REFLECTIONS

Has the loss of Godly values in society impacted your ability to love others?

Please use the space below to write down any thoughts or comments you may have.

"May God Bless You,
As you live your Life for Christ,
Empowered by The Holy Spirit."

September 20

Psalm 86:2 NIV.

[2] Guard my life, for I am faithful to you; save your servant who trusts in you. You are my God...

O Christ, my King of Kings, I bow down before you in humble reverence and awe. You are so generous and gracious. Because of your infinite mercy, you sent Jesus Christ to die on the Cross of Calvary and to bear the sins of the world. O God, the sadness you must have felt hearing the pleas of your Son as the last breaths of earthly life passed from him. Father, the God who created the heavens and the earth, thank you for the sacrifice of your Son, the greatest act of faithfulness to your Word the world has ever known.

In Christ's name, I come before you as a sinner lost in this world full of deception and lies instigated by Satan. O Lord, my God, you are the source of my strength. You are the Shield of Armor that protects me from the cunning manipulation used by Satan to trap me in the ways of the world. I need your help, O Lord. I need your strength. I need the power of the Holy Spirit to aid me in my fight against the forces of evil, so I may be faithful and loyal to your Word.

Heavenly Father, look within my heart and see your struggling servant. O God, I am helpless to be perfect in my walk with Christ, but I endeavor to love and serve Him with all my heart. I yearn to be loyal and faithful to your Word and bring honor and glory to your Holy Name. Extend your infinite mercy and grace upon me and restore me on the path of righteousness so I may once again show you my faithfulness. In Christ's name, I pray. Amen.

REFLECTIONS

As you go about a new day, do you need to call on God's strength to help you in your walk?

Please use the space below to write down any thoughts or comments you may have.

"May God Bless You,
As you live your Life for Christ,
Empowered by The Holy Spirit."

September 21

Matthew 5:9 NIV.

[9] Blessed are the peacemakers, for they will be called children of God.

O Lord, my God, you have all the power and wisdom in the Universe. You stand alone as the Supreme God, the only true God, and the ruler of the heavens and the earth. Thank you for sending your Son, Jesus Christ, as the ultimate atonement for my sins. Father, I bring before you our nation and countries across the world. The need for world peace is much greater than ever before. Hear my prayer that your hand will be firmly grasped by leaders as they turn to you as the trustworthy source of wisdom as they make decisions that can affect world peace.

Across your creation, people are anxious and concerned about decisions made by world leaders. Give them comfort, Heavenly Father, as your children turn their concerns and burdens over to you. Let them rest in the knowledge that all things work together for those that love the Lord. Help us to always keep our eyes and hopes firmly rooted in your Scriptures so together we can draw comfort and peace, secured by faith, in the promises of your Word. Pour out your Holy Spirit upon all your children so they can always know the ease and comfort that comes by being children of God. I ask these things in the name of Jesus Christ, my Lord and Savior. Amen.

REFLECTIONS

Do you take the time to pray for world leaders? What might happen if you did not pray?

Please use the space below to write down any thoughts or comments you may have.

"May God Bless You,
As you live your Life for Christ,
Empowered by The Holy Spirit."

September 22

1 Peter 3:8-9 NIV.

[8] Finally, all of you, be like-minded, be sympathetic, love one another, be compassionate and humble. [9] Do not repay evil with evil or insult with insult. On the contrary, repay evil with blessing, because to this you were called so that you may inherit a blessing. ...

Blessed Father, I thank you for your countless blessings. There is no greater calling than to fulfill Christ's calling. Let me be a blessing to family, friends, and strangers among us. Through the power of the Holy Spirit, I offer up prayers of blessings and prayers that speak to the hearts and souls of all those longings to hear the soft whisper of your voice. It is through prayer that I can share with you my thoughts, fears, and concerns. Through prayer, I hear and feel the gentle nudge of the Holy Spirit that keeps me grounded and on the path of righteousness.

What a blessing, my Lord, to have a personal relationship with your Son, Jesus Christ. Through him, I can cope with the adversities of life, and it is through him I offer up my praise and songs of exaltation proclaiming Jesus Christ as Lord of my life. Father, send your Holy Spirit as I begin my day, so I will be equipped with the spiritual wisdom to touch someone's heart. If there is any unrest or an evil seed within me, purge it now from my heart and mind. Lift my heart and give me the spiritual countenance that will reflect a person who is full of love, compassion, and mercy for all your children. I ask these things in the name of the Great One who knows my heart and is always patient, loving, and kind. Amen.

REFLECTIONS

Do you need to ask God to purge any seeds of unrest as you begin your new day?

Please use the space below to write down any thoughts or comments you may have.

"May God Bless You,
As you live your Life for Christ,
Empowered by The Holy Spirit."

September 23

John 3:16 NIV.

[16] For God so loved the world that he gave his one and only Son, that whoever believes in him shall not perish but have eternal life.

O Holy Father, send now your Holy Spirit upon me. Speak to my heart with the soft whisper of your voice guiding my thoughts and words as I petition you for prayers of comfort. Lord, my heart is heavy for those that doubt the truth of your Word. My heart is heavy for those that struggle to make sense of prayers that seem to go unanswered. My heart is heavy for those that seem to be caught up in a sea of hopelessness. Lord, your Word promises that for those who are in Christ, you are loyal and faithful to your Word. Your Word does not promise that you will provide answers to prayers according to their will but to your will. When faced with doubt, let me remember you are a faithful and loving God who is always honest to His Word. Let me not forget that what seems to be unanswered prayer may in your time be the divine answer to the needs and desires of their heart.

You are the Almighty God, a God of love and compassion, a God that heals the broken-hearted and who can restore their soul no matter the grief that consumes it. Praise to you, O Christ, for the most remarkable healing will come when I enter the gates of paradise in your heavenly kingdom. Thank you, my God, for always being faithful to your Word and for providing the comfort and assurance I need when faced with a life of uncertainty. I ask these things in the precious name of your Son, Jesus Christ, who died for the sins of mankind so I may have eternal life with you. Amen.

REFLECTIONS

When it may seem like God does not answer prayers, what should you remember?

Please use the space below to write down any thoughts or comments you may have.

"May God Bless You,
As you live your Life for Christ,
Empowered by The Holy Spirit."

September 24

1 Corinthians 15:33 NIV.

[33] Do not be misled: "Bad company corrupts good character."

Heavenly Father, I come before you, carrying a burden of sins, sins that have been weighing heavily upon my heart. My heart is tormented by the sins I willfully commit, sins that not only grieve your heart but that impede my relationship with you. Each day I am confronted with personal struggles that are difficult for me to face with the character befitting one in Christ. Each day, I am confronted with obstacles in my life that test my faith and loyalty to your Word. At day's end, I cry out with the pain of a broken heart. I know I have failed you through careless and thoughtless acts toward others who themselves are caught up in the pain and confusion of this world.

Forgive me, gracious Father, through your infinite mercy and unending grace, of my disobedience to your Word, of failing to live out my life faithfully in your service, and of failing to be a faithful witness of your Word to my fellow man. Father, I want to rejoice in the power of your Word, power that can transform my life and make me into the kind of person that reflects the love and character of Jesus Christ. Renew my heart and soul with the power and love of the Holy Spirit, so I may faithfully live out my life in Christ. Through His name, I pray. Amen.

REFLECTIONS

When you think you have failed God, what do you need to remember?

Please use the space below to write down any thoughts or comments you may have.

"May God Bless You,
As you live your Life for Christ,
Empowered by The Holy Spirit."

September 25

Romans 8:10 NIV.

[10] But if Christ is in you, then even though your body is subject to death because of sin, the spirit gives life because of righteousness.

O Father, speak to me now as I receive your Holy Spirit. Take your Truth and plant it deep in my heart so I may bear the fruits of the spirit and live this day faithfully and in righteousness. Shape and fashion me into your likeness so those I encounter today may see the light and love of Christ within me. In all my acts of love, let my deeds of faith lead others to a life filled with the love and the grace of my Lord, Jesus Christ. Position me in situations that will allow me to be a vehicle of your Truth.

Let the hearts of those that may be hardened quickly soften so the Words of your Son, Jesus Christ, may enter their hearts. Keep me in a spirit of humility so pride and arrogance may not grab hold of me. When the forces of Satan threaten my resolve, quickly purge me of Satan's wickedness so the words from my mouth may not be tainted. In all my doings this day, let me rejoice and praise your Holy Name. And as my day ends, let me rest knowing I have been pleasing in your sight. In Christ's name, I pray. Amen.

REFLECTIONS

Is it difficult when you are consumed with personal concerns to reflect God's love to others?

Please use the space below to write down any thoughts or comments you may have.

"May God Bless You,
As you live your Life for Christ,
Empowered by The Holy Spirit."

September 26

Isaiah 38:14 NIV.

[14] I cried like a swift or thrush, I moaned like a mourning dove. My eyes grew weak as I looked to the heavens. I am being threatened; Lord, come to my aid!"

Lord Jesus, you are the light of the world, my hope, and my Salvation. I praise you, Jesus, that you are always there to guide my footsteps down the path of righteousness. From the beginning, I was given the power of free choice, the ability to choose what path in life I would follow. Lord, unfortunately, I have been weak in spirit and have failed to always follow the way that would keep me in your light and basking in the presence of the Holy Spirit. Forgive me, O Lord, for those times I have departed from my walk with you. Forgive me for neglecting the Word of God that is the source of my strength.

Father, it is in you that the hope for mankind shall be revealed. Help me always to live my life preparing for that day when you shall return to fulfill your Holy Word. Let me not be consumed with doubts and fears that undermine the truth of your Word. Let me rejoice with complete knowledge and assurance that you are the Living God, the source of my personal Salvation, and my confidence in eternal life. Praise to you, O Christ! Praise to you! Amen.

REFLECTIONS

How can you prepare to live your life for the day Christ returns?

Please use the space below to write down any thoughts or comments you may have.

"May God Bless You,
As you live your Life for Christ,
Empowered by The Holy Spirit."

September 27

Jeremiah 17:5 NIV.

[5] This is what the Lord says: "Cursed is the one who trusts in man, who draws strength from mere flesh and whose heart turns away from the Lord.

Heavenly Father, awaken in me my spirit of love for your Word. Lord, there are days when it is so challenging to live my life in a way that brings honor and glory to your name. As my day progresses, I am confronted with choices that allow me to choose the path of righteousness or the way of shame that puts a wedge between us. Lord, I do not want to fail in my walk with you. I want to be able to finish my day and rejoice in my victory over Satan. I want to be able to look back over the challenges life put in front of me and be able to say, "Lord, today I have been victorious over sin. I praise you for being there beside me as I faced the temptations of this world."

Father, it helps me to remember when I am confronted with temptations that I have the freedom to reject sinful behavior. Convict my heart and mind and bring me into a state of submission where I not only hear your voice calling out to me but where I choose to honor you in all I do. Let me always be mindful of the price you paid on the Cross of Calvary, and never let me take my Salvation for granted. I love you, Lord Jesus, and need your help in facing the storms in life. Bless me with the assurance of my Salvation. And, despite my sinful nature, grant me a love so deep for you that I live out each day of my life in faithful obedience to your Word. In Christ's precious name, I pray. Amen.

REFLECTIONS

Is there joy to be found when you have been victorious over sin?

Please use the space below to write down any thoughts or comments you may have.

"May God Bless You,
As you live your Life for Christ,
Empowered by The Holy Spirit."

September 28

Psalm 28:6 NIV.

[6] Praise be to the Lord, for he has heard my cry for mercy.

Most Merciful Lord Jesus, I come before you with a heart that longs to be faithful and obedient to your Word. I come before you, as a sinner, cloaked in a veil of shame. I come before you, pleading for your forgiveness and mercy. As I begin this day, O Christ, lead me down the path of righteousness away from any temptation or behavior that dishonors your Word. Let me be mindful of the cost of my Salvation. Let me remember the sacrifice of your life on the Cross of Calvary for my sins.

You, my Lord, are the way, the Truth, and the life. You have blessed me in countless ways and have enriched my life way beyond what I thought was possible. You shield me from my enemies. You give me hope when I have nowhere to turn. You challenge me when I need to dig deeper in my heart to find the love and compassion needed by my fellow man. And you grant me countless blessings when I call upon your name.

All your love, grace, and mercy are undeserved save for the blood of my Lord and Savior, Jesus Christ. Lift me up now, as a child of yours, so I may feel the warmth and scope of your love. And, when I finish my day, let me rejoice that by your name, I can do all things. Praise to you, O Great One! Praise to your Holy Name. Amen.

REFLECTIONS

- *Can you feel God's protection through the Holy Spirit when Satan attacks you?*

Please use the space below to write down any thoughts or comments you may have.

"May God Bless You,
As you live your Life for Christ,
Empowered by The Holy Spirit."

September 29

Job 32:8 NIV.

[8] But it is the spirit in a person, the breath of the Almighty, that gives them understanding.

O God, the Father of my Salvation, I thank you for the garden of life, a garden that you have given me to cultivate and to nourish with the fruits of the Holy Spirit. Lord, you are Master Pruner, the one who knows the branches that need to be pruned and who knows which fruits need to be brought forth in my life. Father, you have promised if I need anything, you are faithful in your provision. Grant me the spirit of wisdom and revelation so I may know the fruits I must bring forth in my life.

Bearing the fruits of righteousness and living a life devoted to service in your name is one of the most significant fruits I could possess. Lord, there are days when I find it difficult to love others as you have loved me. There are days when I am frustrated with life, full of anxiety, and cannot bring forth the fruits of the Holy Spirit to touch the lives of others. In those times, Lord, grant me forgiveness and understanding of my weaknesses, so I may not lose favor in your eyes. Help me, O Lord, to always have the assurance of my Salvation no matter how often I may fail to reflect to others the love of Christ.

O Christ, open my heart to the beauty of your Word. As I remember the garden of my life, provide me with spiritual discernment so I may see the withering branches and wilting flowers in need of nourishment. Grant me then, my Lord, the spiritual food to cultivate and sustain their growth in the light of your love and endless mercies. In Christ's name, I pray. Amen.

REFLECTIONS

In the garden of your life, there may be many thorns. How can you get rid of them?

Please use the space below to write down any thoughts or comments you may have.

"May God Bless You,
As you live your Life for Christ,
Empowered by The Holy Spirit."

September 30

Psalm 6:9 NIV.

[9] The Lord has heard my cry for mercy; the Lord accepts my prayer.

Heavenly Father, I rejoice in the beauty of this day that you have made. I praise you for all the opportunities you give me to extend the love of Christ to others that may not know Him. I thank you, Lord, for the grace and mercies you so generously bestow on me. These are mercies that meet my financial needs, mercies that ease the sorrow in my heart, mercies that heal my body and soul, and your constant mercies of forgiveness.

Father, I am always in need of your grace. I am frequently in need of your divine love and patient guidance as I walk alongside my Lord and Savior, Jesus Christ. Keep me ever so vigilant against those things that will compromise your Word, and that will cause me to stumble along the path of righteousness.

By the power of the Holy Spirit, I claim freedom from all evil influences in this world. I claim freedom from things that compromise the Word of God and tears down the fabric of my soul. It is no easy task, my God, to run an endurance test for you. It is impossible to shed my sinful nature. It is not easy to resist the forces of evil. But, with your Son, Jesus Christ, as my constant source of inspiration and strength, I can claim victory from the shackles that bind me to the sins of this world. Praise to you, O Faithful God, for the daily mercies of love and grace you extend to me. Amen.

REFLECTIONS

Try to recall a time you ran an endurance test for Christ? Did you win, or did God win?

Please use the space below to write down any thoughts or comments you may have.

"May God Bless You,
As you live your Life for Christ,
Empowered by The Holy Spirit."

October 1

Psalm 19:13 NIV.

[13] Keep your servant also from willful sins; may they not rule over me. Then I will be blameless, innocent of great transgression.

My Lord, my God, hear the cry of my heart. I come before you with a repentant heart convicted of my sinful nature and with an earnest desire to live out my life worthy of your love and grace. Bless me today as I read your Word, sing your praises, and feel your presence and joy while in the company of fellow Christians. I am one of your lost children, who, despite knowing the truth of your Word, sometimes abandons your Truth to satisfy my carnal nature and earthly desires. Sometimes, I need your firm hand to place me back on the path of righteousness so I may more fully live in your grace and will for my life.

As your child, you know the secrets and hidden desires of my heart. O Lord, cleanse my soul of all impurities so I may reflect the utmost love, honor, and respect for your Holy Word. Grant me a spirit of wisdom and revelation of one that is truly in harmony with the gifts of the Holy Spirit. Bring to me, O Christ, the peace that can only come by being obedient and submissive to your will for my life. You are the Prince of Peace and the Giver of Eternal Life through Salvation in Jesus Christ. Thank you, my God. Praise to your Holy Name. Amen.

REFLECTIONS

When in the company of fellow Christians, do you reflect the life of Christ to them?

Please use the space below to write down any thoughts or comments you may have.

"May God Bless You,
As you live your Life for Christ,
Empowered by The Holy Spirit."

October 2

Jeremiah 7:28 NIV.

[28] Therefore say to them, 'This is the nation that has not obeyed the Lord its God or responded to correction. Truth has perished; it has vanished from their lips.

Gracious Lord, my Redeemer, and Savior reveal to me, through the power of the Holy Spirit, the infallible Truth of your Holy Word. Your Word is the manna of my soul. It is the source of all righteousness and wisdom from which the validity of your Word is revealed. Lord, I yearn for a better understanding of your Word. Let me be a faithful witness to all those who have not yet come to know you as Lord of their lives. Lord Jesus, so many of your children, look for contemporary language and teachings that fit what they want to perceive as their Truth and not the Truth as revealed in your Word. Help us all, Lord, to understand that the validity of your Word is the same today as it was in the beginning. Help us realize your Word cannot be modified or changed to fit into language that is more inclusive of social behaviors.

O, Father, your children cry out to know you. They desire to be loved by you. And, despite the influences of Satan, they long to spend eternity with you. Your Holy Scriptures are not meant to meet their personal needs or gratifications at the expense of behaviors, thoughts, and lifestyles contrary to the Truths revealed in your scriptures. Grant us all a sincere desire to love and understand your Word, to passionately believe in it, and to find the comfort and guidance we need as we live our lives for you. I ask these things in the name of the One who gave his life for all, Jesus Christ. Amen.

REFLECTIONS

- *Have you ever tried to adapt the Word of God to your personal worldview or to the worldview?*

Please use the space below to write down any thoughts or comments you may have.

"May God Bless You,
As you live your Life for Christ,
Empowered by The Holy Spirit."

October 3

Psalm 4:1 NIV.

[1] Answer me when I call to you, my righteous God. Give me relief from my distress; have mercy on me and hear my prayer.

Faithful Lord Jesus, I come before you with a humble spirit, reconciled that I am sinful and in need of your redemption. If I am to be Truthful, Lord, I often fail in my prayer life. In your Word, you have taught me to pray, not just in bad times but in good times as well. So often, my heart is burdened with fears, anxieties, and frustrations that tear down my will to faithfully live my life for you. Help me, O Christ, to overcome life situations that are impediments to coming before you in prayer with the needs I so desperately yearn to have met. Help me to conquer my failure to pray faithfully. I want my time with you to be my top priority, from the moment I wake up until I lay my head down to rest. Forgive me, Lord Jesus, for not faithfully reaching out in prayer for your divine love and guidance.

Father, I know apart from you, I can do nothing. I try to run my own life with my human intellect and wisdom gained from the world and fail miserably. Develop within me, O Lord, the fruits of the Holy Spirit: love, joy, peace, kindness, goodness, faithfulness, gentleness, and self-control. Wake me up, O Christ, to the love and open arms that have been extended to me from the moment you died on the Cross of Calvary. I want to absolutely love you and demonstrate my love by enjoying a fruitful prayer life with you. Father, prayer is as essential to my spirit as oxygen is to my body. Help me start each morning by embracing your love, enjoying your presence, and receiving your gifts to go through this day empowered by the Holy Spirit. In Christ's name, I pray. Amen.

REFLECTIONS

When you realize you have not been praying faithfully, what should you do?

Please use the space below to write down any thoughts or comments you may have.

"May God Bless You,
As you live your Life for Christ,
Empowered by The Holy Spirit."

October 4

1 Timothy 2:3-5 NIV.

[3] This is good, and pleases God our Savior, [4] who wants all people to be saved and to come to a knowledge of the truth. [5] For there is one God and one mediator between God and mankind, the man Christ Jesus, ...

Blessed Father, send now your Holy Spirit upon me as I venture forth in a new day of service in your name. As I go about my walk with you, whisper to me your divine guidance as I navigate the tumultuous pathways in life. Keep me safe from all danger as I seek to reach out to those who are lost and do not know your Son, Jesus Christ, as their personal Savior. Give me the words to express the depth of your love and grace to them that can ease the pain in their hearts. Give them hearts that are softened, not guarded, so the words I share may enter and give them the peace they so desperately need.

Lord, you are a Great God, one capable of transforming the lives of those you touch through the immense power of the Holy Spirit. As I wait for your direction, prepare the hearts of those you wish for me to touch. Let my spirit be calm, gracious, and full of the love you have blessed me with. Let me rejoice when I come upon one of your lost children as an opportunity to fulfill your Great Commission. Let me not pass judgment on those that turn from you but continue to lift them up in prayers of intercession so one day they may enter the gates of your heavenly kingdom. In Christ's name, I pray. Amen.

REFLECTIONS

How does your heart feel when someone rejects the message of Christ's Gospel?

Please use the space below to write down any thoughts or comments you may have.

"May God Bless You,
As you live your Life for Christ,
Empowered by The Holy Spirit."

October 5

Psalm 36:5 NIV.

[5] Your love, Lord, reaches to the heavens, your faithfulness to the skies.

Almighty Heavenly Father, in you, the breath of life is found. In you, the embrace of love is kindled through your Son, Jesus Christ. Lord, embrace me with the beauty of your love so I may taste the fruit of a life in Christ. Father, all too often, I take your love for granted and neglect to give thanks and praise to your Holy Name.

Hear my voice, O Christ, as I declare my love for you and joyfully rejoice in the warm embrace of your tenderness. It is because you love me so much that you sent your Son, Jesus Christ, to die on the cross for my sins. It is because you love me so much that despite my grievous sins, you are quick to extend mercies and forgiveness for my failure to be faithful in my Christian walk. Lord, let me walk with you, so I will not cause you to shed tears for sins that grieve your heart.

Grant me the wisdom and spiritual discernment to root out the evil in this world so I may reflect the purity of one whose life belongs to Christ. Lord, help me to surrender my stubborn will. Shape my sinful nature into a shining example of one whose heart is devoted to loving and serving you. Grant me the courage to turn from all evil influences that are bent on tearing down my stronghold of faith in you. In Christ's name, I pray. Amen.

REFLECTIONS

If someone attacks your Christian faith, how should you react?

Please use the space below to write down any thoughts or comments you may have.

*"May God Bless You,
As you live your Life for Christ,
Empowered by The Holy Spirit."*

October 6

1 Peter 4:19 NIV.

[19] So then, those who suffer according to God's will and should commit themselves to their faithful Creator and continue to do good.

Gracious God, Lord of the earth and Lord of my life, thank you for the seeds of goodness you have placed in my heart. Thank you for your numerous blessings that have touched each area of my life. Thank you for your abundant grace and meritless mercies you have seen fit to bestow upon me.

Father, I am no longer of this world. When I accepted Christ into my heart, my old self died, and I was crucified with Christ. I no longer live in this body. The Son of God, who preserves me through the resurrection of His body, blood, and power of the Holy Spirit, has taken hold of my heart and soul. Although the Son of God, Christ Jesus, now lives in me, I am still a wretched sinner. I remain caught up in the sins of this world with the forces of Satan consistently exploiting my weaknesses to further his reign on earth.

God of mercy shield me with a coat of armor so I may fend off the forces of evil and be victorious in my battle over sin. Through the Holy Spirit, you have given me the power to bring honor and glory to your name. Father, allow me to be a faithful disciple of Christ. Help me to be a faithful ambassador of Jesus Christ as I spread the message of His Gospel. Praise to you, my God. Praise to you. Amen.

REFLECTIONS

As a child of God, how can you triumph over the forces of Satan?

Please use the space below to write down any thoughts or comments you may have.

"May God Bless You,
As you live your Life for Christ,
Empowered by The Holy Spirit."

October 7

Psalm 116:1-2 NIV.

[1] I love the Lord, for he heard my voice; he heard my cry for mercy. [2] Because he turned his ear to me, I will call on him as long as I live. ...

On this blessed day, Lord Jesus, I give thanks for the beauty of your creation. I give thanks for the power of prayer and all the blessings that can come from my faithful prayers. Father, amid all the beauty you created, there is turmoil and heartache. Yet, in that turmoil, some people embrace the beauty of your love by doing your will. I praise you for each one of them and for the blessing they are to their fellowman.

Lord, it is easy to get caught up in the daily reports of tragedies resulting in the loss of life from violence, natural occurrence, unforeseen events, extreme weather, and natural disasters. At times life can be so overwhelming that your children can be overcome with grief in their efforts to restore their lives. Let me be one of those willing people who help those with personal struggles. Let me minister to those in need of your grace and mercy.

Father, I give thanks to those that reach out in compassion to serve those that are less fortunate. Let me not forget your children's fragile nature, whose hearts and minds need healing when faced with situations beyond their control. And Lord, let me remember that all your children and I are called by you to be faithful ambassadors of your Word. In Christ's name, I pray. Amen.

REFLECTIONS

When you hear of those who are overcome with grief, do you reach out to help them?

Please use the space below to write down any thoughts or comments you may have.

"May God Bless You,
As you live your Life for Christ,
Empowered by The Holy Spirit."

October 8

Psalm 71:22 NIV.

[22] I will praise you with the harp for your faithfulness, my God; I will sing praise to you with the lyre, Holy One of Israel.

Praise to you, O Mighty God! Through your Son, Jesus Christ, you have made me whole again. You have restored my heart and soul. You comforted me when I was distressed. You have protected me with your guardian angels. Whatever the area of my life I needed help with, you have been there. Your presence is a blessing and joy to behold. While I am not worthy of your grace by my doings, you see fit to shower your grace upon me in good and dark times.

Praise to you, O Christ! May I, this day, be a faithful and loving disciple of yours, ready to proclaim your Gospel Message and prepared to reflect the life of Christ to all I encounter. Send now your Holy Spirit so I will be equipped with the Shield of Christ and the Armor of your Word as I go out among your children, steadfast in my faith and devotion to you. And by the end of this day, may I be able to say, I have been faithful and true to your Holy Word. Glory to you, O Christ. All Praise to you. Amen.

REFLECTIONS

How can you equip yourself with the Armor of God's Word?

Please use the space below to write down any thoughts or comments you may have.

"May God Bless You,
As you live your Life for Christ,
Empowered by The Holy Spirit."

October 9

2 Corinthians 9:13 NIV.

[13] Because of the service by which you have proved yourselves, others will praise God for the obedience that accompanies your confession of the gospel of Christ, and for your generosity in sharing with them and with everyone else.

Heavenly Father, thank you for letting me be a child of yours. A child that, through the baptism of the Holy Spirit, has been born anew. Lord, I confess that I have not lived each moment as a faithful child of yours. I admit that sinful thoughts have entered my mind. I admit I have committed sins that grieve your heart. These sins have been either by omission or direct acts of disobedience that have not been pure and faithful to your Word. Father, I do not like to suffer your heart and beg you for the forgiveness of my transgressions.

Father, through the blood of Christ, I can face my enemies and the demons that attack me. Because of your love, the unrest in my heart is calmed, and I can rise above my selfish desires to genuinely love and serve you with reverence and awe. Forgive me, Lord Jesus, when I am weak, vulnerable, and lacking in my faith. Let me be fully committed to serving you and your people with unshakable faith and devotion to your Word.

Cleanse me, O Christ, of all impurities so my heart and soul may be restored to the likeness of you and the model of one in Christ. Father, the world may say I am not worthy of being a child of yours, but I know that I am worthy of being your child through your grace and precious love. I praise your Holy Name for this special gift. Because of the sacrifice of your Son, Jesus Christ, on the Cross of Calvary, I can boldly rejoice in the knowledge and assurance that I have been redeemed by His precious blood. Thank you, Lord. Thank you, my Almighty God. Amen.

"May God Bless You,
As you live your Life for Christ,
Empowered by The Holy Spirit."

REFLECTIONS

How do impurities in your heart defile your model as one living a Christian life?

Please use the space below to write down any thoughts or comments you may have.

"May God Bless You,
As you live your Life for Christ,
Empowered by The Holy Spirit."

October 10

John 1:17 NIV.

[17] For the law was given through Moses; grace and truth came through Jesus Christ.

Gracious Father, in your infinite compassion, you laid down the life of your Son, Jesus Christ, as an eternal sacrifice for the sins of mankind. Father, you know and can see all things. I come before you as a sinner stripped bare of any falsehood that would cloak my presence before you. Forgive me, my Lord, of all my transgressions that have disgraced me and that have offended you. Father, while I deserve swift and just punishment for my sins, I have been redeemed by your grace and infinite mercy.

Lord, you desire all your children to trust in you and to confess matters that weigh heavily upon their hearts. Grant me the honesty to examine my heart, my behaviors, and my thoughts so I can bring them into conformity with your commandments. Enable me, O Christ, to recognize my sins and to feel the guilt of my transgressions, so I may not become insensitive to those things that offend you.

As I go about this day, let me, by example, be a shining light of your love and grace so I may touch the lives of all your children in need of your precious grace. Give me the faith and assurance that as an ambassador of Christ, and through the gifts of the Holy Spirit, I can do all things. Praise to you, my Lord! All glory to you. Amen.

REFLECTIONS

What sins in your life have been weighing heavily upon your heart?

Please use the space below to write down any thoughts or comments you may have.

"May God Bless You,
As you live your Life for Christ,
Empowered by The Holy Spirit."

October 11

Mark 16:15 NIV.

[15] He said to them, "Go into all the world and preach the gospel to all creation.

Most Merciful Lord Jesus be with me today as I look to you for strength and guidance. Be with me as I look for Divine Opportunities to spread the message of your love. Let me do this, O Christ, not only by the words I share but also by my actions. Keep my heart and thoughts in tune with your Holy Word so when I meet the person whose life you want me to touch, I may be faithful and loyal to your calling.

Give me the grace and love that will enable me to bring excitement and joy into someone's life. Let the words you would have me to share come from a contrite heart and one that is guided by the Holy Spirit. Fill me with your love so I, in turn, can bless this person with an abundance of love and joy. Wipe away any sins or evil thoughts from me that may taint my witness. Bless me and guide me as I live out your Great Commission to spread the message of your Gospel. In Jesus's name, I pray. Amen.

REFLECTIONS

- *Can you think of someone God would like you to have a Divine Appointment with?*

Please use the space below to write down any thoughts or comments you may have.

"May God Bless You,
As you live your Life for Christ,
Empowered by The Holy Spirit."

October 12

Psalm 25:12 NIV.

[12] Who, then, are those who fear the Lord? He will instruct them in the ways they should choose.

Heavenly Father, you are my rock and the foundation of all my hope. Thank you for being the fortress of my strength and source of hope for coping with adversities in this world. I am so grateful, Lord, that you have given me the power of your Word to face my enemies and to quell their anger through the power of the Holy Spirit. Because I fear you, my love for you has become more significant. From the depth of my heart, my thirst to know and grow stronger in your Word becomes more critical with each passing day.

When the world is in disarray, you are always there to comfort, guide, and restore my heart. Thank you for providing the strength and sustenance that feeds my heart and soul. You are the trustworthy source of love and righteous power in this world. Grant me the wisdom and fortitude to face life challenges with grace and faith that comes from being in harmony with you and your Holy Word. As I go about this day, lead me down the path of righteousness and instill in me an earnest desire to love and cherish my relationship with your Son, Jesus Christ. Amen.

REFLECTIONS

How can you fear God and still have your love for Him grow stronger?

Please use the space below to write down any thoughts or comments you may have.

October 13

Psalm 86:6 NIV.

[6] Hear my prayer, Lord; listen to my cry for mercy.

O Great Jehovah, Father of my Lord and Savior, Jesus Christ, cast your eyes upon me with love and mercy as I go about this day devoted to serving you. I struggle at times, my Lord, to be faithful in my walk and in my desire to love others as you have so graciously loved me. Do not remove the gift of your mercy from me, for although I am not worthy of your grace, I am a child of yours in need of compassion, love, and forgiveness.

Your love is precious to me, and I once again promise to love you with all my heart and to fight the forces of Satan so I will not succumb to evil. Send your Holy Spirit to guide me, direct me, and whisper to me the knowledge and Truth that will be my source of strength when confronted with the evil ploys of Satan. Praise to you, Almighty God, for you are the Great Jehovah, the Lord of my life, and the Rock upon which I stand. Amen.

REFLECTIONS

Talk with God right now and tell him what grace and mercies you need.

Please use the space below to write down any thoughts or comments you may have.

October 14

Ephesians 6:12 NIV.

[12] For our struggle is not against flesh and blood, but against the rulers, against the authorities, against the powers of this dark world and against the spiritual forces of evil in the heavenly realms.

Gracious Lord Jesus, I come before you a sinner saved by your blood, blood that has paid the price for the sins of mankind. I come before you filled with anxiety and confusion, not knowing if my Salvation is assured. I have engaged in sins that are displeasing and dishonorable to your Word. I have led a life that has been filled with many spiritual shortcomings. I have failed you as a follower of Christ and as an ambassador of your Word. And, I have not been faithful to all your commandments.

Forgive me, Lord, for although I am a wretched sinner, I do love you. I ask that you spare me your wrath and look upon me like a lost child in need of your redeeming grace. For without your love and grace, I would be doomed and subject to eternal damnation. Lift me up now and restore my heart and soul on the path of righteousness so I may once again bring honor and glory to your Holy Name. I pray you will instill in me the assurance of my Salvation so my heart and soul may be at peace. As I go about this day, my Lord, let your light shine from me, and may the people who see me know I am a child of God, not perfect, but forgiven. Praise to you, O Christ. Amen.

REFLECTIONS

How can God love you if you have spiritual shortcomings? Does He expect you to be perfect?

Please use the space below to write down any thoughts or comments you may have.

"May God Bless You,
As you live your Life for Christ,
Empowered by The Holy Spirit."

October 15

1 Samuel 26:23 NIV.

[23] The Lord rewards everyone for their righteousness and faithfulness. The Lord delivered you into my hands today, but I would not lay a hand on the Lord's anointed.

O Gracious Father in Heaven, through the blood, spilled on the Cross of Calvary, your Son, Jesus Christ, has paid the price for the redemption of my sins. I praise you, Father, for this blessed gift of love. I praise you that as a sinner caught up in the evils of this world, your grace and love are sufficient to make me acceptable in your eyes. No matter how grievous my sins are to your heart, your love is so great, so precious, and so endearing to me. I love you, my Lord, and I offer up my prayers of gratitude with the hope that you may see deep within my heart that there is an abiding faith and love for your Holy Word.

As I go about this day, let me be a beacon of hope to your lost children, children who, like me, know the difficulties that life can bring. Someone who has also been caught up in sins that dishonor your name. Let me be that light guided by the Holy Spirit that brings that lost child into a personal relationship with Jesus Christ. And may I be humble and contrite, not prideful, as I profess my faith, profess my joy, and profess the truth of your Word. Send now your Holy Spirit upon me so I may be equipped with spiritual wisdom and discernment to touch the lives of others. Praise to you, O Christ. Amen.

REFLECTIONS

- *What does it mean to be a beacon of hope to the lost? Are you able to be that beacon?*

Please use the space below to write down any thoughts or comments you may have.

"May God Bless You,
As you live your Life for Christ,
Empowered by The Holy Spirit."

October 16

Luke 1:77 NIV.

[77] to give his people the knowledge of Salvation through the forgiveness of their sins,

Blessed Jesus, O how I love you. Your love for me is more precious than anything I have ever known. You love me despite me. You love me even though I grieve your heart with my sins. As I look around, I wonder if your children enjoy a life of joy with you as the center of their lives. I ask myself what I can do to touch their lives with the love you so freely give. I hesitate because people are so reluctant to reach out and have a relationship with you. I do my best to be a witness of your love because I sense so many of them are lost and too wrapped up with the ways of the world that they have no time for you.

Father forgive them and forgive me when I fail to reach out to them with the same love you bestow upon me. Hear now my prayer, O Christ, that I may be genuinely faithful as one of your disciples called by your Great Commission. Let me be filled with the power of the Holy Spirit as I spread the Gospel of your Word. Lift me up when I falter in my witness and set me back on the course of righteousness so I may faithfully reflect the love of Christ to all your children. If a child responds to my sharing of your Gospel, give me the words filled with the Holy Spirit to lead him to Christ. Let their lives forever be changed by your love and grace. Praise to you, my Lord! All glory to you. Amen.

REFLECTIONS

What can you do to touch the lives of God's children today? Describe what you would do.

Please use the space below to write down any thoughts or comments you may have.

"May God Bless You,
As you live your Life for Christ,
Empowered by The Holy Spirit."

October 17

Psalm 33:4 NIV.

[4] For the word of the Lord is right and true; he is faithful in all he does.

O Glorious God, I praise you for the gift of grace. I thank you for your enduring love and the mercy you continuously extend to me. I know I am not worthy of your mercies save for the blood of my Savior, Jesus Christ. Yet you are always there to put me back on the path of righteousness when I falter in my Christian walk. I am so grateful for your love, love that sustains me in my darkest days, and love that lifts me up when I am lost, confused, and weary from life's struggles.

Praise to you, O Christ! For without you, I would remain a wretched sinner. Thank you for being my Salvation. Thank you for shedding your blood on the Cross of Calvary for my sins. Thank you for being my Rock and for the power of the Holy Spirit that leads and guides my thoughts and actions that glorify your name. I lift my voice and rejoice in song for your glorious love. With heartfelt gratitude, I sing, "Alleluia, Praise to your Holy Name." As I go about this day, my Lord, let me be mindful of your great faithfulness. Empower me to be firm in my faith and in my resolve to be obedient to your Word in all I say and do. In Christ's name, I pray. Amen.

REFLECTIONS

Can you recall a time of despair when you cried out for God, and He was not there? If you felt He was not there, why did you?

Please use the space below to write down any thoughts or comments you may have.

"May God Bless You,
As you live your Life for Christ,
Empowered by The Holy Spirit."

October 18

Ephesians 4:29 NIV.

[29] Do not let any unwholesome talk come out of your mouths, but only what is helpful for building others up according to their needs, that it may benefit those who listen.

O Christ, my Lord and Savior, I come to you as a sinner caught up in sins of the flesh. I come before you seeking your forgiveness. I remember those times where I had fallen short of your calling to live my life faithfully and in reverence to my Lord and Savior, Jesus Christ. Lord, there are times when my thoughts and words to my fellow man are not honorable and undermine my witness as a Christian. There are times when I am so frustrated by life situations that I react out of my human condition and not as a child of God. My opportunity to witness then becomes tarnished, and I find myself consumed with guilt and a heart full of grief.

Lord, I seek your Holy Face, yet I remain a sinner that needs your precious grace. Forgive me when unwholesome words spew from my mouth. I need your love to comfort me in times of distress and calm my heart when I speak to others. I praise you, my dear Lord, for I know you are always with me, and because of that, I can rely upon the Holy Spirit. Praise to you for your divine presence in my life. Amen.

REFLECTIONS

When you hear people using foul language, do you succumb to Satan and do the same?

Please use the space below to write down any thoughts or comments you may have.

"May God Bless You,
As you live your Life for Christ,
Empowered by The Holy Spirit."

October 19

Jeremiah 32:17 NIV.

[17] "Ah, Sovereign Lord you have made the heavens and the earth by your great power and outstretched arm. Nothing is too hard for you.

O Gracious God, Lord of the Universe, you are an all-powerful and omnipotent God. From the beginning, you created the heavens and the earth to be a place of beauty and peace where your children could multiply and bring glory to your Holy Name. What a joy it is to be among your creation. I am a child that is loved by the most awesome God. It is with a heart of gratitude that I offer up my praise and offerings to thank you for your eternal gifts of mercy, love, and grace. Let me always be worthy of such love and grace.

As I go about this day, may I be keenly aware that I am responsible for sharing my faith as a child of God. Let me be a shining example of one of God's children. May I be mindful that the lives I touch are to your glory and that I am just an instrument of your love filled with the power of the Holy Spirit. Lord, I have known no greater love than the love you have bestowed upon me. Let me be mindful that as I share the Gospel of Jesus Christ, that I may be met with resistance to His message of love. Open the hearts of those I approach so as I speak the truth of your Word, they may not only hear my words but respond with joy and acceptance to your message of love. And may they receive the same grace, love, and forgiveness you have bestowed upon me. In Jesus' precious name, I pray. Amen.

REFLECTIONS

It is sometimes difficult to be a shining example of God's love. Explain why?

Please use the space below to write down any thoughts or comments you may have.

"May God Bless You,
As you live your Life for Christ,
Empowered by The Holy Spirit."

October 20

1 Corinthians 2:3 NIV.

[3] I came to you in weakness with great fear and trembling.

Glorious Father in Heaven, hear my cry, the cry of a servant's heart. I come to you confused and filled with uncertainty about my path in life. I look to you as I struggle to fight off the forces of Satan as he taunts me when I go about your work. Where am I to turn, my Lord, but to you? I know your Word and how it beckons me to love my neighbor as you first loved me. I know that the fruits of the Holy Spirit are there for me to bless others as you have so richly blessed me. Yet, I break under the stresses of temptation and the physical and spiritual weakness in my human frailty.

Rescue me, my Lord, from the depths of my despair. Awaken in me the strength of the Holy Spirit, so I may be able to conquer all weaknesses in my life and rise like an eagle, confident of my strength in your Word. Grant me now a spirit of calmness as I go about this day looking for Divine Opportunities. Let me be there to bless others with the power of the Holy Spirit so they too may enjoy a life of peace and joy in Christ. And when I am confronted with doubt and fear, purge from me these weaknesses and restore me to a life of joy and confidence as a servant of the most loving God and Savior, Jesus Christ. Amen.

REFLECTIONS

- *Without God, is it possible to soar like an eagle capable of conquering all fears in your life?*

Please use the space below to write down any thoughts or comments you may have.

"May God Bless You,
As you live your Life for Christ,
Empowered by The Holy Spirit."

October 21

Psalm 45:2 NIV.

[2] You are the most excellent of men and your lips have been anointed with grace, since God has blessed you forever.

Holy Father, in your Word, you say victory is ours through Jesus Christ. Lord, there have been so many areas in my life where I have not been faithful and, as a result, could not claim victory in Christ. I have stumbled in my walk. I have failed to love others as you first loved me. I have not been gracious and loving as you have taught me. And, I have not lived a life of purity because of my weakness of the flesh.

Father, I am genuinely a wretched sinner in need of your redeeming grace. Forgive me for all my transgressions and my weakness in spirit. Fill me now with the Holy Spirit so my walk with you may be renewed. Present me with Divine Opportunities to witness others' faith in you and the sanctity of your Word. Lift me up when I am weak and give me the wings of an eagle so I might soar victoriously over Satan's evil ploys. Let me feel the presence of your guardian angels as they form a hedge of protection around me. O Christ, protect me, guide me, and reveal the warmth of your love as I strive to live out my faith in you? Amen.

REFLECTIONS

Describe a conversation you would like to have with Christ. Who would do most of the talking, and what would you talk about?

Please use the space below to write down any thoughts or comments you may have.

"May God Bless You,
As you live your Life for Christ,
Empowered by The Holy Spirit."

October 22

Matthew 21:22 NIV.

[22] If you believe you will receive whatever you ask for in prayer."

Precious Lord Jesus, in your Word, you tell me if I believe, whenever I come to you in prayer, I will receive what I ask for. I praise you, Lord, for this gift of prayer and the knowledge that you are always with me through the power of prayer. I praise you that when I am ill or facing health concerns that are afflicting me and causing despair, you are there to heal me and comfort me.

I praise you when I am faced with financial needs, for you are there to guide my actions and give me the wisdom to make wise choices. I praise you when I am faced with situations that cause me distress in life, for you are there to rescue me, calm my spirit, and restore my soul. I praise you when Satan tempts me repeatedly because I have the power through the Holy Spirit to rebuke him and send him running. Yes, Lord, there is so much to be grateful for by having a fruitful relationship with you. Keep me, I pray, in your care so I may feel your loving arms around me as I go about this day loving and serving you. Amen.

REFLECTIONS

Does God literally mean when you ask for something in His name, he will give it to you?

Please use the space below to write down any thoughts or comments you may have.

"May God Bless You,
As you live your Life for Christ,
Empowered by The Holy Spirit."

October 23

1 Corinthians 10:16-17 NIV.

[16] Is not the cup of thanksgiving for which we give thanks a participation in the blood of Christ? And is not the bread that we break a participation in the body of Christ? [17] Because there is one loaf, we, who are many, are one body, for we all share the one loaf. ...

O Christ, on the day your blood was spilled on the Cross of Calvary, I was blessed with the gift of Salvation. I praise you, my Lord, for this precious gift. I cannot know the depth of your pain as you hung on the cross, suffering for all humanity. But I know because of your sacrifice, my place in Heaven is assured. Because I believe in the redemptive power of your blood for my sins, I know I will one day be among your angels.

I pray now, my Lord, that you will enable me, through the power of the Holy Spirit, to touch the lives of others and to help them come to know the joy of life in Christ. Be with me now by stilling the waters in my heart so I may be at peace with my soul. Bless me as I go forth this day, rejoicing in my faith, my God, and my blessed Savior. Praise to your Holy Name, O Christ, for through you I will enjoy eternal peace and happiness. Amen.

REFLECTIONS

When the waters of your heart are agitated, how can you still them?

Please use the space below to write down any thoughts or comments you may have.

"May God Bless You,
As you live your Life for Christ,
Empowered by The Holy Spirit."

October 24

Psalm 34:3 NIV.

[3] Glorify the Lord with me; let us exalt his name together.

Gracious God, hear my voice as I exalt your Holy Name and bring glory to your kingdom on earth. Hear my voice as I pray for the lost who are drifting further from the truth of your Word. Hear my voice as I plea for those caught up in sins of the flesh and who have no respect for the temple of God. Bring to my lips words that can touch their lives, words that can open their hearts, and a conversation that will lead them to a personal relationship with Jesus Christ.

Let the power of the Holy Spirit enable them to embrace the calling of God for their lives. Wherever my walk may take me today, let me mindful that we are all children of God who need the redemptive power of our Lord and Savior, Jesus Christ. You are the Almighty God, my personal Savior, and the One in whom I place my hope and trust. Bless me now with the power of the Holy Spirit and with the spirit of wisdom and revelation as I seek out those whom I have a divine appointment. In Christ's precious name, I pray. Amen.

REFLECTIONS

What does the temple of God mean to you? What is it referring to?

Please use the space below to write down any thoughts or comments you may have.

"May God Bless You,
As you live your Life for Christ,
Empowered by The Holy Spirit."

October 25

Psalm 51:1 NIV.

[1] Have mercy on me, O God, according to your unfailing love; according to your great compassion blot out my transgressions.

My Lord, my God, and my Savior, glory to your Holy Name! When this day unfolds, bless me with your constant presence. Bless me with the spirit of wisdom and revelation so I may be in tune with the needs of others. Help me to have a willing heart to love and serve those lost and looking for hope. Awaken in me the desire to reach out and share the Gospel of my Lord and Savior. Let me be faithful to your Word as I tell others about your great love, compassion, and mercy. And if they are in turmoil, let my words through the power of the Holy Spirit calm and soothe their souls so they may be at peace.

Lord, I want nothing more than to bring your lost children to a personal relationship with you. I want nothing more than to be an ambassador of your Word, one who can, through the Holy Spirit, minister to those that are lost and wandering in seas of discontent. And when I find my Divine Appointments, open the door of their hearts. Through your Word and the Holy Spirit, may they be moved to know with certainty that you are a loving God, one that has always loved them and one that will never forsake them. Amen.

REFLECTIONS

What does it mean to be a minister of God's Word? Are you a minister of God's Word?

Please use the space below to write down any thoughts or comments you may have.

"May God Bless You,
As you live your Life for Christ,
Empowered by The Holy Spirit."

October 26

Acts 4:12 NIV.

[12] Salvation is found in no one else, for there is no other name under heaven given to mankind by which we must be saved."

Gracious God, you have set me free through the power of the Holy Spirit to break the shackles of Satan over my life. You have given me the free will to make choices that will either dishonor you or bring glory to your precious Name. And you have given me the gift of prayer to communicate with you when I need your continued strength to remain healthy and faithful in my Christian walk.

I thank you, Father, for this gift of prayer. Let me remember that prayer provides an opportunity to give you adoration, praise, and honor for all you do for me. Let me remember prayer is a means of confession for the sins I have committed and grieve your heart. Let me remember prayer is a way of giving thanks for all I am grateful for in my life and in the world about me. Let me not forget that prayer is a means of supplication, so I may petition you for the needs of others and myself.

For all these gifts, I praise and adore you. I am so grateful to you for the gift of Salvation, a gift paid for by the blood of Christ. A gift that has been provided to all your children because of your great love for us. Let me go forward this day with the knowledge and joy of your Word. Because of your great love for me and the gift of Salvation that I have accepted, I can rest assured I will spend eternity with you in Heaven. Amen.

REFLECTIONS

As a believer, how can you be assured you will spend eternity with God?

Please use the space below to write down any thoughts or comments you may have.

"May God Bless You,
As you live your Life for Christ,
Empowered by The Holy Spirit."

October 27

Luke 24:38 NIV.

[38] He said to them, "Why are you troubled, and why do doubts rise in your minds?

O Christ, the Light of the World, it is into your hands that I commend my soul. Lord, I am a wretched sinner whose life fails to faithfully reflect your light to my fellowman. I struggle to fight off the forces of Satan and pray you will give me the victory over him I so desperately want. Yet during my struggle, I fail to do so because of my sinful state and worldly desires. Where can I turn to, my Lord, when I need the strength and moral fortitude to live my life faithfully for you? Who can I rely on when I need the personal assurance I am loved despite my grievous sins? And when I am consumed with doubts and fears, are you still there to love me and to be the Rock I want to cling to?

Yes, Father, I remember your promises and the gift of Salvation paid for by the blood of Christ. Who am I to doubt your Word? Who am I to not forgive myself when your Son paid the ultimate price for my Salvation? Open my eyes, O Christ, so no matter what struggles I face, I can rest assured you will always be with me. Open my heart, O Lord. Let me be confident that my heart can be blessed with grace and the power to rise above all my sins through the Holy Spirit. I plea for these things, Lord, and ask them to be granted to me in the name of the Father, Son, and Holy Spirit. Amen.

REFLECTIONS

- *Why is it so important to forgive yourself? Can you truly forgive others if you do not forgive yourself?*

Please use the space below to write down any thoughts or comments you may have.

"May God Bless You,
As you live your Life for Christ,
Empowered by The Holy Spirit."

October 28

2 Corinthians 1:5 NIV.

[5] For just as we share abundantly in the sufferings of Christ, so also our comfort abounds through Christ.

O Faithful God, Lord of the Universe, you have created opportunities for your children to go out and pronounce the Gospel Message of Jesus Christ. You have given us hearts full of love and compassion to touch the lives of those in turmoil. You have given us opportunities to comfort hearts that are broken and whose lives are devastated by disease, famine, and natural disasters. You have given me, a child of the most loving God, a life full of both spiritual and material blessings. I praise you for these gifts, O God. I praise you that your love and grace have unfolded many benefits upon me no matter what my need.

I ask now that you extend to me through the Holy Spirit the heartfelt desire to reach out and touch the lives of those less fortunate. Let me not become tired of circumstances across my nation and the world where lives are being disrupted and torn apart. Let me be a force of good, willing to share my resources, ready to extend my compassion, and willing to extend the same love and grace you have extended to me. I praise you, Father, that I can petition you to intervene in the plight of others. May your grace and love be showered upon them so that their pain and suffering may be alleviated. In the name of the Father, the Son, and the Holy Spirit. Amen.

REFLECTIONS

What are some spiritual and material blessings you are grateful for?

Please use the space below to write down any thoughts or comments you may have.

"May God Bless You,
As you live your Life for Christ,
Empowered by The Holy Spirit."

October 29

Ephesians 4:31 NIV.

[31] Get rid of all bitterness, rage and anger, brawling, and slander, along with every form of malice.

Gracious God, awaken me from my slumber so I may go about my day seeking your divine plan. Make me mindful of my neighbors' needs so I may be a faithful ambassador of your Word. Cultivate within me a caring heart, one that knows no prejudice or malice towards others.

When I come across a neighbor that looks different from me, let me only see a child of God, one that needs the redemptive power of your Son, Jesus Christ. Give me the countenance I need to reflect the love of Christ. Lift my voice so I may be confident in my witness and joyful in praising my God. Remove from me all hindrances in my heart and soul that may impede the exaltation of Jesus Christ. And if Satan should try to gain a foothold in my life, spill your Holy Spirit upon me so I can squash Satan's evil ploys.

I praise you, O Christ, for through you I can do all things. I thank you for the overflowing love you have for me. And I am eternally grateful for your gifts of grace, love, and forgiveness. Entrust me now with the endowment of the Holy Spirit, so I may accomplish your will. Amen.

REFLECTIONS

Are you harboring prejudice toward those who are different from you? How can you free yourself of this racism or hatred?

Please use the space below to write down any thoughts or comments you may have.

"May God Bless You,
As you live your Life for Christ,
Empowered by The Holy Spirit."

October 30

Romans 3:24 NIV.

[24] and all are justified freely by his grace through the redemption that came by Christ Jesus.

Holy Father, you have blessed me with the gift of Salvation because of your great love for all your children. As a child of God, I come before you today, praising you for the redemptive power found in Jesus Christ. I come before you as a wretched sinner that can know no peace unless I am one in Christ. I come before you, seeking your forgiveness for my grievous sins, sins that have wreaked havoc in my life. Yet, thanks to your abiding love, I can claim freedom from the torment and anguish they have caused me.

What a blessed God you are! Your love is so precious and so enduring I need only to cry out your name when confronted with trials I have difficulty coping with. Praise to you, O Christ, for the knowledge that you are always with me even when I am lost and struggling to find my way back to you. Let me give love and kindness to my fellow man. And, with the same grace, ease the discord in all your children. Empower them through the Holy Spirit so they too can bless another with this precious gift of grace. Amen.

REFLECTIONS

How has sin wreaked havoc in your life, and what did you do about it?

Please use the space below to write down any thoughts or comments you may have.

*"May God Bless You,
As you live your Life for Christ,
Empowered by The Holy Spirit."*

October 31

Psalm 4:3 NIV.

[3] Know that the Lord has set apart his faithful servant for himself; the Lord hears when I call to him.

Blessed Father, what a glorious day you have made. From the moment I awoke, I felt your presence around me. The gifts of love and kindness. The blessings of family and friends. And the gift of Salvation, paid for by my Savior, Jesus Christ. True blessings from a great and loving God.

As I go about my day, let me be a true reflection of your love and grace to my neighbors. Let all I say and do be in harmony with the truth of your Word. Let my heart sing your praises so I may lift the spirits of the downtrodden. May I be filled with the power of the Holy Spirit so I may be a faithful witness of yours. Let me be firm in my resolve to live the righteous life of one empowered to conquer evil forces in this world.

You are my God! You are my Savior! You are the King of Kings! I bow before you with great humility in service to your Holy Name. Bless me now in the name of the Father, Son, and Holy Spirit, so I may be renewed through the love of Christ to be a Holy and righteous servant of God. Amen.

REFLECTIONS

What gives you, as a child of God, the power to conquer the forces of evil in this world?

Please use the space below to write down any thoughts or comments you may have.

"May God Bless You,
As you live your Life for Christ,
Empowered by The Holy Spirit."

November 1

Philippians 2:14-16 NIV.

[14] Do everything without grumbling or arguing, [15] so that you may become blameless and pure, "children of God without fault in a warped and crooked generation." Then you will shine among them like stars in the sky [16] as you hold firmly to the word of life. And then I will be able to boast on the day of Christ that I did not run or labor in vain.

Most Merciful God, send your Holy Spirit upon me so as a child of God I may embrace the fruits of the spirit. Give me a heart full of compassion and kindness for the oppressed, especially for the homeless, who find themselves unable to provide for their food, shelter, and medical needs because of overwhelming life situations. Allow me to bless those less fortunate with timely resources to alleviate their pain and suffering. Help me remember that the homeless are children of God and no less deserving than I or any of your other children in dire need. Let me be a faithful steward of my resources so I may give freely and without remorse for my acts of kindness.

Lord, you are a Great God, a God of love and compassion. A God that understands the needs of the homeless, both emotional, mental, and physical. Bless each of these children who have not been able to profess their love for Christ. Bless them so they too may be blessed with the gift of Salvation. As this day goes on, my Lord, let me be mindful as a child of God that I can love because you first loved me. Amen.

REFLECTIONS

When you see a homeless person, do you turn your back and say someone else can help them? What do you think their biggest need is?

Please use the space below to write down any thoughts or comments you may have.

"May God Bless You,
As you live your Life for Christ,
Empowered by The Holy Spirit."

November 2

Isaiah 53:4-5 NIV.

[4] Surely, he took up our pain and bore our suffering, yet we considered him punished by God, stricken by him, and afflicted. [5] But he was pierced for our transgressions, he was crushed for our iniquities; the punishment that brought us peace was on him, and by his wounds we are healed.

Holy Father, the Alpha, and the Omega, through your Son, Jesus Christ, my life has been blessed beyond anything I could have ever imagined. From the moment I was baptized, I was sealed with the blood of Christ as a child of yours. From the moment I accepted the gift of Salvation, I was given the promise of eternal life among your angels in Heaven. From the moment I became a child of God, I became a vessel of the Holy Spirit that could touch my neighbors' and strangers' lives through the fruits of the spirit.

What more could a child of God want? What could be a more incredible blessing than to be used by God to bless the lives of others? Is there any God greater than you? You are the only true God and the Almighty God, a God who, through his infinite love and compassion, sacrificed his only Son on the Cross of Calvary for my sins. Bless you, Father, for although I am a wretched sinner, I am redeemed through the blood of Christ and made anew as a child of the Living God. All glory and praise to you, O Christ, my Lord, my Savior, and my Redeemer. Amen.

REFLECTIONS

When you accepted the gift of Salvation, did you think all your problems would go away?

Please use the space below to write down any thoughts or comments you may have.

"May God Bless You,
As you live your Life for Christ,
Empowered by The Holy Spirit."

November 3

Psalm 119:132 NIV.

[132] Turn to me and have mercy on me, as you always do to those who love your name.

Blessed Lord Jesus, how thankful I am for the gift of faith. When people fail me and leave me confused, you, Lord, are always loyal and faithful to your Word. Because of the sacrifice of your Son, Jesus Christ, and because I have given my life to Christ, I have the assurance of eternal life with you in Heaven. Father, I recognize many of your children are completely lost and do not believe in your Son. I realize there are many of your children who struggle with their faith. In your mercy, O Lord, cover those that are lost and distraught with your grace. Cover them with your blessed understanding so they will feel the warmth of your love. And Lord, speak to their hearts. Reveal to them the truth of your Word. Help them come to know you personally so they may have the divine assurance that you are present in their lives no matter what trials or confusion they must live with.

As I go about this day, let my walk with Christ reflect the love and grace that has been showered upon me. Let me be a beacon of hope and light that you are the Almighty God, a God that loves his children and will never forsake them. Bless me now with the Holy Spirit's power so I may bring forth the fruits that will allow me to touch the lives of those in need. In the name of the Father, the Son, and the Holy Spirit. Amen.

REFLECTIONS

Has anyone you trusted ever failed you and left you confused? How did you feel?

Please use the space below to write down any thoughts or comments you may have.

"May God Bless You,
As you live your Life for Christ,
Empowered by The Holy Spirit."

November 4

Galatians 5:13 NIV.

[13] You, my brothers, and sisters, were called to be free. But do not use your freedom to indulge the flesh; rather, serve one another humbly in love.

Precious Father, I come before you, crying out for your love. I have slipped into an abyss where the darkness is consuming me. The sins I have committed weigh heavily upon my heart. I have faltered in my walk with Christ and allowed Satan to wreak havoc in my life. Where am I to go, my Lord? Who am I to turn to? I have sought out your face but have been overwhelmed by the guilt of my sins. Why, Lord, must I be in this bottomless pit? Your promise of Salvation is there for me to claim. Your assurance of love has never left me. Your angels look over me and cry when they see the despair I have allowed myself to fall into.

Rescue me, my Lord! Come and pull me out of this dark hole so I may once again see your light. Bring my stubborn will into submission and make me bow with humility before your Holy Throne. Cleanse my heart and soul from all impurities so I may once again be seen faultless in your eyes. Take my hand, and pull me into the bosom of your chest, not gently, but with an urgency that shows your great love. Forgive me, O Christ, for wandering like a lost sheep on slippery slopes. Renew my heart and soul through the power of the Holy Spirit, so I may be vital in my faith and in my ability to run the race of freedom through Christ Jesus. Amen.

REFLECTIONS

When you find yourself in a bottomless pit, how can you escape from it?

Please use the space below to write down any thoughts or comments you may have.

"May God Bless You,
As you live your Life for Christ,
Empowered by The Holy Spirit."

November 5

Job 34:22 NIV.

[22] There is no deep shadow, no utter darkness, where evildoers can hide.

Blessed Lord Jesus, my heart awakens this morning with fear and trepidation upon it. Across our nation, violence is taking place in various forms. Satan has been actively working to gain a foothold in the hearts and minds of those bent on destroying the lives of innocent people. Satan has preyed upon the weak who have never known the love of Jesus Christ or, because of a lack of faith, have never known the assurance of God's love in Christ Jesus. Hear my plea, O Christ, for all those victims of terrorism and other forms of violence. Hear my appeal for those suffering physical and emotional turmoil due to hatred and senseless acts of violence. Comfort them, my Lord, and give them peace in their hearts that their suffering may soon be relieved.

Lord, it is difficult to pray for those that are perpetrators of evil. You command me to pray for my enemies. With a heavy heart that longs to be at peace with your Word, hear my prayer. I pray for the hearts and souls of those that perpetrate evil acts. Find a crack in their armor, O Lord, that will allow the Holy Spirit to find a permanent dwelling place within their hearts. Let them be filled with the fruits of the Holy Spirit rather than the evil fostered by Satan. Bless them, Lord, with a spiritual countenance that will unmask their identity, one that is a child of God. May they cry out to you to forgive their evil acts and find true peace in Christ Jesus. And finally, may the power of the Holy Spirit bind the forces of Satan that are fermenting in the hearts of your lost children. Amen.

REFLECTIONS

- *When you hear of senseless evil perpetrated on God's children, how should you respond?*

Please use the space below to write down any thoughts or comments you may have.

"May God Bless You,
As you live your Life for Christ,
Empowered by The Holy Spirit."

November 6

Ezekiel 35:11 NIV.

[11] therefore as surely as I live, declares the Sovereign Lord, I will treat you in accordance with the anger and jealousy you showed in your hatred of them, and I will make myself known among them when I judge you.

O Christ, my Savior, Redeemer, and Shepherd of lost sheep, my heart cries out for all those who are lost and do not know you. My heart is sad because they do not see the beauty and comfort a personal relationship with you can bring. Lord, the evil in this world is wreaking havoc in my heart. The sadness in my heart is overwhelming each time I hear reports of your children being killed. Some of them are maimed by those bent on perpetuating the evil of Satan. There is no hope of change in our nation if people continually turn from your Word.

I pray, O Christ, for Divine Opportunities to touch the lives of those that harbor hatred or malice toward innocent children of yours. I pray I may be a vessel of hope to those that need comfort, hope, and the assurance of a Savior that can quell any unrest instigated by Satan. You are the Almighty God. You are all-powerful, omnipotent, and you know beforehand the intentions of evildoers. Lord, I pray you will put an end to this senseless violence. Cause the hearts of those bent on violence to turn from hatred to love, from evil to kindness, and from Satan's evil to a personal relationship with Jesus Christ. In the name of the Father, Son, and Holy Spirit. Amen.

REFLECTIONS

What is the best way to get perpetrators of evil to turn to God?

Please use the space below to write down any thoughts or comments you may have.

"May God Bless You,
As you live your Life for Christ,
Empowered by The Holy Spirit."

November 7

Job 1:12 NIV.

[12] The Lord said to Satan, "Very well, then, everything he has is in your power, but on the man, himself do not lay a finger." Then Satan went out from the presence of the Lord.

O Most Merciful God, hear my Words of joy and exaltation for the gift of Salvation. My heart is overflowing with thanksgiving, knowing I am loved by the true God — the God of Abraham, Isaac, and Jacob. When the world throws chaos and confusion into every corner of my life, you are my refuge and hope for a brighter future. When the world is consumed with hatred and evil perpetrated by Satan, you are the way, the Truth, and the life.

Make way, evil one, for the Lord my God will squash any effort by you to tempt me beyond my ability to resist your satanic influences. Make haste, you snake of the earth, for you shall crawl on your belly while I soar like an eagle above the majestic mountains.

Through the power of the Holy Spirit that dwells within me, I can do all things through Christ Jesus, my Lord, and Savior. Praise to you, O God, for your strength sustains me. Your wisdom guides me, and your love will grow in my heart so I can love others with the same passion and grace you shower upon me. Praise to you, O Faithful Christ, for through your bloodshed on the Cross of Calvary, I am free of the tyranny and evil of Satan. Praise to you, O Lord. Amen.

REFLECTIONS

How can you build up your shield of armor to find victory over Satan?

Please use the space below to write down any thoughts or comments you may have.

"May God Bless You,
As you live your Life for Christ,
Empowered by The Holy Spirit."

November 8

Luke 20:21 NIV.

[21] So the spies questioned him: "Teacher, we know that you speak and teach what is right, and that you do not show partiality but teach the way of God in accordance with the truth.

O Father, my God, and my Creator, there is so much I do not know about your written Word. My heart yearns to understand your Truths more fully. I know it is meant to reveal the extraordinary love and grace you have for me and humanity. I pray, my Lord, that you will open my heart and ears to hear the truth of your Word as revealed in your Holy Scriptures. Give me the clarity and understanding that will allow me to fully grasp the lessons and Truths revealed in your Word.

Bless me so I may grow in spiritual maturity. Do not let my mind be filled with sinful thoughts that can mask your revelations. I pray I do not fall into a slumber where my thirst for your Word is clouded. Free me of any fatigue and confusion that may inhibit the Holy Spirit from revealing the blessings of your love. As I go about this day, O Christ, let me remember I am a child of God.

This child must be mindful of the temptations promulgated by Satan that are intended to cause doubt in my mind about the truth of your Word. I love you, my God, and ask that a cloak of armor be placed around me to shield me from Satan's influences so I may bear the fruit of a life in Christ. May your blessings sustain me, protect me, and allow me to glorify your Holy Name. Amen.

REFLECTIONS

When you are physically tired, what can you do to maintain your spiritual strength?

Please use the space below to write down any thoughts or comments you may have.

"May God Bless You,
As you live your Life for Christ,
Empowered by The Holy Spirit."

November 9

Matthew 26:41 NIV.

[41] "Watch and pray so that you will not fall into temptation. The spirit is willing, but the flesh is weak."

Precious Savior, I awaken this morning with joy in my heart for all the blessings you have showered upon me, gifts that have touched every area of my life. You are a gracious God, one who loves me despite my failings as your child. You give me hope when everything seems to be hopeless. You give me strength when I feel too weak to resist the temptations of Satan. You give me faith as a precious gift to remind me that I can do all things if I remain in Christ.

Praise to you, O Faithful Lord, for my life would be empty without your loving presence within me. How can I honor you, my Lord, for these precious gifts? Hear me, Satan, you shall have no dominion over me. Hear me, Satan, you shall be rebuked every time I call upon the Name of the Most High God. My life belongs to Christ, who dwells within my heart, restores my soul, and is the Savior of mankind.

When I drift from my Christian walk, my Savior who walks beside me will pull me back as a wandering sheep to the path he lights before me. What joy there is in following Christ! What joy there is in living a righteous life! What joy there is in prostrating myself before God. I recognize I am nothing without Him, and I am willing to say, "Lord, shape me into the child you mean for me to be." I give all that I am, O Lord, for you to shape me into your image. Let me reflect on the life of Christ and His great love to all that I meet this day. Amen.

REFLECTIONS

How are you like a wandering sheep who follows the shepherd but wanders from the path?

Please use the space below to write down any thoughts or comments you may have.

"May God Bless You,
As you live your Life for Christ,
Empowered by The Holy Spirit."

November 10

Jeremiah 33:8 NIV.

[8] I will cleanse them from all the sin they have committed against me and will forgive all their sins of rebellion against me.

O Christ, my faithful Redeemer, I come before you today seeking your continued presence in my life. I come before you with a grateful heart. I have been blessed beyond measure by the shedding of your blood on the Cross of Calvary. As I go about this day, my Lord, let me be mindful of all the lost souls wandering through life with no desire to draw close to your loving arms. I worry about them and friends and family that have pulled away from a personal relationship with you.

Draw them back into your arms, O Christ. If they need trials in life to prune their stubbornness, let it be so. If they need Christian friends to help them grow closer to you, bring them into their lives. If they are confused and need clarity in thought and reason, give them a fruitful understanding of your Holy Word. Whatever is required to help them shed the shackles of rebellion, bring this upon them so they may break free of Satan's grip.

You are a loving God, one that is patient and merciful. What joy there is in giving my life to you. I pray that these lost souls may find the same joy and assurance of your Word that I know. Bless them, Father, with the spirit of wisdom and revelation, so when Divine Opportunities come their way, they may seize the moment and claim you as their Lord and Savior. Amen.

REFLECTIONS

Have you ever had trials that brought you closer to Christ? If you have more, will you lose faith in God?

Please use the space below to write down any thoughts or comments you may have.

"May God Bless You,
As you live your Life for Christ,
Empowered by The Holy Spirit."

November 11

Galatians 5:1 NIV.

[1] It is for freedom that Christ has set us free. Stand firm, then, and do not let yourselves be burdened again by a yoke of slavery.

Most Merciful Lord Jesus, through the sacrifice of your blood on the Cross of Calvary, I can claim freedom from the burden of sin. Thank you, Lord, for this Veteran's Day, where I have the privilege of honoring all the Veterans who have faithfully served our country. I recognize my freedoms were paid for at a high cost. My heart is full of gratitude and appreciation for all the men and women who laid down their lives for my fellow countrymen and me.

Throughout our nation's history, the men and women who have served in our military forces have given their best to preserve the freedoms we enjoy. I praise you, Lord, for their sacrifice that has allowed me to live in a country free of tyranny and oppression. And I am so overwhelmed by the blessings of living in a country founded on Christian principles.

Awaken the sleepy souls, my God, who fail to acknowledge that our freedoms were paid for by our veterans. May they realize that despite our differences and the social environment at times of conflict, our daily lives would be profoundly different if not for their sacrifice. Bless them, Father, and may our veterans always know they have their country's gratitude for their selfless service. Amen.

REFLECTIONS

When you see veterans this Veteran's Day, what would be an excellent way to honor them? Do you have family or friends who are veterans you could honor today?

Please use the space below to write down any thoughts or comments you may have.

"May God Bless You,
As you live your Life for Christ,
Empowered by The Holy Spirit."

November 12

1 Peter 1:3 NIV.

[3] Praise be to the God and Father of our Lord Jesus Christ! In his great mercy he has given us new birth into a living hope through the resurrection of Jesus Christ from the dead, ...

Gracious Lord Jesus, it is a joy to rise in the morning and feel the presence of my Almighty God. From the moment I wake, I know you are with me. From the moment I wake, the Holy Spirit has taken His place in my heart and soul, so I may have the fruits of the spirit to guide my thoughts and actions during the day. Praise to you, O Christ, for your sweet love. Praise to you for blessing me with Divine Opportunities where I may be a faithful witness of your love and grace.

As I go about my day, Lord Jesus, continue to walk beside me. Keep me on the straight and narrow path, so when Satan attempts to lure me into wayward behavior, I can have the power to rebuke him and his evil ploys. You are my God, the Rock upon which I stand. Use me today for your glory so I may be the instrument of your love to all those I encounter. Bless me in the name of the Father, Son, and Holy Spirit with all the spiritual gifts that will enable me to be a faithful child of yours. And when a divine opportunity presents itself, allow me the privilege to lead others to a personal relationship with Jesus Christ. Amen.

REFLECTIONS

As an instrument of God's love, what are you going to focus your attention on today?

Please use the space below to write down any thoughts or comments you may have.

*"May God Bless You,
As you live your Life for Christ,
Empowered by The Holy Spirit."*

November 13

1 Timothy 4:15-16 NIV.

[15] Be diligent in these matters; give yourself wholly to them, so that everyone may see your progress. [16] Watch your life and doctrine closely. Persevere in them, because if you do, you will save both yourself and your hearers. ...

O Lord, my God, how great Thou Art! From the moment I rise until I lay down my head, you are with me. Your love and your strength sustain me. When I go about my day filled with uncertainty, I look to you as the one constant in my life that provides the love and assurance I need to weather any storms that may cross my path. You are my Savior, O Christ! You are my Deliverer! I praise you for your eternal blessings. I sing praises to you for the forgiveness of my sins that are covered by the blood of Christ. Praise to you, O Lord. Let me be fruitful in my walk today as I face the temptations of this world. Let me have the strength and moral fortitude to fight off the sins of the flesh Satan places in my path.

Fill me with the power of the Holy Spirit so I may discern the truth of your Word and live the life of one who strives to be righteous. Strip from me any falsehoods that may cloak the intentions of my heart. Father, God, whether it be friends, family, or strangers, let my devotion to serving you be paramount in my life. Help me to bring their receptive hearts to a lasting personal relationship with your Son, Jesus Christ. And free me of my stubborn nature by bringing me into total submission to your will by removing any pride that hinders my sharing of your Word. In the name of the Father, the Son, and the Holy Spirit. Amen.

REFLECTIONS

What are the falsehoods in your life that may be cloaking the intentions of your heart?

Please use the space below to write down any thoughts or comments you may have.

"May God Bless You,
As you live your Life for Christ,
Empowered by The Holy Spirit."

November 14

Acts 1:8 NIV.

[8] But you will receive power when the holy spirit comes on you; and you will be my witnesses in Jerusalem, and in all Judea and Samaria, and to the ends of the earth."

O Lord my God, the Risen King of Kings, I come before you today seeking your guidance. Bring to me Divine Opportunities to share the love and forgiveness of Jesus Christ. There is no greater calling to fulfilling the Great Commission than by communicating with the lost, the love of Christ. Where would I be, O Lord, if not for your mercies and grace? Where would I be without the comfort of my Savior? Where would I turn to if I were not able to seek refuge in your arms?

My Father, I want to share these gifts of grace with those lost and caught up in what they think are hopeless situations. Let me be your instrument of love to them, so they will know you are a God of love and a God capable of calming any storm in their life. Let their hearts be receptive to the words I share, and may the Holy Spirit work within them as they give their hearts and minds to Christ.

All things are possible with you, O Lord. Through the power of the Holy Spirit, bring the lost into newness of life so they may receive the promises in your Word. As I seek out the lost, let me reflect on the character of Christ, free of evil influences, so I may glorify the name of the Great Comforter. Amen.

REFLECTIONS

Is there really hope for those that do not know Christ? Who or what can change their hearts?

Please use the space below to write down any thoughts or comments you may have.

"May God Bless You,
As you live your Life for Christ,
Empowered by The Holy Spirit."

November 15

Psalm 141:9 NIV.

[9] Keep me safe from the traps set by evildoers, from the snares they have laid for me.

Blessed be your name, O Christ. By your stripes, I have been healed and set free from the evil of Satan. No longer does he have dominion over me. For as long as I remain in Christ, I have the power through the Holy Spirit to rebuke him and to cast him down among the snakes of the earth. He wants nothing more than to enslave me to my sinful nature. Praise to your name, Son of God, for through your grace, I have been set free to enjoy your love and the assurance of eternal life.

Bless me now this day, so I will remain strong in the face of Satan and be able to rebuke any attempt by him to control me. You are the light of the world, faithful Christ, who lights a path of righteousness before me so I may bring honor and glory to your name. As I go about my day, may I be blessed and filled with the Holy Spirit so I may continue to faithfully do God's will? Praise to you, Light of the World! "I will give thanks to the Lord with all my heart in the company and assembly of the just." Amen.

REFLECTIONS

How can you rebuke attacks by Satan that try to control you?

Please use the space below to write down any thoughts or comments you may have.

"May God Bless You,
As you live your Life for Christ,
Empowered by The Holy Spirit."

November 16

Psalm 37:8 NIV.

[8] Refrain from anger and turn from wrath; do not fret — it leads only to evil.

My Lord, my God, my Jehovah, you are the Creator of all the Universe. I praise you for the glorious life I have been blessed with. You have blessed me beyond measure and see to it that my strength is renewed when my days are weary. Your power enables me to do your will, reach out to the lost in Christ, witness to them, and tell them the Good News in Jesus Christ. Let me be fruitful as I go about your calling to love and serve my neighbors.

This day, grant me the grace to lift those influenced by Satan and who are bent on spreading anger and discord around them. Let me be a force that will calm them, not agitate them, or arouse their fury. Give me the understanding and empathy so I may see who they are in Christ. For the sake of their souls, lean their hearts toward you so they may receive the promises of your kingdom. In the name of the Great Peace Maker, Jesus Christ. Amen.

REFLECTIONS

It can be challenging to see the good in those who are evil. Can Salvation still be found through Jesus Christ if you are consumed with evil?

Please use the space below to write down any thoughts or comments you may have.

November 17

Colossians 1:11 NIV.

[11] being strengthened with all power according to his glorious might so that you may have great endurance and patience, ...

Heavenly Father, send now your Holy Spirit upon me. My patience is frayed with life circumstances that test my character and cause me to succumb to frustrations unbecoming of my Christian witness. I long to be steadfast in my faith, grace, and understanding of situations I cannot control. But I lack the spiritual strength to walk the path of righteousness. Forgive me, Lord Jesus, for this flaw in my Christian character.

Help me through the power of the Holy Spirit to remain calm when faced with situations that are frustrating and that undermine the true nature of a Disciple of Christ. Guide my thoughts and actions so I may make the best choices when faced with adversity. Purge my heart and soul of any evil influences that Satan has over me. Lead me down the path of righteousness so I may enjoy your peace and love as a part of my daily walk with Christ.

And when this day has passed, let me reflect on the power of your mercies and grace. Bless me through the Holy Spirit with the strength to calm the roughest waters in my life. In your Holy Name, I pray. Amen.

REFLECTIONS

We all have character flaws. How do we free ourselves from them so Christ can prevail?

Please use the space below to write down any thoughts or comments you may have.

"May God Bless You,
As you live your Life for Christ,
Empowered by The Holy Spirit."

November 18

James 4:7-10 NIV.

[7] Submit yourselves, then, to God. Resist the devil, and he will flee from you. [8] Come near to God and he will come near to you...

Precious Lord Jesus, the sound of your name brings joy and comfort to my soul. I am so grateful for the gift of Salvation. A precious gift paid for by the shedding of your blood on the Cross of Calvary. What greater joy is there in life than to proclaim the name of the Risen Christ. You are my Savior, the Great Physician, my Great Comforter, and my Shield of Armor when I am faced with ploys by Satan to destroy my witness.

Lord, I want to fulfill the message of your Gospel. Let me live true to your Word as I pursue a life of righteousness. Give me the strength and courage to resist the temptations Satan places before me. Help me to live a life committed to spreading the Word of your Gospel. Praise to your name, O Christ. For it is through your grace and the power of the Holy Spirit that I can rise above my failings in life and soar like an eagle above any difficulties I may face.

As this day unfolds, let me be faithful to your Word. Let me be true to my Christian faith. May I always remember if I have a repentant heart, remain humble, and contrite in my heart for the sins I have committed, I can do all things. Let me go forth this day with a heart that is eager to show the power of a life that can be transformed by your love and grace. Amen.

REFLECTIONS

Wanting to face your failures in life is honorable. Can you really do it without the Holy Spirit?

Please use the space below to write down any thoughts or comments you may have.

"May God Bless You,
As you live your Life for Christ,
Empowered by The Holy Spirit."

November 19

Psalm 22:19 NIV.

[19] But you, Lord, do not be far from me. You are my strength; come quickly to help me.

Holy Father, your Son, is the Risen King of Kings. Blessed is this day as I glorify His name. With Christ as my Breast of Armor, I can rout the forces of Satan and trump their lies with the truth of your Word. With Christ by my side, I can overcome any difficulties in life by trusting in the Lord my God for the spiritual sustenance I need.

O Father, your gifts of mercy and grace never cease. You wake me in the morning and give me the strength to persevere during the day. And when night falls, it is only by your grace that I can proclaim it is still well with my soul. For my joy is in the Lord. My strength and my comfort are cradled in your loving arms. I no longer must go down a path of uncertainty, for my God lights the way of hope and righteousness.

Praise to your name, O Precious Christ! For I am lost when I am not covered by your blood. I am lost when I forsake the truth of your Word. I am lost when I refuse to be pruned of my wayward branches. What a joy it is to be loved by the Almighty God. For it is through your showering of grace and love upon me that I can rise and declare to the world, "My God is an awesome God." Amen.

REFLECTIONS

When you wake up in the morning, do you pray to God for spiritual strength? If not, He is waiting to hear from you.

Please use the space below to write down any thoughts or comments you may have.

"May God Bless You,
As you live your Life for Christ,
Empowered by The Holy Spirit."

November 20

Romans 11:31 NIV.

[31] so they too have now become disobedient in order that they too may now receive mercy as a result of God's mercy to you.

Father, through your grace, you have taught me to trust and obey. As a disobedient child, full of pride and indulgent behavior, I have been caught up in sins that have grieved your heart. I praise you that I can come before you with a true spirit of thanksgiving for your continuous outpouring of love and grace. When my heart and mind were full of confusion and despair, you saw me through with your gentle prodding and pulled me close in an embrace of warmth and love. What a glorious Savior you are, proper to your Word and faithful to the promises you made to me and to all your children who have accepted the precious gift of Salvation.

As I go about this day, O Christ, bless me with Divine Opportunities to express my love and appreciation to you for your grace and guidance along my Christian walk. When I encounter a wandering soul caught up in confusion, let me be a calming force of peace and love. Allow me to be instrumental in sharing the Gospel of Jesus Christ, so he can know his Savior. Let me forsake any temptation by Satan that would compromise my witness. Give me the strength and power through the Holy Spirit to rebuke any instigation by Satan designed to undermine my faithful obedience to your Word. At day's end, O Lord, may I look back upon my day and be able to say, "I have fought the good fight and have prevailed through the grace of the Almighty God." Amen.

REFLECTIONS

- *At the end of your day, do you praise God for being able to fight the good fight for Him?*

Please use the space below to write down any thoughts or comments you may have.

"May God Bless You,
As you live your Life for Christ,
Empowered by The Holy Spirit."

November 21

Job 4:4 NIV.

[4] Your words have supported those who stumbled; You have strengthened faltering knees.

Precious Father, I come before you with a heart full of gratitude and love for my Christian brothers and sisters in Christ. You have brought them into my life to help guide my Christian walk and build me up in the faith. When I look back over my life, I can see how instrumental they have been in drawing me closer to my Lord and Savior, Jesus Christ. Let me be an ambassador of yours. Bless me with the truth of your Word. Protect me with your Shield of Armor. And let me be sincere in my witness of your love and grace.

You are my Almighty God! Without you, I can do nothing but flounder in a sea of murky water. With you, I can persevere through the most challenging storms. Give me the strength to pull myself out of any dilemma that threatens to devour me. Give me the strength to always look to you when my heart is heavy and weak from Satan's demonic influences. Fill me with the power of the Holy Spirit so with your Word of Truth, I can conquer any adversity that may cross my path. Praise to you, O Christ! All glory and honor are yours. Amen.

REFLECTIONS

How does the truth of God's Word help you in your daily walk with Christ?

Please use the space below to write down any thoughts or comments you may have.

"May God Bless You,
As you live your Life for Christ,
Empowered by The Holy Spirit."

November 22

Proverbs 22:5 NIV.

[5] In the paths of the wicked are snares and pitfalls, but those who would preserve their life stay far from them.

My God, my God, hear the cries of my heart. I have been so foolish as to think I could travel down the path of sin, and there would be no repercussions. Yes, I have accepted the gift of Salvation that was paid for by my Lord and Savior, Jesus Christ. Yet, the sanctification of my life has been a slow and arduous process. Everywhere I turn, I come face to face with temptations flaunted by Satan. Everywhere I turn, his demonic snares lay in waiting, bent on entrapping me to sin.

Your Word says that the wages of sin are death. I do not want to be separated from you, my God. I do not want to be trapped by evil snares that want to cut me off from your love and grace. Rescue me, O Christ, not only from myself but also from all the bad influences in society that try to entrap me. You are my Almighty God! I claim your promises and pray you will place a hedge of guardian angels around me so I may triumph over Satan. Let me finally be able to break the shackles of sin.

Praise to you, O Lord. I trust in your Word, and I trust that I can do all things with the armor of the Lord. In Christ's precious name, I pray. Amen.

REFLECTIONS

If you see yourself about to step into one of Satan's snares, what can you do to avoid it?

Please use the space below to write down any thoughts or comments you may have.

"May God Bless You,
As you live your Life for Christ,
Empowered by The Holy Spirit."

November 23

Malachi 2:2 NIV.

[2] If you do not listen, and if you do not resolve to honor my name," says the Lord Almighty, "I will send a curse on you, and I will curse your blessings. Yes, I have already cursed them because you have not resolved to honor me.

Great God and my Savior, Jesus Christ, today I am reminded of all the blessings you have bestowed upon me. I praise you for being the center of my life, my Rock, my Strength, and my Redeemer. When those I have placed my hope and trust in fail me, you are faithful and true to your Word. When I am weary from my daily struggles, you provide comfort and peace to calm my soul. When the world is full of chaos and discord, you will always mediate and bring about reconciliation.

What a glorious God you are! You are always looking after your children, being patient, loving, and firm. What a glorious God you are! When Satan attempts to strip me of my honor, your Holy Spirit empowers me to rebuke the evil one. You are the All-Powerful and Loving God, who has freed me from my slavery to sin through your forgiveness and grace. What more could I ask of my loving Savior?

Thank you, O Christ, for the opportunity to serve you. Bless me this day with a divine opportunity to touch the life of someone who is searching for the love and peace only you can provide. In Christ's precious name, I pray. Amen.

REFLECTIONS

When you are weary from your daily struggles, how do you renew yourself?

Please use the space below to write down any thoughts or comments you may have.

"May God Bless You,
As you live your Life for Christ,
Empowered by The Holy Spirit."

November 24

Zechariah 7:9 NIV.

[9] "This is what the Lord Almighty said: 'Administer true justice; show mercy and compassion to one another.

Glorious Father, I come before you with a contrite heart, one that has not been as gracious to my neighbors as I should have been. You look upon me with loving eyes that are filled with understanding and compassion. I am truly blessed by your unconditional love — love that has sustained me in my darkest hours. Yet, when I am called upon to show others grace, I sometimes get caught up in a swell of anger and retribution for their failure to meet the expectations I set for them.

Father, help me remember I am not perfect and that we all fall short of your glory. Your capacity for forgiveness is so great, so remarkable, and so complete that I should be willing to shout out to others the great love you have for me. Forgive me, Lord, for not faithfully reflecting the love of Christ to those I meet in my daily walk. Cleanse my heart from this ungodly behavior and let me go forth this day with a new attitude of love and forgiveness for my neighbor.

As this day comes to an end, I pray you will be pleased with the spiritual growth I have gone through. For it is only through your mercy and grace that I can escape the seeds of discontent that displeases you. Bless me now as I endeavor to grow in love, understanding, and grace for others. Amen.

REFLECTIONS

- *Showing grace to others can sometimes be challenging. What can make it easier?*

Please use the space below to write down any thoughts or comments you may have.

"May God Bless You,
As you live your Life for Christ,
Empowered by The Holy Spirit."

November 25

Psalm 40:1-3 NIV.

[1] I waited patiently for the Lord; he turned to me and heard my cry. [2] He lifted me out of the slimy pit, out of the mud and mire; he set my feet on a rock and gave me a firm place to stand. [3] He put a new song in my mouth, a hymn of praise to our God. ...

O Lord, my Almighty God, you are the Master of all creation and the source of all wisdom. Your Holiness compels me to look inside myself for spiritual strength and wisdom to master the areas of my life in disarray. I am so grateful for your blessings and your willingness to walk beside me as I navigate confusing areas of my life. Grant me the moral fortitude and courage to resist the temptations Satan sets in my path, so I will not dishonor you. Grant me mercy and kindness of heart so no matter what I am confronted with, I will always reflect the love of Christ to my fellowman.

When I am weary and lack the clarity of vision to see the Truth, remove the fog of confusion from me so I may see and do your will. My heart longs to faithfully serve you, O Christ, and I pray that through my Baptism as a child of God, I may go forth this day full of joy in my heart and unwavering in my passion to love and serve you.

All glory is yours, my Lord, for I am just a child with a servant's heart that pleads for your understanding, compassion, and strength when my walk brings discontent. Bless me now, this day, in the name of the Father, Son, and Holy Spirit. Amen.

REFLECTIONS

Describe the qualities of one with moral fortitude that God can use to His Glory.

Please use the space below to write down any thoughts or comments you may have.

"May God Bless You,
As you live your Life for Christ,
Empowered by The Holy Spirit."

November 26

Mark 8:34 NIV.

[34] Then he called the crowd to him along with his disciples and said: "Whoever wants to be my disciple must deny themselves and take up their cross and follow me.

Holy Father, I give glory to the redeeming blood of my Savior, Jesus Christ. Your Son who paid the heavy price on the Cross of Calvary so I might be freed from Satan. Yes, Satan, you can taunt me day-in and day-out, but you will not be able to rule over me. You can tempt me with sins of the world, but again you will lose because I am a child of God.

The Cross is my reminder that I can and will survive your insidious onslaught into my life. You have no control over me unless I cave in and do your will. That will not happen, Satan, because I wear the Armor of Christ, and through the Holy Spirit, you will be defeated. I have the Lord my God as my refuge and a hedge of guardian angels to protect me from your evil plans. With the Word of God as the Belt of Truth, I can fend off your lowly promises of a more prosperous life by being part of the world. That will not happen, Satan, because I love the Lord my God too much to succumb to your demonic influences.

Yes, Satan, I love Jesus Christ, and no temptations or worldly snares will pull me away from my Savior. Through the power of the Holy Spirit, I will rise victorious and shred any control you have over me. Praise to you, O God! Amen.

REFLECTIONS

Have you ever felt Satan was setting a trap for you with snares of the world? Describe them.

Please use the space below to write down any thoughts or comments you may have.

"May God Bless You,
As you live your Life for Christ,
Empowered by The Holy Spirit."

November 27

Hebrews 7:28 NIV.

[28] For the law appoints as high Priests men in all their weakness; but the oath, which came after the law, appointed the Son, who has been made perfect forever.

Great God, you reign supreme over the universe. You created me in your image and breathed life into me, that was formed from dust. Despite my human intellect, the truth of your Word remains strong. Your grace is eternal when I see the blood of Christ as an atonement for my sins. What a glorious God you are — powerful, omnipotent, and full of love and grace for your wayward children.

Lord, I come before you today with a heavy and sad heart because of losses in my life I do not understand. Your Words say all things work together for those that trust in the Lord. Father, I trust in you, yet situations in my life remain unchanged. I pray for reconciliation and peace, but it does not come. I beg that your wisdom will persevere and pave my way with a cloak of righteousness, but I fail to grasp it. What am I to do, my God? There is no one else to turn to. While my faith and trust are steady, I need your reassurance that the answers to my needs will be provided.

O Lord, how I have failed you! My doubt breeds a firestorm that is sure to destroy my witness if I do not persevere. Grant me the strength of Christ to look constantly for your presence. Grant me the forgiveness I need for doubting your Word. Renew my soul, lift my heart, and allow me to rejoice in the power of your Holy Word. And when the day is done, let me look back over the day and be able to say, "Yes, Lord, you were with me all the time." Praise to you, O Christ. Amen.

REFLECTIONS

When you experience loss in your life, it is easy to blame God. Is that fair to God?

Please use the space below to write down any thoughts or comments you may have.

"May God Bless You,
As you live your Life for Christ,
Empowered by The Holy Spirit."

November 28

Acts 2:38 NIV.

[38] Peter replied, "Repent and be baptized, every one of you, in the name of Jesus Christ for the forgiveness of your sins. And you will receive the gift of the holy spirit.

O Christ, my Majestic God, send now your Holy Spirit upon me. Give me the grace I need to faithfully forgive others as you have forgiven me. Give me the wisdom to recognize true believers in Christ and give me the insight to remember those yearning for your loving embrace. As this day unfolds, be with me every hour as I walk rocky paths so I may not stumble and fall. When those who refuse to acknowledge you as the only true God run from you, please forgive them. Bring upon them someone who has the wisdom and discernment needed to break the hold of Satan on their lives.

You are the Almighty God — the God who sent His Only Son to die on the Cross of Calvary. Because of this precious gift, I can claim freedom through Christ and defeat the armies of Satan. Thanks to your patience, and unconditional love for all your children, you welcome them into the family of God. Your love is so great that no matter what sins are in their lives, you only see the blood of your Son, Jesus Christ. Thank you, Father, for the blessings you extend to me. Bless me as I go about my day, in the name of the Father, Son, and Holy Spirit. Amen.

REFLECTIONS

When you intentionally sin, will God forgive you? Will He love you any less?

Please use the space below to write down any thoughts or comments you may have.

"May God Bless You,
As you live your Life for Christ,
Empowered by The Holy Spirit."

November 29

Psalm 23:6 NIV.

[6] Surely your goodness and love will follow me all the days of my life, and I will dwell in the house of the Lord forever.

Most gracious Heavenly Father, your love surpasses anything I have ever known. It is gentle, kind, merciful, and provides an enduring love that enables me to cope and meet daily life challenges. Without you, I would be lost and would wander from circumstance to circumstance without your constant presence and assurance of your love. I thank you, Lord, for your continued existence. Thank you for your love and the gift of Salvation, which was paid for on the Cross of Calvary.

I lift you up this morning as I embark upon another day in service to you. There is no more tremendous honor, no more significant way of showing my love for you than to love others as you have loved me. Your presence in my life is what sustains me through the trials in life I encounter daily. I need not question where you are. I need not doubt your love. I need not doubt your presence. Despite those that question your existence, I know the truth of your Word. I see the power it has over my life and that it can have for those who need your grace. And when I conclude, another day in service to you, may your blessings overflow. May they touch every aspect of my life. And may they bless me as I strive to be an effective ambassador of your Word. Amen.

REFLECTIONS

- *As a disciple of Christ or ambassador of God's Word, what is your primary mission?*

Please use the space below to write down any thoughts or comments you may have.

"May God Bless You,
As you live your Life for Christ,
Empowered by The Holy Spirit."

November 30

Proverbs 22:11 NIV.

[11] One who loves a pure heart and who speaks with grace will have the king for a friend.

Blessed Christ, what a joyous day this is. You have given me so much to be thankful for that I am speechless and deeply touched. Your grace is overflowing. Your love is so extraordinary and precious that I shed tears of gratefulness. What can I do for you, O Christ? Give me a task to fulfill so I may put my faith in action.

Today, I want to seek Divine Opportunities to share my love with others, no matter who they are and their circumstance in life. Let me be a beacon of hope and love to them. The need for hope and faith among my brothers and sisters can only be fulfilled by surrendering their lives to Christ. The need for grace and mercy among those lost and forgotten by their fellow man can only be met by giving one's fruits of the Holy Spirit.

I ask that you send your Holy Spirit upon me so I might share the beauty of Christ with those who are yearning for peace in their lives. Take my hand, O Christ, and lead me down the path of righteousness so I may be a faithful witness of your love and grace. Bless me now as I seek to be a blessing to those in need. Amen.

REFLECTIONS

What can you do for Christ today as an example of one putting his faith in action?

Please use the space below to write down any thoughts or comments you may have.

"May God Bless You,
As you live your Life for Christ,
Empowered by The Holy Spirit."

December 1

Psalm 116:5 NIV.

[5] The Lord is gracious and righteous; our God is full of compassion.

O Holy Father, you are the creator of the heavens and the earth, the Almighty God whom I worship and adore. Thank you for your constant grace, precious love, and the incredible forgiveness you have bestowed upon me. In my foolishness, I have been naive and held captive to the lust in my heart. I engaged in sins that defiled my body, corrupted my heart, and that demeaned the beauty of your Word. Even though I had accepted you as my Lord and Savior, I did not live or reflect on the life of Christ. Yet, as I have grown, the seeds of faith planted in my youth have finally been pruned and are ready to blossom into one who absolutely loves and wants to serve my precious God.

Praise to you, my Lord, for without your presence in my life, I would not be able to love and serve you with a heart full of gratitude. As this day goes forward, know that I will continuously look for Divine Opportunities to lead the lost to Christ. For without the forgiveness of my sins, I would have a hardened heart devoid of any compassion. Bless me now as I pray for your blessings so I may give my love in service to my fellow man. In Christ's name, I pray. Amen.

REFLECTIONS

Describe the seeds of faith from your youth that have blossomed through God's grace?

Please use the space below to write down any thoughts or comments you may have.

"May God Bless You,
As you live your Life for Christ,
Empowered by The Holy Spirit."

December 2

Matthew 18:15 NIV.

[15] "If your brother or sister sins, go and point out their fault, just between the two of you. If they listen to you, you have won them over.

O Lord, I am faced with another day where my patience is being tested. Coping with frustrating situations is not something I am particularly good at. I try to show grace, yet my inner voice wants to shout out and say inappropriate things. Help me, Lord, to find the strength and wisdom to contain myself and to remember I am a child of God and need to reflect the life of my Lord and Savior, Jesus Christ.

As I continue through this day, let me be seen as a Disciple of Christ -- patient, loving, kind, and slow to anger. Let me be forgiving of my fellow man when I am tested and want to act out in ways that are not Godly.

You are my God, and I love you. I am here to serve you. I need your grace. I need your love. I need your forgiveness. Build me up in my character, in my faith, and in my willingness to lead others to Christ by my faithful example. Should I go astray, place in front of me a reminder that I, too, am fallible. Caution me to not judge others' behavior and actions when I am no better than they are. You are the final judge, and I am here to obey your Word and to be a beacon of hope and light to others in need. Praise to you, O Faithful God. Amen.

REFLECTIONS

If you go astray today, what kind of reminder would set you back on the right path?

Please use the space below to write down any thoughts or comments you may have.

"May God Bless You,
As you live your Life for Christ,
Empowered by The Holy Spirit."

December 3

Isaiah 18:5 NIV.

[5] For, before the harvest, when the blossom is gone and the flower becomes a ripening grape, he will cut off the shoots with pruning knives, and cut down and take away the spreading branches.

Praise to you, O Christ, for this season of hope and blessings. Hallelujah to you for coming as a newborn babe to save humanity from its sinful state. Thank you for dying on the Cross of Calvary so I will no longer be a wretched sinner but as a child of God, pure as snow, basking in the warmth of a loving God. As I go about this new day, lift me up in your grace so I will grow in love and character as a child of the Highest God. Reveal to me, O Christ, areas of my life that need pruning so I may indeed reflect the life of one in Christ.

Take my sins and blot them out as I confess them and do my best to repent. I am weak in trials, while I am strong in faith. Lord, grant me the strength and moral fortitude to expose my faults, hidden thoughts, hidden sins, and hidden fears. Let me be honest with myself as I bow before you with a humble and contrite spirit. Let me always be aware of my failings, so I may correct them and be able to turn from those things that dishonor your Holy Name. And when this day ends, let me look back so I may see how your love and grace have sustained me, made me strong in my witness, and blessed me throughout my day. Praise to you, the Lord of Life, and the Redeemer of my soul. Amen.

REFLECTIONS

As a wretched sinner, is God's grace still available to you? If so, how is that possible?

Please use the space below to write down any thoughts or comments you may have.

"May God Bless You,
As you live your Life for Christ,
Empowered by The Holy Spirit."

December 4

Psalm 103:13-14 NIV.

[13] As a father has compassion on his children, so the Lord has compassion on those who fear him; [14] for he knows how we are formed, he remembers that we are dust. ...

Gracious Lord Jesus, before long, I will be celebrating your birth as a fully human and fully God on this earth. Your birth represented new hope and grace from my Almighty God. Your coming led to the ultimate sacrifice of your life. You hung on the Cross of Calvary to pay the debt of my sins, even though I am not deserving of such grace and love. I am a sinner that longs to be forgiven and be cleansed of the guilt I feel. Your grace and love provided me with the ultimate new regeneration through my Savior, Jesus Christ. What a blessing it is to partake of such great love! What a blessing it is to know and to have the assurance of eternal life through my Savior, Jesus Christ.

As I go about this day, O Father in Heaven, open the doors of love and grace where I can be a faithful disciple of yours. Let me have a heart of compassion and kindness towards those children of yours that are in need. Let me faithfully reflect the character of Christ to all those whose paths I cross this day. Let me pause and remember that you were born as a fully human man and a fully God that can bring peace, harmony, and love into my life. Thank you, Lord, for your continued guidance and patience with me as I seek to do your will. Amen.

REFLECTIONS

If you find yourself caught up in sin today, how can you free yourself of the guilt?

Please use the space below to write down any thoughts or comments you may have.

"May God Bless You,
As you live your Life for Christ,
Empowered by The Holy Spirit."

December 5

Isaiah 30:21 NIV.

[21] Whether you turn to the right or to the left, your ears will hear a voice behind you, saying, "This is the way; walk in it."

My Lord, my God, my Great Jehovah, thank you for your love. Through your grace, you have brought Christian brothers and sisters into my life. Through the power of the Holy Spirit, they have blessed me with the freedom found in the blood of Christ. Without the guidance they provided, I would not be here today, strong in my faith and firm in my devotion to you.

As my day goes forward, O Christ, lead me down the path of righteousness so I will be honorable in all I say or do. Do not let me stumble or become arrogant in my human condition, for I am a slave to your will and divine guidance. I praise you, my Lord, and I willingly sacrifice the material things of this world to be able to spend eternity with you in paradise. Grant me a pardon for my sins, through my Savior, so I may faithfully love and serve you as I strive to love and serve my fellowman. Bless me in my coming and goings as I lift and praise your name to all the world. Amen.

REFLECTIONS

How have brothers or sisters in Christ helped you to grow in your faith?

Please use the space below to write down any thoughts or comments you may have.

"May God Bless You,
As you live your Life for Christ,
Empowered by The Holy Spirit."

December 6

Psalm 89:1 NIV.

[1] I will sing of the Lord's great love forever; with my mouth I will make your faithfulness known through all generations.

Almighty God, you are the Supreme God, the One whom I turn to for consolation when I am in despair. You are my Creator, the One who made me in your image. I am so profoundly grateful for the greatest act of love mankind has ever known — the sacrifice of your Son, Jesus Christ, on the Cross of Calvary.

As this day unfolds and I enter the Christmas season to celebrate my Savior's birth, let me be mindful that the price paid for my sins was the cost of your Beloved Son, Jesus Christ. Nowhere in history has there been such an incredible demonstration of love, grace, and forgiveness. I praise you, my Lord, for this gift. I ask now that you send your Holy Spirit upon me. Equip me with the fruits of the spirit that will enable me to demonstrate the power and glory of my Almighty Savior. Let me be that beacon of hope and light to those that do not know the Christmas story so I may bring them to a personal relationship with Jesus Christ.

Glory to you, O Mighty God! Praise your name! And praise the truth of your Word that is the food that feeds my soul. In Christ's Holy Name, I pray. Amen.

REFLECTIONS

It will soon be Christmas. How can you prepare your heart to celebrate Christ's birth?

Please use the space below to write down any thoughts or comments you may have.

"May God Bless You,
As you live your Life for Christ,
Empowered by The Holy Spirit."

December 7

Luke 11:13 NIV.

[13] If you then, though you are evil, know how to give good gifts to your children, how much more will your Father in heaven give the holy spirit to those who ask him!"

O Promised One, Lord of my life and the Redeemer of my soul, your grace has enabled me to be mindful of your love. Your grace has instilled in me the fruits of the Holy Spirit, so I may be an instrument of your love and great mercy.

Today is a new day. A day to look with fresh eyes upon my fellow man and to see the beauty within their hearts. These are children of yours whose lives I need to touch with God's love. Empower me through the gifts of the Holy Spirit, so I may truly reflect upon my fellowman the Truth of your Holy Word. Bring them to their knees as I bow before you with a humble spirit so together, we will be able to love and serve our Lord.

As I look upon my Divine Appointments, Lord, let me acknowledge that their Salvation and freedom from sins came not from me but from your grace and precious love. Through the Great Redeemer, Jesus Christ, all glory belongs to you. Amen.

REFLECTIONS

Today is a new day. Are there children of God whose lives you can touch today?

Please use the space below to write down any thoughts or comments you may have.

"May God Bless You,
As you live your Life for Christ,
Empowered by The Holy Spirit."

December 8

John 1:14 NIV.

[14] The word became flesh and made his dwelling among us. We have seen his glory, the glory of the one and only Son, who came from the Father, full of grace and truth.

Dear God, the wisdom from your Word is infinite. The truth of your Word is eternal. From the birth of Jesus Christ over 2000 years ago, your Son has been the greatest blessing mankind has ever known. As I enter this Christmas season, let me be constantly aware of the price Christ paid on the Cross of Calvary for my sins.

Father, your love has always been there for me. Because of my faith in Christ, I can claim freedom from the claws of Satan. As the day of Christ's birth draws near, let me rejoice in the knowledge that my Salvation is not earned by works but by faith in the Living God.

Give me the grace, my God, to have compassion and mercy upon people who are suffering and do not know the joy that can be found in Christ. Give me the patience to weather any storm that may come up that attempts to defile the blessing of Christmas Day. And when Christmas is upon me, let me reflect upon the year and rejoice with genuine gratitude, the love and grace that has always been there for me. Amen.

REFLECTIONS

- *As the Christmas season comes upon us, what blessings of Christmas do you value the most?*

Please use the space below to write down any thoughts or comments you may have.

"May God Bless You,
As you live your Life for Christ,
Empowered by The Holy Spirit."

December 9

Romans 1:28-29 NIV.

[28] Furthermore, just as they did not think it worthwhile to retain the knowledge of God, so God gave them over to a depraved mind, so that they do what ought not to be done. [29] They have become filled with every kind of wickedness, evil, greed and depravity. They are full of envy, murder, strife, deceit, and malice...

Precious Christ, my Lord, and my Savior, your blessings continue to unfold as I begin each new day. Today, I am reminded of your grace, love, and forgiveness that lifts me up in peace and continues to sustain me each moment of my life. Thank you, Father, for walking beside me and for guiding me along the footsteps of life. There is so much joy in committing my life to you. Your love is the fulfillment of all my needs and provides all the strength needed to weather any storms that may come my way. Blessings abound when I devote my life to serve you and my fellow man.

Hear my promise, O Lord. I will uphold the truth of your Word and be obedient to your plan for my life with true faith and devotion to Jesus Christ. Lord, let me always be mindful of your Word. When wickedness abounds around me, seal my heart and soul with an impenetrable hedge of protection strong enough to fight off the evil one. Give me the wisdom and spiritual discernment to withstand all attacks by Satan. And, Lord, grant me, through the power of the Holy Spirit, the knowledge to discern your will for my life. Give me the moral courage and fidelity to your Word so I may be your faithful child. In Christ's name, I pray. Amen.

REFLECTIONS

What promises are you prepared to make to God as you go about your day?

Please use the space below to write down any thoughts or comments you may have.

*"May God Bless You,
As you live your Life for Christ,
Empowered by The Holy Spirit."*

December 10

Psalm 1:1-2 NIV.

[1] Blessed is the one who does not walk in step with the wicked or stand in the way that sinners take or sit in the company of mockers, [2] but whose delight is in the law of the Lord, and who meditates on his law day and night. ...

My Lord, my God, I give thanks to you for your unfailing love. You continue to lift me up, to comfort me when I am in distress, and to guide my footsteps through the power of the Holy Spirit. I am not worthy of such love save for the blood of your Son, Jesus Christ. Let me always be worthy of your grace and the gift of Salvation.

As I begin a new day in service to you, may my heart be humbled and hopeful as I look for Divine Appointments to share the Gospel of Jesus Christ. Let your Holy Spirit flow through me so what I profess with my mouth is truthful to your Word and serves as a blessing to those whose lives I touch. I cannot do this on my own, O Christ. I need your presence as I talk with your children. If they are people who do not share my faith, let my words open the doors of their hearts so your Holy Word may enter in. If they are warm Christians, let my words remind them of the tremendous responsibility that real children of God need to be mindful of the truth of your Word.

Grant all your children the spirit of wisdom and revelation they need to love and faithfully serve you. And may I always be aware of my own sinful nature and capacity to lead people astray. Instill a hedge of guardian angels around me so I may be a vital force in declaring my faith and unwavering devotion to service in your name. Amen.

REFLECTIONS

How do you know if the words you share with someone are inspired by the Holy Spirit?

Please use the space below to write down any thoughts or comments you may have.

"May God Bless You,
As you live your Life for Christ,
Empowered by The Holy Spirit."

December 11

Psalm 31:7 NIV.

[7] I will be glad and rejoice in your love, for you saw my affliction and knew the anguish of my soul.

O Christ, my Lord, and my Savior. My heart is heavy with something that has impacted my life for quite some time. With the changing mores of our society, social issues have taken their toll on traditional values and beliefs. I praise you, Lord, that I can share this burden with you. I ask that you send your Holy Spirit upon me so I may hear your whisper and have the wisdom to respond appropriately to your Word.

Lord, I do not understand why so many Christians persecute those whose lifestyles are contrary to what their religious beliefs dictate. Please forgive me, O Lord. Is the sin of homosexuality any more grievous to your heart than the hidden sins I have committed? Father, you are a God of love! You are a God of compassion! You are a God of forgiveness! Through the death and resurrection of your Son, Jesus Christ, I am free of the burdens of my sins. I am free of all the guilt that causes my heart to grieve. I pray that you will extend the same forgiveness and love to all your lost children, especially those in the homosexual lifestyle. Lead them to lasting repentance through the Holy Spirit so they may experience the joy and peace found in Christ.

Father, I know the sin of homosexuality grieves your heart. It suffers mine as well. But why, my God, do people push those in need of your love further away from your blessings. You are the omnipotent God. You know all things. You know the hearts of your children. Regardless of their lifestyle or sexual orientation, they need and want your love. I have struggled with understanding those I do not understand. I have come to realize with new clarity that the truth of your Word and the message of love and forgiveness is not for a select few.

"May God Bless You,
As you live your Life for Christ,
Empowered by The Holy Spirit."

REFLECTIONS

Does God love the homosexual? If so, is it difficult for you to do the same?

Please use the space below to write down any thoughts or comments you may have.

"May God Bless You,
As you live your Life for Christ,
Empowered by The Holy Spirit."

I remember the Words of Christ and the message of love He preached for all your children. It was not a message of hate — it was a message of love. Make no mistake, my God, I know your Word says homosexuality is an abomination. I pray, Lord, through the power of intercessory prayer, that you forgive those caught up in this sin. I pray if they do not repent and turn from what grieves you, that through your infinite mercy, and for the peace of mind of their loved ones, that you will welcome them into your kingdom. Grant this, I pray, through your great compassion and my intercessory prayer.

Thank you for the insight and the spirit of wisdom and revelation you have bestowed upon me. Thank you for opening my eyes to the truth of your Word — Love! Bless me now, my Lord, as I share the validity of your Word with my fellow man. May their hearts and minds be open to your Truths, so if they embrace hatred, they may be freed from this sin. And, Father, let me not be of this world. Let me always embrace the truth of your Word as I embrace the spirit of love, grace, and forgiveness. Your Word is the constant answer to the questions of my heart. Praise to you, O Christ, for this gift of love. Amen.

REFLECTIONS

- *If you have a family member or friend in the gay lifestyle, what would be the best way to demonstrate your love for them?*

Please use the space below to write down any thoughts or comments you may have.

"May God Bless You,
As you live your Life for Christ,
Empowered by The Holy Spirit."

December 12

Psalm 18:2 NIV.

[2] The Lord is my rock, my fortress, and my deliverer; my God is my rock, in whom I take refuge, my shield and the horn of my Salvation, my stronghold.

Blessed Father, Lord of my life. Your hand is evident in all areas of my life. From the gift of Salvation to this very moment, your love has preserved me through your infinite mercy and grace. Whether I am walking in your will or struggling to free myself from Satan's grip, you still love me. Why you love me is no longer a question for me. I understand your will for my life. I know that even though I go through adversity, it is so you can prune me to be more like Christ. And I understand love is not merely a word you throw out carelessly to gain favor. It is a matter of the heart. It is the embracement of Agape love for all people no matter who they are or what station in life they may find themselves.

Your love is so great and so powerful that it transcends any love a mortal human can embrace. Thank you, my Lord, for this gift of revelation. Thank you for implanting your passion and your Word upon my heart. As I go about this day, wrap me in your arms and draw me close to your bosom so I may embrace you as well. I love you, my God! Stay with me as I walk down the path of life until the moment you bring me home. Amen.

REFLECTIONS

Do you understand God's will for your life? How would you describe it?

Please use the space below to write down any thoughts or comments you may have.

*"May God Bless You,
As you live your Life for Christ,
Empowered by The Holy Spirit."*

December 13

Psalm 5:3 NIV.

[3] In the morning, Lord, you hear my voice; in the morning I lay my requests before you and wait expectantly.

O my Great Redeemer, your presence is needed in my life. I find myself among the lost. I find myself among those that take your name in vain who are vexations to your spirit. I struggle to close my ears and to find peace in your Word, but the noise is so great in my head that I find myself discouraged and full of anxiety.

Rescue me, O Lord, and cleanse this noise that keeps me from hearing and living according to your Word. Lift me up with your loving arms and hold me close until this noise becomes silent. Your love and continuing guidance give me the strength and the power to resist being pulled into their clamor. Spill your Holy Spirit upon me so I can remain firm and diligent in my commitment to living my life for Christ.

Keep me from sliding into a pit of darkness where Satan can have his way with me. You are my God. You are my Strength. You are my Helper who is always there to pull the thorns from my side. All Praise and power to our Holy Name. Amen.

REFLECTIONS

- *Have you ever been caught up in worldly confusion that has kept you from hearing God's Word?*

Please use the space below to write down any thoughts or comments you may have.

"May God Bless You,
As you live your Life for Christ,
Empowered by The Holy Spirit."

December 14

Colossians 1:16 NIV.

[16] For in him all things were created: things in heaven and on earth, visible and invisible, whether thrones or powers or rulers or authorities; all things have been created through him and for him.

O Great Jehovah, the pain within my heart is lifted when I pause and reflect on your great love and mercy. Wherever I go, whether it is for a walk through your majestic forests, the city streets, or my local place of worship, your constant love reassures me. It allows me to face the trials in my life with the confidence that all will be well. It is only through your grace I can have this confidence.

Father, your love for me is so great that you sent your only begotten Son, Jesus Christ, to die on the Cross of Calvary for my sins. Who am I to question the beauty of this gift? Who am I to cast off the freedom that is found through my Lord, Jesus Christ? Who am I to turn and run from your arms when there is nothing but fear and turmoil in the world? The strife born of Satan must end. I must be strong in my faith and devoted to your service even to the point of my death. No matter how difficult the seasons may be, I can survive because of your great love.

As I go about this new day, O Christ, let me lend my ear as you whisper to me your soft Words of encouragement. Speak to me through the power of the Holy Spirit so I might have crystal clarity and knowledge of your will for my life. And when the light has passed, and the darkness begins to descend, may you find me jubilant in my love and devotion to your Holy Word. Always faithful and always grateful for the gifts of love, grace, and forgiveness. Amen.

REFLECTIONS

Have you ever found yourself facing the choice of intentionally sinning? Were you able to defeat Satan's trap?

Please use the space below to write down any thoughts or comments you may have.

*"May God Bless You,
As you live your Life for Christ,
Empowered by The Holy Spirit."*

December 15

Isaiah 25:1 NIV.

[1] Lord, you are my God; I will exalt you and praise your name, for in perfect faithfulness you have done wonderful things, things planned long ago.

Precious Father, your Word is my constant assurance that all things work together for those that trust in the Lord. No matter what challenges in life I may be facing, I must only look to you for deliverance from my fears. Your Son, Jesus Christ, paid the ultimate sacrifice on the Cross of Calvary for my sins. Sins, my God, that have grieved your heart. Sins that have caused me to wallow in a sea of confusion and despair. Wherever I go in my daily walk, I know your Word will sustain me and give me the hope, through Christ, that all will be well with my soul. Praise to you for the gifts of love, grace, and forgiveness that have blessed me beyond anything I could have imagined.

Let me go forth this day full of hope and with a heart full of love for my fellow man. Let me extend forgiveness to those that have offended me. Give me the grace and courage to forsake my pride and to simply do the right thing so those whom I have offended may know, through my witness, the love of Christ. And when I succumb to my weaknesses, remind me with a jolt that will awaken me and make me mindful that I am a child of God called to reflect the life of Christ in all I say and do. Amen.

REFLECTIONS

- *When you pray to God for deliverance from your sins, do you trust that He will?*

Please use the space below to write down any thoughts or comments you may have.

"May God Bless You,
As you live your Life for Christ,
Empowered by The Holy Spirit."

December 16

Psalm 119:81 NIV.

[81] My soul faints with longing for your Salvation, but I have put my hope in your word.

My Lord, my God, it is with a humble heart that I come before you. Although I am weary and in need of rest, I jump for joy at the sound of your name. I tune my heart into songs of praise that lift my heart and soul. You are my God, my Redeemer, and my Refuge and Strength in times of need. You protect me with your guardian angels and lift me up when Satan's power overcomes me. What a loving and merciful God you are.

As this day goes on, my Father, know my heart belongs to you. Know that although I am a sinner, my hope for forgiveness can only come from you. I do not want to sin, O Christ, for you set the example of living a life of purity on this earth. I cannot be as pure as you, but I will try my best to honor and love you by the way I live my life. And if I should falter and be led down the path of the evil one, pull me back into your loving arms by awakening within me the power of the Holy Spirit. Care for me when I am weak. Admonish me when I sin. Love me despite my faults. Most of all, keep me within the fold of sheep that tend to wander yet always come back to you.

I love you, my God. You have instilled in me the power of the Holy Spirit. Let me always be mindful of sharing the fruits of the spirit with my fellow man. Thank you for the continuing blessings that have enriched my life and have drawn me closer to your Holy Word. Amen.

REFLECTIONS

Because of your sinful nature, you will sin. What is your best defense against Satan?

Please use the space below to write down any thoughts or comments you may have.

"May God Bless You,
As you live your Life for Christ,
Empowered by The Holy Spirit."

December 17

Psalm 59:16 NIV.

[16] But I will sing of your strength, in the morning I will sing of your love; for you are my fortress, my refuge in times of trouble.

Holy Father, the day your Son, Jesus Christ, was born is approaching. Let me remember He came to earth for a glorious purpose. He fulfilled a divine purpose that resulted in the sacrifice of His life on the Cross of Calvary. I know, Father, that His death was the greatest gift mankind has ever known. Yet, His life on earth demonstrated the power of love and compassion I need to have for my fellow man.

I am grateful, O God, that you provided such a wonderful example of love and compassion. As much as I want to follow the example you gave, I often fail in my Christian walk. I get caught up in the sins of mankind and often do things that reflect poorly as a child of God. I need your help, O Lord. I need you to prune the withering branches from my life. I need you to instill in me, through your Holy Spirit, an earnest desire to always say and do the right thing so I may reflect the life of Christ faithfully.

While I am a sinner with the propensity to sin, I can, through your grace and love, rise above the noise and clamor that longs to drag me down and cause me to fail you once again. Lord, I love you so much and do not want to disappoint you. Bless me now as I go about this day with the spiritual strength and moral fortitude to always be a faithful and loving child of God. Amen.

REFLECTIONS

What are some of the things you do that reflect poorly upon you as a child of God?

Please use the space below to write down any thoughts or comments you may have.

"May God Bless You,
As you live your Life for Christ,
Empowered by The Holy Spirit."

December 18

Psalm 34:19 NIV.

[19] The righteous person may have many troubles, but the Lord delivers him from them all...

O Christ, the Son of God, your mercies never cease. The gratefulness in my heart is overwhelming. Whenever I need your guidance, you send the Holy Spirit to guide my way. Whenever I am consumed with sadness and grief about the sins I have committed, you extend the forgiveness and grace I do not deserve.

Father, it is only through your Son, Jesus Christ, that I become worthy of such great love and mercies. Although I am consumed with grief and sadness about the sins I have committed, I can claim freedom from those through my Lord and Savior. No longer do I need to feel guilt and shame. Now, I can live for you and know that true peace and love come from my Almighty God.

As I go about this day, my Lord, let me be faithful in my walk with you. Let me be mindful that my Salvation was paid for at a great price — the crucifixion of your Son, Jesus Christ. Let me face the challenges that come my way with the patience I need so my actions and words reflect the character of Christ, not my human condition. And let me be strong when Satan uses his diabolical schemes intended to strip me of my faith and trust in you.

I belong to you, Almighty God. Let me not fail you as I walk down the paths that are dangerous to my Christian faith. Do not let my failures perpetrated by Satan threaten my relationship with you. I will remain strong. I will stay faithful. And I will honor your Word that feeds my soul. Amen.

REFLECTIONS

Building up a character strong in Christ can help you face the challenges in life. Why?

Please use the space below to write down any thoughts or comments you may have.

"May God Bless You,
As you live your Life for Christ,
Empowered by The Holy Spirit."

December 19

John 10:28-30 NIV.

[28] I give them eternal life, and they shall never perish; no one will snatch them out of my hand. [29] My Father, who has given them to me, is greater than all; no one can snatch them out of my Father's hand. [30] I and the Father are One." ...

O Lord, my God, I come before you with the faith of a child. Through the shedding of Christ's blood on the Cross of Calvary, I have accepted the gift of Salvation. If I believe in you, you have promised me I would inherit the promise of eternal life with you in Heaven.

Father, I am faced with choices that can fan the flames of Satan in my life. Choices that go against your commandments and that dishonors your name. Forgive me, O Lord, and help me to ban any influences of Satan in my life. Restore my desire to live out my faith in you and to be able to find the strength and wisdom to turn from all sin that dishonors your name.

I am your child, O Mighty God. Satan must not have any hold on me. I can only resist him through the power of the Holy Spirit. I must fight him, O Christ, because I long to be strong in my faith and in my ability to turn from sin. I will resist him, Faithful One, because I am your child, and I belong to you. No one can snatch me out of the hand of the Almighty God. Praise to you, O Christ. All glory belongs to you. Amen.

REFLECTIONS

Satanic influences can wreak havoc on your spiritual life. How do you fight them?

Please use the space below to write down any thoughts or comments you may have.

"May God Bless You,
As you live your Life for Christ,
Empowered by The Holy Spirit."

December 20

1 Corinthians 15:18 NIV.

[18] Then those also who have fallen asleep in Christ are lost.

Most merciful Christ, when you walked this earth, you were the glorious example of one who epitomized the life of a righteous man. You spread the message of your Gospel, so I may know the love and life of one who is in Christ. Your love and grace are so great that no matter how sinful I am, you are there to forgive me and to restore my footsteps onto the path of righteousness. Thank you for your guiding hand as I traverse the complex challenges that life presents.

As I begin this day, let me be mindful of those who do not know the love you have for them. Let me be a faithful reflection of your love, grace, and forgiveness so they may see in me one who is trustworthy and who reflects the love of Christ. I am a sinner, my Lord, and I do not deserve your grace. Because of your great love for me and your endless mercies, I can live with confidence that I will enjoy eternal life with you in Heaven. When I meet the lost, let my sinful nature be quiet, so I may not lead them astray. Let me be filled with the power of the Holy Spirit, so the words I utter to them are loyal and faithful to your Holy Word.

Bless me now, O Lord, so I may be vital in my witness and unwavering in my devotion to your Holy Scriptures. Now, through the power of the Holy Spirit, let me go forth confident of my victory in Christ, faithful in all things, so I may lead those that are lost into your loving hands. Amen.

REFLECTIONS

When your sinful nature refuses to be quiet, what do you do? How strong are you in your Christian faith to fight off Satan?

Please use the space below to write down any thoughts or comments you may have.

"May God Bless You,
As you live your Life for Christ,
Empowered by The Holy Spirit."

December 21

John 17:3 NIV.

[3] Now this is eternal life: that they know you, the only true God, and Jesus Christ, whom you have sent.

O Christ, the Christmas Child, the day of your birth is fast approaching. All over the world, your children are waiting with heartfelt joy so they may be able to celebrate and sing praises to your Holy Name. As a child of yours, let me be mindful of the true meaning of Christmas. Let me not get caught up in the worldly desires of so many of your children. Let me remember you were born to save all your children from the penalty of sin. Let me recognize it is only through your love and grace that I can enter the kingdom of my Heavenly Father. Let me be an instrument of your love. Let me bring your lost children to the realization that without their accepting the gift of Salvation, they cannot enter the kingdom of God.

Empower me through the power of the Holy Spirit to hear your gentle whisper and to be able to touch the lives of those who are yearning for peace in their hearts. Bless me now, O Father, as I go about my day, confident of my victory in Christ and secure in the knowledge that through Christ I can do all things. Amen.

REFLECTIONS

- *With all the commercialization of Christmas, how do you keep Christ in Christmas?*

Please use the space below to write down any thoughts or comments you may have.

"May God Bless You,
As you live your Life for Christ,
Empowered by The Holy Spirit."

December 22

Matthew 2:13 NIV.

[13] When they had gone, an angel of the Lord appeared to Joseph in a dream. "Get up," he said, "take the child and his mother and escape to Egypt. Stay there until I tell you, for Herod is going to search for the child to kill him."

Precious Christ, my Lord, and my Savior, the day you came into this world was the beginning of a new life for those who embrace the gift of Salvation. Do not let me forget that your birth was one of a full man and a fully God. Do not let me forget that you experienced temptations and turmoil in your life beyond anything I or any other child of God has ever had to endure. Despite the pain and suffering you had to take, you still embrace your children with love, grace, and eternal mercies. And when you drew your last breath on Cross of Calvary, my transgressions were paid for by your precious blood.

Thank you, my Lord, and thank you for coming into this world as a new babe that brought hope and eternal life to all of mankind. As I go about this new day, let me be joyful and excited in this Christmas season so all those whose lives I cross today may see the Son of God within me. Let me be a beacon of hope to those who are lost. Let me be a symbol of strength to those that are weary. Let me be a light that reflects the Truth of your Holy Word to all those that yearn to have a personal relationship with you. And, for those that do not accept you as the Son of God, may the Holy Spirit work through me as I attempt to share with them the love of Christ and the fruits of the Holy Spirit. All glory to you, O Christ! Amen.

REFLECTIONS

- *How could Christ love you so much that He was willing to die for you? Would you do that for Him?*

Please use the space below to write down any thoughts or comments you may have.

"May God Bless You,
As you live your Life for Christ,
Empowered by The Holy Spirit."

December 23

Luke 1:31 NIV.

[31] You will conceive and give birth to a Son, and you are to call him Jesus.

Precious Christ, my heart is full of love and gratitude as the day of your birth arrives. All over the world, your children are preparing to celebrate Christmas Day. Let me remember your coming was the beginning of your life on earth as the Son of God. Father, there is joy in my heart and sadness for those who do not recognize you as the Living God. Let my faith be a light to those who are at crossroads in their lives. Let my joy be reflected in my face as I sing praises to your Holy Name. You are my God. You are the Prince of Peace. You are the Great Jehovah.

During this Christmas season, let me be an ambassador of Christ, one who is strong in his faith and committed to carrying out the message of your Gospel. Be with me so I do not falter in my walk. Strengthen me in the areas of Holiness I need to grow in. Prune all the branches in my life that are not bearing the fruits of the Holy Spirit. And bless me through the power of the Holy Spirit so I may be a caring, compassionate, and loving child of God. And when the day of your birth arrives, may it remind me of the joy that can be found through Christ Jesus. Praise to your name, O Precious Christ. Praise to your Holy Name. Amen.

REFLECTIONS

During this Christmas season what sadness consumes your heart the most? Why?

Please use the space below to write down any thoughts or comments you may have.

"May God Bless You,
As you live your Life for Christ,
Empowered by The Holy Spirit."

December 24

Mark 10:17 NIV.

[17] As Jesus started on his way, a man ran up to him and fell on his knees before him. "Good teacher," he asked, "what must I do to inherit eternal life?"

Blessed Jesus, the three wise men are on their way to Bethlehem to honor your birth. They bring Gold as a symbol of your Kingship on earth—Frankincense as a symbol of your Deity. And Myrrh as a symbol of your death on the Cross of Calvary. Your birth represents the beginning of a new life and relationship with my Holy Father.

All over the world, people are preparing their hearts and souls to celebrate your birth and the promise of eternal life your arrival brings. As a child of God, I praise your Holy Name. Father, I see the joy in the faces of your children who are waiting expectantly for the day your mother, Mary, and our Father in Heaven brought you into this world. What joy there is in my heart! I am so grateful you came into this world to teach your children how to love their neighbors. I am so thrilled with the examples of love, compassion, and kindness that exemplified your life while on this earth. What more can I give you on the day of your birth? Let my gift to you be by living my life as a reflection of your life on earth.

Help me, Lord, to always be mindful that you paid the ultimate price for my grievous sins. Help me in my daily walk by keeping me on the path of righteousness and correcting me when I wander off course. Love me, O Christ, despite my sinful nature, so I can always have the assurance that I can find absolution from the sins that grieve your heart. As I go about this day, let me prepare my heart by honoring the day of your birth with a spirit of holiness and thankfulness for all the blessings you have bestowed on me. In Christ's name, I pray. Amen.

"May God Bless You,
As you live your Life for Christ,
Empowered by The Holy Spirit."

REFLECTIONS

💡 *Describe the joy in your heart during this Christmas season. How will you share your joy?*

Please use the space below to write down any thoughts or comments you may have.

"May God Bless You,
As you live your Life for Christ,
Empowered by The Holy Spirit."

December 25

Isaiah 9:6 NIV.

[6] For to us a child is born, to us a Son is given, and the government will be on his shoulders. And he will be called Wonderful Counselor, Mighty God, Everlasting Father, Prince of Peace.

Almighty Father, let the whole world know that today marks the birth of your Son and my Lord and Savior, Jesus Christ. Let your angels proclaim through the lips of all your children that Christ the Savior was born this day. He came to bring new life and hope to all those that are lost and without hope. Let your angels proclaim that Christ has come to pay the penalty of our sins so we might enjoy eternal life with you. The birth of my Savior fills my heart with joy and gratitude.

How great is my God! Even though I am a sinner, I now have the promise of a Savior that can restore my heart when torn apart by difficulties in life. I now have a Savior that can restore my walk on the righteous path when Satan leads me astray. Blessed be your name, O Christ! Blessed be your glorious name! You are the everlasting light. You are the light that brightens my path and gives hope for all of mankind. You are my God! You are the eternal hope for all those that are lost and in need of a personal Savior.

Lead me, O Faithful Lord, as I navigate the days ahead. Let my voice be heard that you are the Son of the Living God. From a babe in a manger to the Cross of Calvary, you are the hope of the world. You are the King of Kings! You are my everything. Praise to your Holy Name. Fill me now with the presence of the Holy Spirit so, on this glorious day, I may use the fruits of the spirit to awaken the lives of all those whose paths I cross. Thank you, Father, for the gift of the Christmas child. Amen.

REFLECTIONS

The Christ child is born. How will you celebrate the true meaning of Christmas?

Please use the space below to write down any thoughts or comments you may have.

"May God Bless You,
As you live your Life for Christ,
Empowered by The Holy Spirit."

December 26

1 John 4:19-21 NIV.

[19] We love because he first loved us. [20] Whoever claims to love God yet hates a brother or sister is a liar. For whoever does not love their brother and sister, whom they have seen, cannot love God, whom they have not seen. [21] And he has given us this command: Anyone who loves God must also love their brother and sister.

Blessed Christ, as the new year approaches, let me always be mindful that you came into this world as a Living Sacrifice for the sins of mankind. Your love, grace, and forgiveness are gifts I will always be grateful for. As I go about this day, let me be faithful in my walk and confident in my ability to be victorious over Satan's cunning ploys. You are my God! No matter what my day may bring, I serve only you. Even if there is turmoil, frustration, or overwhelming depression. I know your hand is upon me and will bless me with everything I need to rise above my life difficulties.

As a child of God, I am called to love my neighbor as you first loved me. Lord, help me be faithful to this calling no matter how difficult the challenges may be. Help me to be a faithful steward of my resources so when the opportunity arises, I may be able to bless others as you have blessed me. Help me to rise above my sinful nature where I can use the gift of free will to honor you with the choices I make. I love you, O Christ. My heart sings praise to your Holy Name. Let the joy in my heart spill over like a fountain of Living Water so the people whose paths I cross today may be touched by your eternal love and grace. Amen.

REFLECTIONS

The day after Christmas can sometimes be depressing. How can you find joy in God's child?

Please use the space below to write down any thoughts or comments you may have.

"May God Bless You,
As you live your Life for Christ,
Empowered by The Holy Spirit."

December 27

Isaiah 66:2 NIV.

[2] Has not my hand made all these things, and so they came into being?" declares the Lord. "These are the ones I look on with favor: those who are humble and contrite in spirit, and who tremble at my word.

Most Holy Father, glory to your Holy Name. From the moment you created the heavens and the earth, I was a child of yours. From the moment of Christ's birth, I was one of your chosen children. From the moment Christ died on the Cross of Calvary, I was forgiven of my sins and redeemed by His precious blood. No matter how grievous my sins are to your heart, you still love me. Furthermore, you forgive me when I come before you with a contrite and repentant heart—what a precious gift it is to have a personal relationship with my Lord and Savior. No matter what despair may be consuming me, you are always there to rescue me and to lift me up into your loving arms.

As I begin this day, O Christ, let me be faithful and honorable in all I do. Fill me with your Holy Spirit so I might hear your sweet whisper and be able to respond in a way that brings glory to your name. I love you, Heavenly Father. I rejoice amid your presence. I am grateful you blessed me with opportunities to share with others the love of Christ. I am thankful for the Divine Opportunities that cross my path and allow me to connect with others in a way that speaks to their hearts. Let me always be kind and loving to those whose paths I cross. Let me always be forgiving of those that offend me. And, my Lord, let me always be willing to stand up for the truth of your Word no matter the consequences that may occur to me. In Jesus' name, I pray. Amen.

REFLECTIONS

Being a child of God is a tremendous privilege. How can you honor God with this blessing?

Please use the space below to write down any thoughts or comments you may have.

"May God Bless You,
As you live your Life for Christ,
Empowered by The Holy Spirit."

December 28

Isaiah 12:2 NIV.

[2] Surely God is my Salvation; I will trust and not be afraid. The Lord, the Lord himself, is my strength and my defense; he has become my Salvation."

O Faithful Redeemer, your presence in my life has been a true blessing. Without you, I would be lost. I pray for those that are followers of Satan. Because you love me so much, you have forgiven me of my sins and made it possible for me to enjoy eternal life with you in Heaven. Lord, my heart is full of gratitude for the opportunity to have a personal relationship with you. One that allows me to enjoy your presence in every area of my life. Through your grace, I am free of areas of my life that bind me to the falsehoods of this world. Whenever I find myself slipping into the darkness perpetrated by the evil one, I can always count on you to rescue me and to lovingly admonish my behavior. Your love, mercy, and forgiveness will always be there for me to claim. I no longer need to drown in murky waters of self-pity and become depressed over circumstances that overwhelm me.

Because of your great love for me, I am free of the bondage of depression. Those circumstances have caused me to be ashamed of myself and full of regret for the sins I have committed. I am a child of the Almighty God who loves me and is faithful to the promises in His Word. Praise to you, O Christ! Let me always be worthy of your great love and mercies. As I go about my day, let me be mindful that my strength is in the Lord and not of myself. I can do all things with Christ as my Shield of Armor. Bless me now, in the name of the Father, Son, and Holy Spirit. Amen.

REFLECTIONS

If our loving God were to admonish you for sinful behavior, what would you do?

Please use the space below to write down any thoughts or comments you may have.

"May God Bless You,
As you live your Life for Christ,
Empowered by The Holy Spirit."

December 29

2 Corinthians 1:3-4 NIV.

[3] Praise be to the God and Father of our Lord Jesus Christ, the Father of compassion and the God of all comfort, [4] who comforts us in all our troubles, so that we can comfort those in any trouble with the comfort we ourselves receive from God.

Blessed Father, send now your Holy Spirit upon me. Bless me with the truth of your Word, so I may faithfully profess the Gospel of my Lord and Savior, Jesus Christ. Purge me of any sins that may taint my witness and that would dishonor your name. Fill me with love for my fellow man, and do not let me falter in my love and grace towards them. As I go about my day, let me be mindful that a cheerful heart is quick to soothe a heart yearning for comfort.

Lord, let the words of my mouth bring comfort and peace to those in need of your grace. If someone is caught up in a maze of personal conflict, bless me with the spirit of wisdom and revelation so I may say the words needed to bring comfort and peace to their heart. Lord, I cannot serve you faithfully without the Holy Spirit upon me. Let me always be faithful to your Word. Let me be ever faithful in my witness to others. And let me be mindful that your love is so great, so powerful, and so enduring I do not need to be fearful of living my life for you. You are my God. Your Son is my personal Savior. Your love sustains me through my darkest hours. And your grace is truly a gift of love. What more can a child of God want? In the name of our Most Gracious Lord, Jesus Christ. Amen.

REFLECTIONS

Are you comfortable enough in your faith to witness to someone in need of God's love?

Please use the space below to write down any thoughts or comments you may have.

"May God Bless You,
As you live your Life for Christ,
Empowered by The Holy Spirit."

December 30

Psalm 20:6 NIV.

[6] Now this I know: The Lord gives victory to his anointed. He answers him from his heavenly sanctuary with the victorious power of his right hand.

As this year ends, Gracious Father, let me praise you for all the blessings you have showered upon me. Your love, grace, and forgiveness have sustained me during my darkest hours. Your love has given me so much joy and happiness that my cup is overflowing. I am thankful for my family and friends who have stood by me and have given me the support and affirmation that has truly blessed me.

All through this past year, there have been situations that have tested my faith. There have been situations that have sent me spiraling into the depths of depression. Problems that have caused me to falter in my walk. Yet, no matter how far I have wandered from your presence and despite how grievous my sins are, you have been there to welcome me back into your loving arms. Your love is so great, my Lord, that I rejoice and sing praises to your Holy Name. Your grace and mercies have blessed me beyond anything I can comprehend.

Who am I, O Christ, that you would love me so much that you would bless me despite my sinful nature? You are my Lord! You are the King of Kings! You are the Prince of Peace! And you are the Christ, the Son of the Living God. Yes, Lord, you have been there for me every day of this past year. I am so grateful for your presence in my life and the compassion you have shown me. As I go about this new day, let me reflect on all the blessings you have anointed me with. Fill me now with the Holy Spirit, so I may glorify you in all that I say and do this coming year. Amen.

REFLECTIONS

As you look forward to the New Year, is there some way you can honor God?

Please use the space below to write down any thoughts or comments you may have.

*"May God Bless You,
As you live your Life for Christ,
Empowered by The Holy Spirit."*

December 31

Proverbs 16:9 NIV.

[9] In their heart's humans plan their course, but the Lord establishes their steps.

O Christ, my Majestic King, you have blessed me with your presence every day of this past year. Your love and grace sustained me, increased my faith, filled me with the truth of your Word, and enabled me to have victory over Satan through the power of the Holy Spirit. As I enter the new year, my faithful Lord, I ask for a continuation of those blessings. But more than that, I pray for increased knowledge of your Word so I may be an effective Disciple of your Great Commission.

As the New Year is ushered in with anticipation of new beginnings, let me be more passionate about my faith. Grant me grace as I become more devout in my devotion to the study of your Word. Let me be more passionate about sharing the Gospel of Jesus Christ with those children of yours that cross my path. Through the power of the Holy Spirit, let me grow in my faith. Allow pruning of the branches in my life, keeping me from a closer relationship with my Savior, Jesus Christ.

Father, this New Year will enable me to reflect on my relationship with you and increase my joy in serving you and my fellow man. Please bring me Divine Opportunities to touch the lives of weary souls who have lost hope in themselves and the future before them. Let me be a powerful instrument of your love so I may bring the lost to a personal relationship with Jesus Christ. In the name of the Father, the Son, and the Holy Spirit. Praise to you, O Christ. Amen.

REFLECTIONS

As this year ends, praise God for His blessings and the strength He has given you. Commit to a more faithful prayer life and the strength and courage to live a live reflective of Jesus Christ. Describe how you can do that.

Please use the space below to write down any thoughts or comments you may have.

"May God Bless You,
As you live your Life for Christ,
Empowered by The Holy Spirit."

About the Author

George H. Brooks

Raised as a Lutheran in Brooklyn, New York, George H. Brooks holds a BA in Journalism from Texas State University. He is not an ordained minister, nor does he have any credentials in biblical theology. He is simply a sinner saved by the blood of Jesus Christ and the grace of the Almighty God. He accepted Jesus Christ as his Savior as a child at the age of 8 years old. As with any child at that age, he did not understand the scope of his decision that day. Subsequently, he entered his teen years and then adulthood unprepared for the onslaught of temptations Satan was about to rain upon him.

During his life, he served in the United States Army as a Combat Medic/Medical Corpsman on Korea's DMZ in 1969. He then served as a Medical Corpsman in an Evacuation Hospital in Vietnam in 1971. His adult life found him succumbing to many temptations of this world and other sins that are offensive to God. While he went through these temptations, he was constantly reminded of his mother's faith in God's promises and the need for a personal relationship with Jesus Christ. He always felt God had a particular purpose for his life but struggled to find his true calling. It took years of personal trials and obstacles before he allowed himself to be pruned by God so the fruits of the Holy Spirit could spring forth in his life.

This devotional, *"From the Cradle to the Cross, A 365 Day Morning Prayer Devotional,"* is a testimony of his life. A life riddled with sin but found redemption and forgiveness through his Lord and Savior, Jesus Christ. He has said this devotional could not have been written if the Holy Spirit was not present within him. While still facing temptations of this world, his hope for you, as you read the prayers in this devotional, is that you will come to see the reality of sin in *his* life. And how it may be present in *your* life as well. His hope for you is that you will surrender your heart and will over to Christ. And to allow yourself to become an instrument of God's grace and love not only to yourself but also to your fellow man.

Printed in the United States
by Baker & Taylor Publisher Services